Pleasure Packing

Pleasure Packing

by Robert S. Wood

Illustrations
by Warren Dayton III

Ten Speed Press

Other Books by Robert S. Wood

Desolation Wilderness
★Mountain Cabin
Good-Bye, Loneliness!
★The 2 Oz. Backpacker
★Whitewater Boatman
Homeopathy, Medicine That Works!
★Dayhiker

★Available from Ten Speed Press

Ten Speed Press
Box 7123
Berkeley, CA 94707

Library of Congress Cataloging-in-Publication Data

Wood, Robert S. (Robert Snyder), 1930-
    Pleasure packing / Robert S. Wood. — Rev.
      p.   cm.
    Includes bibliographical references (p.) and index.
    ISBN 0-89815-476-8
    1. Backpacking.   I. Title.
GV199.6.W66   1992   92-8323
796.5'1—dc20   CIP

Printed in the United States of America

1 2 3 4 5 — 95 94 93 92 91

For Deanne,
my favorite trail companion,
best friend . . . and wife

ACKNOWLEDGMENTS

First and foremost I'm grateful to Jack Stephenson for patiently trying to educate me. I also want to thank the crew in the Sacramento REI: Boyd, Louise, Christine, Win, Dennis, and Ken. And I appreicate help from Laurel, Carol, and Mike at Back Country Traveler here in Pollock Pines. I also want to thank Bob Galbreath of the Lake Tahoe Outdoorsman, Wayne Gregory, Chuck Kennedy, fly fisherman Sam Ragent, and *Backpacker, The Magazine of Wilderness Travel*. Without their help I wouldn't have made it.

Bob Wood

STARTING OFF

Awakened in the dark
by the purling of Robins
I set myself deeper
in the frost stiff bag
and sink into sleep
as the day takes hold.

With new melted ice
from a rock bound pool
we wash back the night
from our cobwebbed faces
and breakfast on apples
from my father's farm.

As the sun breaks free
from the shadowed trees
and the stillness gives way
to the clamor of day
we gather our gear
and make ready to go.

Then with tentative steps
under unaccustomed loads
we set forth out the trail
in the growing light
through the warming air
on the first long trip
of the new found summer.

Contents

Pleasure Packing??

Anyone can backpack in comparative misery—and many people regularly do. Every summer I shudder at the number of people struggling through the wilds, plagued by poor equipment and a lack of experience, unable to enjoy the coutry around them. Backpacking becomes ridiculous when the misery clearly outweighs the pleasure. But when a trip can be made in relative comfort, all the joys of living and traveling in the wilds will unfold. My hope is to help the reader achieve the level of comfort that turns backpacking into *Pleasure Packing*.

Pleasure Packing is anything but simple, especially for the highly civilized, city-oriented individual. The first problem is weight. Comfort means equipment and equipment means weight. Comfort in camp (ample equipment) often means sacrificing comfort and mobility on the trail. And comfort on the trail (a light pack) often comes at the expense of comfort in camp. The backpacker seemingly must choose between the freedom and mobility of a small pack and the shelter and comfort of a happy camp.

But weight is not the only problem. All the gear in the world will not ensure comfort for the hiker who knows nothing about conditioning, trip planning, efficient walking, choosing a campsite, wilderness cookery—in short, technique.

So comfort in the wilds comes from carrying just the right gear and knowing precisely how to use it. And that is exactly what *Pleasure Packing* is all about: taking some of the work out of the wilderness so the beauty and happiness are free to shine through.

—Berkeley, January 1972

Introduction to the Third Edition

Spawned by the backpacking boom of the early seventies, *Pleasure Packing* has been helping avid hikers for 20 years. With only word-of-mouth promotion, its several editions have sold over 100,000 copies. Now the children of those boomers are discovering for themselves the joys of wandering the wilds with their homes on their backs, creating in the nineties a mini-boom of their own. They know there still is no vacation more rewarding or inexpensive. Helping this new generation of backpackers find its way is the principal aim of this new revised edition.

Today's hikers face more difficult conditions than their parents enjoyed. Nowadays there are dirt bikes, mountain bikes, gear thieves, irate farmers, dope growers, and armed jeepers to contend with. Once-pristine wilderness is often overgrazed—and overpopulated with deer, cows, sheep, and hungry bears. Increasing government regulations limit group size and length of stay and prohibit wood fires (but rarely guns and horses). Wilderness Permits for when and where you want to go may well be unobtainable. Possibly polluted water may require boiling, filtering, or chemical treatment.

The local backpacking gear firms you once loyally supported are now owned by multinational Hong Kong holding companies that make competing products in the same Korean factory. And the population explosion in the last 20 years has increased competition for a shrinking supply of choice wilderness. Fortunately the savvy backpackers of the nineties know more about the hazards and more about paraphernalia than their parents did 20 years ago.

I won't pretend that everything in this book is brand new, because it isn't. There's no reason to fix what ain't broke! Some things simply haven't changed. Woods lore, for instance, is virtually timeless. But in 20 years time backpacking gear (clothing and equipment) has changed radically. In many cases the fundamental concepts and design principles behind that gear have altered dramatically.

And the makers of all this gear, with some notable excpetions, continue to come and go—like the styles—every year. Speaking of style, backpacking clothing, like skiwear and yachting attire, has again become stylish—because it suggests healthy, rugged, outdoorsy independence. This trendiness has contributed to the backpacking renaissance.

Because there are hundreds of manufacturers—making thousands of products—and because the scene is constantly changing, it's no longer possible for any one person—or even a team of testers—to evaluate even a fraction of the offerings that a backpacker might logically consider. There's just too much gear out there nowadays for unbiased, objective analysis and comparison. A comprehensive catalog would look like the phonebook. And you probably couldn't trust it!

Even *Backpacker* magazine, whose subsidiary *Wilderness Camping,* I used to test gear for, has ceased rating equipment in its annual *Buyers Guide.* There's just too much of it. Instead, it merely lists boots, bags, tents, packs and stoves—by maker—providing critical specs but letting the maker (a likely advertiser) describe the wonders of its gear. Two more comprehensive sources of the widest range of gear are CAMPMOR and Recreational Equipment (REI), the leading mail order houses. Their prices, guarantees, and nononsense free catalogs are impressive (see Sources).

People shop differently in the nineties than they did in those lazy innocent days 20 years ago. Few of us today have time to comparison shop extensively. What counts nowadays, it seems to me, are the choices actually available to the individual shopper, whether in an Army-Navy store, a chic mountain shop, discount house, convenience store, outdoors emporium, mail-order catalog—or any combination of sources.

Readers of my earlier editions have sometimes beaten their brains out searching for a particular item I raved about—and sometimes come up empty when its maker went bankrupt or changed its line. And the gear that works for me on my turf might be totally unsuitable for your particular purposes. The fit, specific use, or cost might be unacceptable.

So in this new edition I've avoided commenting on individual items—unless they're clearly superior, new or irresistibly unusual, or ripoffs or dangerously inferior. Instead, I concentrate on educating you to make wise choices by generically describing basic gear, how it works, approximate weights, different design schools of thought, the concepts and principles behind the design, and the available choices, rather than pointing you to the comparatively small segment of equipment I happen to know intimately.

This book will give you fundamentals, advantages and drawbacks, things to be wary of, ways to check workmanship and conduct tests, tips for obtaining the proper fit, and so forth. It'll bolster your good judgment and help you make informed decisions. But ultimately it's up to you. You'll have to make the final choices from the selection available where you choose to shop.

So don't get hung up on the "right" backpacking gear. Gear junkies, style-followers, faddists—people who need desperately to know they've got the very best—have usually lost sight of what backpacking's all about. Gear is just a part of the means, not the end.

As I wrote in the 1981 edition, "Our ultimate goal is simply to have fun, see the country and escape our cares—experiencing the excitement, freedom, peace and contentment that seem easier to find when we're walking in the wilds with our homes on our backs."

—Bob Wood, Spring 1992, Pollock Pines, CA

ONE

Backpacking Basics

How the Body Works... Two Kinds of Sweat...
Wind Chill Hypothermia... The Breathability Myth...
Vapor Barrier Warmth... A Simple Experiment... Blotters...
Fabrics... Fabric Coatings... Insulation

The more you know about backpacking gear and the human body's peculiar idiosyncrasies, the easier it is to plan richly satisfying trips. Since the dawn of mountaineering, man has searched diligently for ways to shield his highly vulnerable body from heat and cold, wind and rain. The quest continues today as modern outdoorsmen—aided by the magic of space age technology—seek comfort and protection in the selection of their clothing, packs, boots, bedding, and shelter. Since the walker must carry all he needs on his back, often over difficult, dangerous terrain in uncertain weather, his gear must be light, functional, versatile, compact, and, above all, dependable. Ideally it should also be weatherproof, durable, fireproof, and inexpensive. That's a tall order. No wonder so many backpackers are still uncomfortable.

By taking the mystery and myth out of design concepts, I hope to help today's backpackers go lighter, safer, and happier than ever before. But before one can wisely select backpacking gear, it is vital to understand the qualities of the materials out of which that gear is made. But to understand materials and how they will function, it is essential to be familiar with the design principles behind them and how they apply, in the wilderness, to the needs and idiosyncrasies of the human body. The body's peculiarities, sensitivities, and strange demands easily double the difficulty of producing gear that works. So the place to begin is the human body—its requirements and preferences and the myths that surround them.

HOW THE BODY WORKS

The body is a highly sensitive organism: Meet its complex needs or pain will swiftly follow! Just what does it want, this mysterious creature in which we live but know so little about? For one thing it wants air temperature at the skin to be about 75°F, ranging from 72°F in the hands and feet to about 78°F in the head and trunk. Take away body heat faster than it's generated and the body turns dramatically defensive. To protect crucial head and trunk temperatures it swiftly cuts down blood circulation to the skin by constricting capillaries. If cooling continues, it severely shuts down blood flow to the arms and legs, chilling hands and feet. By allowing skin temperature to drop 20 degrees and reducing blood circulation to

the feet by up to 95%, the body can cut overall heat losses by a startling 75%. When the body is threatened it doesn't fool around!

Incidentally, it pays to keep in mind that the body's thermostat is located in the chest area. If you chill the chest while trying to vent excess heat, you're liable to trigger the production (and resultant energy loss) of massive amounts of heat and moisture. So if you want to cool off without threatening the body, keep your front zippers closed and rely on venting at the shirttails, neck, cuffs—and armpits if your garments have underarm zippers.

The head is the only part of the body in which the capillaries do not contract, because the body knows survival depends on continued alert functioning of the brain. So when your skin turns cool and your hands and feet grow cold, pay attention. The body is trying to warn you that heat production can't keep up with heat loss. No mittens in the world will keep your hands warm if the body believes trunk temperature is threatened. So if your feet get cold, put on a hat and jacket—especially when sleeping with the head exposed.

Body heat loss occurs in five different ways: (1) radiation (heat pumped out through the skin like warmth from a stove); (2) respiration (the steady exhaling of water vapor—visible as steam in cold air); (3) conduction (by skin contact with a good heat conductor, especially water); (4) evaporation (as water evaporates it takes massive amounts of heat with it); and (5) convection (heat stolen from the skin by moving air).

Almost as important to the body as maintaining an average 75°F temperature is the maintenance of moist—but not wet—skin. Comfort, to the body, is a surprisingly high relative humidity of 70–95%, despite the mind's belief that comfort means dry skin. This isn't the contradiction it seems. What the mind calls dry skin, really isn't. Truly dry skin quickly turns chapped, stiff, cracked and flaky. Open sores and bleeding follow. Properly moist, humid skin, on the other hand, isn't wet, either. What the body wants is a quarter-inch thick cushioning layer of moist warm air, like an invisible second skin, shielding and lubricating but not wetting the skin. Humor the body by providing 70°F air with a normal 90% relative humidity, and it will easily maintain this suit of invisible armor with as little as a pint of water a day. Destroy this protective layer by exposure to a harsh environment and the body goes wild in an effort to restore it. Sweat glands open wide and the body goes all out to pump heated water vapor through the skin. Until the layer is rebuilt, heat and water loss from the body will be a terrific 6–800% above normal—though at the time the mind may notice nothing

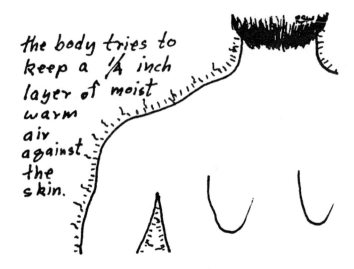

the body tries to keep a 1/4 inch layer of moist warm air against the skin.

because evaporation is immediate. But after hiking in dry or cold air for several hours you'll suddenly discover an insatiable thirst. Your body is signaling dehydration and demanding replacement of water—by the quart!

From the body's standpoint, the loss of water vapor by evaporation means inevitable heat loss, a fact that drives clothing designers crazy. In dry conditions (say 10% relative humidity) a walker might easily lose a gallon of water a day. But if you stop water loss by raising humidity to 100%, you also stop heat loss.

TWO KINDS OF SWEAT

When the skin is below 75°F and the humidity is less than 100%, water vapor passes off unnoticed as "insensible perspiration"—after doing its job: keeping the skin moist. But when skin temperature climbs much above 75°F the body reacts to what it considers uncomfortable overheating by opening the sweat glands wider and pouring out heated water to wet the skin with what we regard distastefully as sweat. So in reality there are two kinds of sweat: the one you don't feel or see that keeps your skin comfortably moist and alive, and the wet one produced by overheating.

The insensible perspiration rate jumps dramatically under a variety of conditions commonly encountered outdoors. When relative humidity drops much below 40%, for example. It isn't widely known that the colder the air the less water it can hold. From the body's standpoint winter ski touring conditions are as dry as those in the desert: it's a struggle to get enough water. At 30°F the relative humidity on bare skin is an arid 15%—even though there's nothing but frozen water (snow) in sight! And liquid water can be just as hard to come by as in the desert. The body may need a gallon a day!

Though dry air sucks up ample moisture (and with it body heat), the two greatest threats to body heat are wind (convection) and water (conduction) because each has the capacity to swiftly obliterate that layer of moist warm air that shields the body. Water's great conductivity—20 times that of still dry air—instantly destroys the air layer and enormous heat loss follows. Ten minutes exposure of the body to 34°F water (if you fall through thin winter ice on a pond) means likely death by freezing! But the water doesn't have to be frigid to chill you. Air temperature of 68°F in a heated home is comfortably warm, but the same 68°F in a swimming pool water feels freezing. Why? In the house the body easily maintains its cushion of moist 75°F air. In the water it can't, and the sudden 7° drop on bare skin is a shock.

Slicing it even finer, if you work up a sweat jogging and return to that 68°F house after you've cooled down, the dampness of your clothes and skin produces chilling evaporative heat loss that will make the house seem chilly, no matter what else you do. But take a shower and put on dry clothes and presto! the 68°F house is warm again.

WIND CHILL HYPOTHERMIA

Wind chill may be even more threatening to the exposed body because the danger is less evident. Most deaths from hypothermia (brain and body core chilling) occur in deceptively mild (above freezing) air temperatures which have been drastically lowered (in chilling effect) because wind has blown away the body's protective layer of still, warm air, permitting rapid heat loss by convection. And it doesn't take much wind. On a 30°F day with mild 10 mph wind, the effective air temperature on bare skin is a chilly 16°F. If the wind freshens to a moderate 25 mph, the effective temperature drops to zero. And on a zero winter day a 30 mph wind is equivalent to a dangerous 50°F below on bare skin!

Combine the threats of wind and water and you multiply the danger by adding the terrible cooling power of evaporation. Although water has 20 times the conductivity of dead air, add evaporative super cooling and that exposed wet skin loses heat more than 200 times as fast as dry protected skin! Stand wet and naked in the wind after a swim on a cool summer day and you'll experience severe chilling in a matter of seconds. Even after you dry and dress it will take a long time to get warm. Sweat up your sleeping bag on a warm autumn evening and you're headed for trouble in the cool before dawn.

When you climb into your bag at night, in any season, insensible perspiration and respiratory water loss continue. Most of that water is driven by body warmth into your bed, and all of it enters your tent, if you have one. Though few campers are aware of it, it isn't uncommon for the weight of your sleeping bag to mysteriously jump $1\frac{1}{2}$ to $2\frac{1}{2}$ pounds in the space of a single summer night from accumulated condensed water vapor given off by the sleeping body.

But the cooling effect of evaporation can be put to work in warm climates. Soak your hat and shirt (or everything but your boots) every time you pass a stream, for blessed relief. If water is scarce, take advantage of what's known about blood circulation to the head and neck. Veteran desert travelers know the most effective use of precious water to combat overheating is repeated wetting— for evaporative cooling—of the back of the neck and the forehead.

The body's ability to generate heat when needed is far from constant. Since vigorous production is vital in cold, dry, or wet conditions, body comfort, if not safety, is dependent on the ability to produce heat at least as fast as it's lost. It is therefore important to be aware of conditions that sabotage heat production. Such stresses as fatigue, wet skin, altitude, poor health, hunger, anxiety, and lack of adequate prior conditioning will all make it harder to get warm once chilling occurs. So if the body is under stress or conditions are extreme, take extra precautions against chilling and pay attention to the body's warning system.

Just what is body comfort? The definition I like is "a blissful unawareness of unpleasant sensation," which means the body is content with conditions—for the moment.

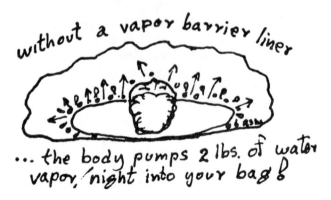

without a vapor barrier liner

... the body pumps 2 lbs. of water vapor/night into your bag

The body's great sensitivity, wild fluctuations, and varied responses—all the while pumping out troublesome water vapor—have posed staggering problems for designers of clothing, tents, and sleeping bags. Small wonder they've been largely frustrated in their attempts to meet the exacting needs of modern hikers. Most of their serious efforts can be broadly classified under three different design principles: breathability, vapor barrier, and temporary moisture storage.

THE BREATHABILITY MYTH

Breathability seems to have its roots in a backlash against the sweat and condensation that so often soaks clothing, tents, and bags from within. Condensation is defined as the reduction of water vapor by cooling into liquid water. Since it seems to be worse beneath sealed (waterproof) fabrics, designers decided—with more hope than science—that open porous fabrics (being the opposite of closed sealed fabrics) would somehow let body vapor escape before it could condense.

Manufacturers began to advertise "breathable" equipment, people bought it, and before long this shaky thesis had been elevated to the level of fact. Water vapor from the body, it was flatly declared, can be satisfactorily dispersed, before it condenses simply by putting porous (i.e., breathable) materials next to the body and by avoiding sealed (waterproof) fabrics. The theory depends on four assumptions: (1) sweating means wetting and occurs at a constant rate, (2) for comfort the skin must be dry, (3) sealed fabrics inevitably produce condensation, and (4) the volume of water vapor produced by an active body will find its way through the pores in unsealed fabrics.

Since all four of these assumptions are false it's not surprising that breathability has never worked—except under ideal conditions when it's not needed. In wet, cold, or humid conditions it fails badly. And when it does work, severely high convective and evaporative heat loss is overlooked or ignored. Even its most feverish adherents admit rain is a problem. Obviously, fabrics porous enough to let body moisture out will let rain in even faster.

Over the years a succession of miracle fabrics have been developed to solve this problem. The latest of these is Gortex and its various imitators (like VersaTech). Despite massive advertising, all of them have failed, as will be seen when fabrics and insulators are individually scrutinized. The fact is, no fabric is capable of "breathing" out the amount of water vapor generated by an average person doing moderate exercise under normal conditions. Not even with the help of "vapor pressure," which is supposed to actually drive water vapor through porous materials. Under field conditions where breathability would be useful, vapor pressure is so faint it can barely push water vapor through the gaping quarter-inch holes in a fishnet shirt.

VAPOR BARRIER WARMTH

In stark contrast to the breathability myth, which steadfastly ignores the workings of the body and the physics of water vapor diffusion, the vapor barrier approach takes clever advantage of body function. Instead of unrealistically trying to rid the body of moisture while ignoring accompanying heat loss, vapor barriers contain body moisture and reduce its production while stopping heat loss. In short, breathability tries in vain to keep you dry. Vapor barriers aim to keep you warm and comfortably moist while your clothes and insulation stay dry.

A vapor barrier is simply a sealed or waterproof fabric *worn close to the skin* to keep body moisture in instead of trying to drive it out. Don't groan with visions of steamy streaming skin. That needn't happen. Though sealed garments worn *away* from the body over clothing (like waterproof parkas) *can* cause oceans of condensation, sealed fabric worn *close* to the skin produces a startlingly different effect. Body heat makes the difference. Because the fabric is warmed by the body, condensation does not occur. Because it protects that moist layer of water vapor covering

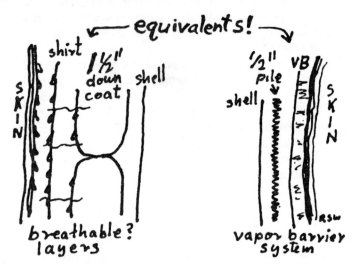

the skin, optimum humidity is easily maintained with minimal vapor output. Given ideal conditions of moisture and heat, the body gratefully closes sweat glands and shuts down vapor production up to 85%.

It's ironic that striving for dry skin only makes it pump more moisture, while permitting skin humidity shrinks production of perspiration! Not only does the wearer escape the steam room condensation associated with sealed garments, clothing worn over the vapor barrier stays completely dry. The severe heat loss that always accompanies sweating is prevented, and the body's water needs (thirst) are proportionally reduced. With the efficient retention of body heat, the outdoor traveler enjoys remarkable warmth with far less of the heavy, bulky, expensive insulation we've come to think is vital in cold weather. In fact the colder it is, the better vapor barriers perform. And there isn't the slightest reduction in efficiency when conditions turn wet and humid. It isn't until the weather grows warm that vapor barriers begin to lose their value, and that's simply because they're so effective at retaining heat.

Radical as the vapor barrier principle sounds, informed consideration of body behavior shows it to be perfectly logical. Not only is the principle scientifically sound, there is proof in the form of practical application. The vapor barrier principle is precisely what keeps well-designed houses warm and comfortable in winter: a plastic or aluminum vapor barrier on the inside of the insulation seals in heat and humidity, and an indoor humidifier adds needed moisture to dry inside air. And during World War II, ski troops were heavily afflicted with trenchfoot and frostbite from continuously wet, cold feet—until both problems were spectacularly solved by providing vapor barrier socks. Furthermore, Mickey Mouse boots employed vapor barriers to solve the frozen foot problem way back in the Korean war.

A SIMPLE EXPERIMENT

Skeptics, I know, will insist that vapor barriers just *have* to produce massive condensation and dismiss the idea without trying it. But there's a very simple experiment the open-minded reader can conduct to see for himself. If you suffer from chronically cold feet, you won't even have to go outdoors. Simply take a large plastic Baggie from the roll in the kitchen (or the market produce section) and slip it over one bare foot when you get up in the morning. Fold the top around your ankle, put on normal socks and shoes, and in the course of the day subject your feet to conditions that normally chill them. Not only should your Baggied foot stay dramatically warmer than the other one, at the end of the day instead of the bagful of sweat you expect there will be nothing more than faint dampness, and your sock will be totally clean and dry! (If the thought of damp plastic on the skin is too repulsive, thin socks can be worn underneath with scant loss of efficiency.)

Extraordinary as it sounds, properly used vapor barriers will increase body warmth by 20°F. I recently went off for an all-day climb in the January Sierra at 8–9000 feet with Baggies on my feet and nothing to protect my torso but a 6-ounce vapor barrier shirt, a 6-ounce fishnet shirt and a 7-ounce nylon windshell—no sweater, wool shirt, or insulated parka. Though it was after sunset when I returned to the cabin, by staying relatively active and carefully controlling my skin temperature by ventilation, I had managed to stay comfortable and warm all day.

Sound too good to be true? The only catch, as already mentioned, is that a vapor barrier must be kept close to the skin, with no more than one thin layer underneath. If the fabric is not kept comparatively warm, the temperature differential will invite condensation, as with waterproof outer garments. Because the vapor barrier principle contradicts all we've been told about keeping dry it takes some getting used to in the field, and when temperatures are mild the system's great efficiency makes overheating easy. But that's not the sodden problem it is with breathability. When you cross the line from water vapor to sweat, you know it instantly inside a vapor barrier. But since coated fabrics absorb no moisture,

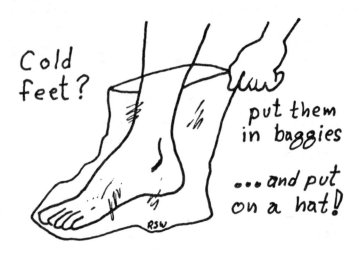

ventilation quickly dries both fabric and body, and outer clothing remains perfectly dry.

VB Virtues

Not only do vapor barriers work best when conditions are worst, they are featherweight, cheap, low on bulk, and versatile. The best applications are socks, shirts, sleeping bag liners, gloves, and pants, most of which can be made at home. And while marvelously adjustable VB shirts can be bought, a plastic dry cleaning or garbage bag (with appropriate holes snipped for head and arms) will work wonders beneath a sweater when skiing in the wind. A VB shirt will double as a windbreaker and even triple as raingear in an unexpected shower, and I know of no more valuable emergency or survival garment.

The role of ventilation in breathability and vapor barrier principles tends to contrast them further. Ventilation is essential to the escape of any significant amount of moisture in breathable fabrics, but it does so at the expense of body heat and dampened insulation. The colder it is, the more insulation and ventilation are needed, and the greater the heat loss. Vapor barriers, on the other hand, require ventilation only in mild weather or when exertion raises skin temperature near the sweat level. But at no time does this ventilation cost needed body heat or dampen insulation.

BLOTTERS

The third strategy employed by clothing designers is temporary moisture storage (the blotter). Materials have varying capacities for storing the water vapor continually exuded by the body. In order of increasing capacity, cotton, wool, and open-celled foam can sponge up considerable quantities before saturation occurs and body wetting takes place. This capacity is often represented as an asset, ignoring the fact that the fabric must be dried and water weight must be carried in the meantime. It is likewise overlooked that once saturation occurs the slow drying that follows (especially in wool and cotton) can mean severe evaporative chilling with enormous heat loss.

But blotters aren't all bad. When you're not wearing vapor barriers—they're only useful when it's cold—dampening of clothing by perspiration is inevitable. So it makes good sense to try and wick it away from the body, to disperse it as widely as possible to speed drying. Cotton and wool are good blotters but give up water slowly and reluctantly. Avoid them like the plague! Much better are mesh liners or nylon tricot laminates built into your garments.

But the best blotters are polyesters treated to make them "hydrophilic," i.e., to make them attract instead of repel water. For instance, Patagonia's Capilene and REI's MTS (Moisture Transport System), among others, don't absorb water, but they rapidly spread it out along the fabric by wicking action. This swift water dispersal greatly speeds up drying as body heat and ventilation evaporate the damp (not drenched) fabric.

Having observed the body's needs and its strategies for self-protection, as well as the principles devised to cope with them, it should now be easier to understand and evaluate the fabrics and insulators out of which outdoor clothing and equipment are made.

FABRICS

COTTON is without doubt the most comfortable fabric on the skin, and the most popular and familiar. But part of its appeal comes from its gradual absorption of sweat, and the comfort only lasts until the fabric is wet. Unfortunately cotton's water holding capacity is low and when cotton becomes saturated it sticks wetly to the skin, loses all its insulating value and is slow to dry, often chilling the body for hours by evaporative cooling. Cotton is comparatively heavy and weak, tears easily, and rots or mildews readily if allowed to stay wet. Although it sews easily and accepts most water repellents, it is usually a poor choice for either clothing or equipment where the climate is difficult or conditions demanding.

WOOL is best known for its warmth and springiness. The stiff, resilient fibers resist crushing and compaction from wetting, giving wool a reputation as a good insulator even when wet. It absorbs more water before saturation than cotton or any other fabric, but when finally wet (like cotton) its comfort drops and its extremely slow drying can mean a long period of uselessness or chilly evaporative cooling. The net result is negative as far as wool's value for outdoor clothing (except socks) is concerned, except in moderate and dry climates (or over vapor barrier shirts). Compared to other insulators, wool is heavy and bulky to carry.

NYLON has become the premier outdoor fabric because it offers great strength, toughness, light weight, elasticity, permeability, and freedom from mildew. Its smooth uniform fibers makes possible tight weaves that are windproof without coatings. Once slippery and unpleasant against the skin, nylon now can be made as comfortable as the finest cotton flannel. Among its remaining drawbacks, nylon's smoothness makes it hard to sew, it is subject to quick unraveling if edges are not heat sealed, it resists repellents, and even tight weaves pass rain quickly. But since the fibers are non-absorbent, nylon dries quickly with minimal heat stealing evaporative cooling.

RIPSTOP NYLON is a weave designed for increased tear resistance. Every 200 threads a group of larger, stronger fibers make a ridge to somewhat inhibit long tears, accounting for the characteristic checkerboard pattern. NYLON TAFFETA, now more common than ripstop, is used where light weight and tight weave are most important. Most light nylon fabrics are either ripstop or taffeta, and the minor differences between them are insignificant. NYLON DUCK or PACKCLOTH is a heavier weave fabric, often with a waterproof coating, for tent floors, pack bags, and gaiters. It has largely been replaced by CORDURA in recent years, a nubby nylon weave designed to look like cotton duck and resist abrasion. Cordura's success is due mostly to its cosmetic appeal since it is weaker than duck and harder to waterproof. TASLAN is a new light fabric of kinky nylon fibers designed to look and feel like sueded cotton and thus improve nylon's image and comfort. TRICOT is still another nylon knit, used mostly as a liner.

POLYESTERS (like Dacron) are nearly as strong as nylon and their lower elasticity makes them ideal as a mildew-proof thread for stitching all types of fabrics. They are also used in various forms and blends to produce fabrics of all sorts. They do not wet, absorb, or wick water. Polyester is commonly blended with cotton to provide greater strength, rot resistance, and reduced cost.

FABRIC COATINGS

GORETEX is a film, not a fabric. Because it is thin and fragile it must be laminated (sandwiched) between two conventional fabrics for protection in most applications. This makes the laminates comparatively stiff and heavy, and the glue inside sometimes makes them crinkly. Because claims for Goretex are extravagant and because it's being sold for everything but underwear, it merits a close look. To obtain the magic film, all manufacturers must purchase the fabrics to be sandwiched and ship them to the Goretex factory in Maryland for lamination. By the time it's shipped back and made into gear the cost has risen 2–300% above that for conventionally coated fabric! And the weight has doubled! Goretex in a parka commonly adds $50 to the price and a pound to the weight.

The claim for Goretex is that it's impervious to liquid water's large molecules, but readily passes the much smaller water vapor molecules. And as various tests demonstrate, it does exactly that—in the lab. The mistake is in projecting this level of performance to clothing and equipment used by humans in the outdoors. It's one thing to say Goretex film *can* pass water vapor; it's quite another to say a significant portion of insensible perspiration from the body *will* find its way through. As far as breathability is concerned, Goretex is no better than the fabrics it's glued to, in fact it's usually only half as good. Since none of the fabrics we've examined is really breathable to begin with, Goretex cannot pass significant amounts of body-generated water vapor. And neither partial nor diffusion pressure have a fraction of the force necessary to help it along. The sad truth is that so-called breathable fabrics often pass moisture in a cruder fashion. Vapor condenses to water on the inside of the fabric, wicks its way through, then evaporates on the outside, stealing considerable body heat in the process.

Fabrics worn well beyond the range of body heat are generally cold, causing water vapor to condense, which means Goretex (like vapor barrier clothing) must be worn close to the body to stay warm enough to prevent condensation. Put several layers of clothing (or several inches of insulation) between Goretex and the skin and all the problems of breathability are magnified, not solved. Goretex also fails to breathe when wet. Those tiny pores which won't pass water are (not surprisingly) sealed closed when the fabric is covered by a film of water in hard rain, trapping body water vapor inside.

The claim that Goretex is waterproof stands up better. Goretex made before 1978-9 often leaked like a sieve for no apparent reason, and many kinds of contamination (food, dirt, bug dope, sweat, and sunburn cream, etc.) also caused it to pass water. But a new improved product (unofficially known as Goretex II) apparently has solved the contamination problem, though at the expense, it is reported, of a further decrease in the porosity of the film.

Despite these limitations, Goretex laminates generally shed water, are exceptionally windproof, and permit the passage of some water vapor under ideal conditions and in reasonable applications.

Gore's monopoly on what is essentially a film of stretched, glued Teflon has come to an end. There are several other brands with the same attributes and drawbacks. All are worthwhile in such limited applications as bivy sacks, gaiter tops, unlined mild weather rain and wind shells, and waterproof protective coverings for down sleeping bags and garments—providing the buyer is willing to accept the substantial extra cost and weight.

SEALERS (fabric coatings) such as urethane, polymer fluorocarbons, and neoprene do not claim to breathe. Their continuous films are tougher than Goretex and therefore do not need to be sandwiched between fabrics. They are largely waterproof until punctured or abraded. Double-coated fabrics are better sealed and tougher, but half again as heavy. REPELLENTS do not seal fabric pores. Like Goretex they allow some water vapor to pass (and usually some water, too). Unfortunately, the best repellents (like Zepel), which are applied at the factory, will survive only 2–3 washings, and aerosol silicone-based spray-ons (like "Campdri") last only a few weeks in heavy weather. Fortunately, however, they can easily be renewed with a quick spray job. The spray can even make old leaky Goretex garments usable in the rain!

INSULATION

While fabrics have various functions, insulation has just one: prevention of body heat loss in the cold. Since motionless air effectively prevents conductive and convective heat movement, all insulating materials for weight-conscious backpackers are built on the principle of small dead air spaces (since both the weight and price of air are low). It has been accurately determined that each pocket of air should have no dimension greater than $\frac{1}{4}$ inch. Larger pockets in materials that flex permit detrimental convective air circulation. (The quarter-inch rule explains why air mattresses, which allow free air circulation, transmit ground cold while foam pads don't.) The effectiveness of any insulation is determined by its thermal conductivity and thickness. In declining order of efficiency, they are closed-cell foams (dead air), Thinsulate, microopen foams, large-cell foams, polyesters, wool, kapok. Since there is little variation between these materials, effective thickness is what counts, with the emphases on "effective."

Using a rough rule of thumb, at 20°F it takes a quarter inch of insulation to keep a laborer warm while working. When he's loafing it takes an inch, and when he's sleeping he needs 2–3 inches. WOOL we've already looked at as a fabric. Its weight and bulk prevent it from being seriously considered for more than medium weight clothing. DOWN, however, has long been the standard of excellence in backpacking beds and parkas, a position it has gradually been relinquishing as prices soar, quality drops, and synthetics improve.

While synthetics are largely uniform, down varies widely. Carefully refined goose down from mature European birds might fill 900 cubic inches per ounce, while commercial grades are now closer to 500 inches. Quality is determined by down pod size as well as filling power in cubic inches, so since duck pods average smaller, duck down is generally inferior, although good duck down is better than low grade goose down. Down quality is state regulated and bedding labels on every bag give a vague idea of filling quality, but the best measure of quality is loft/weight. On clothing, the buyer should rely on feel and weight.

When it comes to lightness, compressibility, resilience, long life, and bulk, down is unexcelled as an insulator. But the drawbacks are not limited to quality and price. Down's great compressibility, a virtue when cramming a sleeping bag in a stuff sack, is a huge drawback in clothing. Just the weight of light sleeping bag fabric cuts filling power and therefore insulation thickness by 50% on the top layer of a good bag. Because fabric pressure in clothing is far greater, down must be packed so tightly to produce insulating thickness (loft) that it often loses its weight advantage to the more resilient synthetic fills. And that part of a down sleeping bag underneath the body is squashed so flat, thanks to down's compressibility, that insulative value is virtually nonexistent.

But down has other disadvantages. Besides providing zero cushioning, it is difficult to clean, mats when wet and becomes dangerously useless as insulation, is hard to dry, leaks through all but the most tightly woven fabrics, and tends to migrate if not carefully contained, producing unsuspected thin or empty places in the insulating layer. The small enclosures (5–9 inches maximum in any dimension) required to keep an insulating layer even halfway uniform, involve complex construction which increases weight,

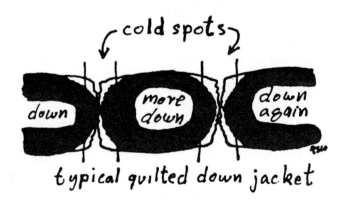

typical quilted down jacket

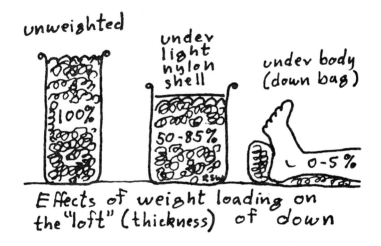

unweighted

under light nylon shell

under body (down bag)

100%

50-85%

0-5%

Effects of weight loading on the "loft" (thickness) of down

and cost. Because of down's sensitivity to weight and tendency to migrate, bag design and construction are often more important to sleeping comfort than the quantity of fill or total bag weight. A 20°F degree slim mummy may need only 20 ounces, while a semi-rectangular bag requires 34 ounces. for the same temperature rating.

POLYESTER fill (better known by such trade names as Dacron, Kodafil, Polarguard, and Hollofil) has made steady inroads in down's markets in recent years for a variety of reasons. Polyester is cheaper, more uniform, water resistant, and more cushioning than down. It retains substantial insulating value when wet, dries faster, is easily cleaned, and non-allergic, and it's far less sensitive to weight loading. However, in most applications, it takes 2–4 times the weight of polyester to match down in loft, and polyester has only three quarters of down's compressibility (making bags bulkier—but warmer and slightly more cushioning on the bottom).

Polyester batting tends to be better than down for clothing but troublesome and weak in sleeping bag construction. Down pods, by comparison, are individual and free. Down is easily blown or stuffed into pre-formed sleeping bag tubes but is difficult to manage in garments, suggesting why down is more effective in bags (on top, at least) while polyester is often superior in insulated clothing. Though polyester's history is still short, there is solid evidence that its effective lifespan is short. Bags are often returned after only a season or two of use because the filling has matted and flattened to a uselessly thin layer that refuses to expand; and the price of polyester moves steadily upward.

In the early 1970s down's drawbacks stirred sleeping bag makers to seriously investigate two synthetic alternatives: polyester and polyurethane foam. When the time came to tool up they put their money on polyester. I think they made a mistake, but foam may yet have its day. This spongelike material (which has largely replaced air mattresses because of its excellent cushioning and insulating characteristics), springs back to its original loft more quickly than polyester or down, and is virtually unaffected by fabric weight loading. Weight for a given loft is comparable to polyester, even though existing foams are far from the materials' potential. Foam is ridiculously simple to fabricate into bags and its insulative value is less affected by wetting. When soaked it wrings out easily and evaporation completes the drying process rapidly. But foam's greatest virtue is its uniformity. Combined with its stubborn springiness this provides dependable insulation without thin or cold spots. I have slept in the snow without a tent, in the wind, in perfect comfort in a foam bag no more than one inch thick, top and bottom. Veteran winter travelers know that a better bag can be made at home from one-inch foam, plastic sheeting, and glue than the most expensive down bag on the market! See Chapter 5, Beds.

Why did bag makers choose polyester? Foam's drawbacks are its considerable bulk and stiffness. Style and fashion–conscious Americans, it was felt, would resist a bulky bag that destroyed the slim profile of their pack. And foam does not nestle cozily around the sleeper like down. It tends to stand out stiffly from the body, and like a vapor barrier shirt it takes some getting used to.

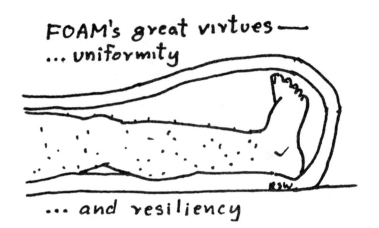

FOAM's great virtues —
... uniformity

... and resiliency

New and unfamiliar concepts are often rejected, even if they work, because their great difference promotes insecurity—and wilderness travel provides more than enough of the unfamiliar for most people.

One of the newest insulators, appearing back in the late seventies, is FIBERPILE (technically "needlestacked fiberfill"), an imitation sheepskin of completely non-absorbent synthetics (acrylic and polyester). Actually, pile is the same stuff used in the cheap winter jackets we wore as kids, but in those days it was made of wool. Climbers and North Atlantic commercial fishermen have been using the synthetic version for years, in preference to wool, because it won't soak or hold water. Shake a fiberpile sweater dry and you can put it on immediately with no discomfort. In 15 minutes it's completely dry.

Although pile is three times the weight and bulk of a down garment of similar loft, it has characteristics that make it competitive in the lightweight world of backpacking. Its ruggedly resilient uniformity provides dependable insulation thickness, even at sewn-through seams. There are no gaps or cold spots in this half-inch thick layer. Unlike down or polyester batting, it can be sewn into a garment without inner or outer nylon shells. Pile garments may be bulky and far from light, but they're 100% insulation. Without the cold nylon shell, fiberpile offers instant luxurious warmth on bare skin. (Of course, without nylon, pile is no more windproof than wool.) In addition pile is durable, tough, and drapes nicely. Best of all it is comparatively cheap. Unlike polyester batting, there is no liability to matting.

The newest entrant in the insulation derby is a micro fiber called THINSULATE, a new polyester from 3M that claims to break the insulation barrier. Just when we understand that insulation efficiency is strictly a function of thickness, no matter what the material, we are told that Thinsulate provides nearly double the insulation of down, wool, fiberpile, or other polyesters for a given thickness of insulation. And it does. The fibers are so small and closely packed that a "vacuum bottle effect" is produced and there is a big drop in heat conductivity.

But where fiberpile's virtues are magnified when applied to backpacking gear, Thinsulate's are diminished, or so it seems. It's still too early to tell. Having been burned by the failings of other polyester batting, clothing makers are wary. Thinsulate is expensive and it remains to be seen whether it will prove more durable than its polyester cousins. It has no weight advantage despite its greater insulative value because it is comparatively dense and there-fore heavy and bulky for its loft. It comes in three batting weights, all of them thin. Bag makers are skeptical of its use in beds for backpackers. DuPont has a comparable product.

Ironically, there is consumer resistance, despite the verification of insulation claims, because Thinsulate jackets are so thin. They look skimpy and chilly to a public that has come to equate warmth with bulk. And this isn't entirely irrational. Bulky jackets nestle cozily against the wearer, blocking unwanted drafts. Thinsulate jackets, no more than a quarter-inch thick, are highly vulnerable to excessive "bellows effect" ventilation unless they are carefully designed and snugly fit. So while Thinsulate is largely windproof, water resistant, and almost twice as insulative as its competition, its future is thought to lie in the stylist world of downhill skiing where slim, sleek clothing is the fashion. Its weight, cost, and unknown durability seem to make it inferior to other insulators for backpacking gear, although it may have a future in gloves and socks.

Being a booster of foam, I cannot overlook the "wet suit" foam used in skiwear, even though it may be too heavy for backpacking use. This thin closed-cell foam (like ensolite) sandwiched between two bonded nylon layers insulates better than Thinsulate, is com-pletely wind and waterproof, dependably uniform, resilient, and tough. Though stiffer than Thinsulate it is stretchier and provides greater compression resistance. Like Thinsulate its thinness makes it vulnerable to unwanted ventilation, but a comfortably snug fit can overcome that. Being snug and watertight, foam clothing func-tions as a vapor barrier as well as providing insulation. With all these virtues, wet suit foam may well be valuable to the backpack-ers of the nineties.

As fiberpile and Thinsulate have demonstrated, the qualities of fabrics and insulators can be deceptive. What at first seems a virtue may turn out to be a liability when materials are made into backpacking garments and sleeping bags for use on that temper-amental humid furnace, the human body. Specific application is what counts. Theoretical results become meaningless unless they result in effective comfortable gear in the field—as will be seen in the chapters that follow.

TWO

Clothing

Protection Against Cold... Three VB Tests...
Jack's "No Sweat" Shirt... Triple Threat Protection...
Net Shirts... Underwear... Fiberpile and Fleece... Goretex
Unfrocked... Parka Insulation... Shirts... Vests...
Rain Gear... Don't Wear Jeans!... Walking
Shorts... Headgear... Handgear

Armed with the data in Chapter 1, you should now be able to evaluate both your personal needs and the clothing available wherever you shop. Backpacking togs get better every year—lighter, tougher, and more versatile, but clothing suitable for camping is where you're lucky enough to find it. I rely on the widest range of sources—from Goodwill castoffs to chic outdoor shops—in my neverending search for ideal apparel. Nosing around is half the fun.

But before we examine individual garments, we need to consider a vital and often overlooked design consideration: moisture and heat control through ventilation.

Ventilation is by far the most effective way of getting rid of unwanted heat generated by the body. It is far easier to get rid of warm air and excess humidity by causing it to flow out apertures in garments (from an open neck, for instance) than it is to hope for diffusion through porous clothing. As we have seen, when there are several layers of fabric and one or two of insulation, chances are that very little if any warm humid air will escape—especially since the outer layers are cooler than the inner ones. Smart designers like Jack Stephenson of Warmlite employ vapor barriers and rely on ventilation, not breathability, to carry off excess heat and moisture. Jack is a former aerospace engineer who turned mail-order manufacturer to produce unique and original equipment that is available nowhere else—except when copied.

Instead of ignoring body function or trying to fight it, Jack takes advantage of it. The body generates heat, but heat always rises. So if air is permitted to flow vertically through a garment, cool air will enter at the bottom and warm air will escape at the top. That's what carries smoke up a chimney so it's called the "chimney effect." To experience it, simply put on a pullover shirt or sweater that fastens tightly around the throat and tuck it into your pants. Then exercise until excess body heat is generated. Now untuck your shirt and open the collar and note how much cooler you rapidly become. You can feel the cool air entering at the waist and the warm air flowing up around your throat.

Far more heat has escaped through chimney venting than could ever be dissipated through even a single layer of the most breathable of fabrics.

In a somewhat different test, Jack discovered there was no noticeable difference in sweating inside chimney vented jackets of Goretex and conventional waterproofing, when both were open at the neck. When venting was prevented the Goretex performed

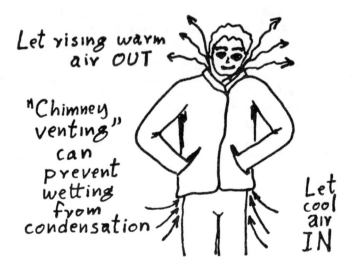

Let rising warm air OUT

"Chimney venting" can prevent wetting from condensation

Let cool air IN

better, but when both jackets were vented the breathability of the Goretex was too negligible to be a factor. This suggests that clothing manufacturers of the nineties should make controllable vertical ventilation a prime objective in their garment design.

PROTECTION AGAINST COLD

The first consideration when selecting backpacking clothing is protection against cold, wet, windy weather. In my experience, for harsh conditions, vapor barrier clothing is unexcelled. In the early 1970s Jack Stephenson, proprietor of Warmlite, provided me with a vapor barrier shirt and an explanation of the theory that made it work. I was then a columnist and editor of *Wilderness Camping* magazine (now merged with *Backpacker*). After exhaustive testing of vapor barrier applications of all sorts, I wrote a series of articles, the first published on the subject. As a result of my experiments I have come to rely heavily on vapor barriers for warmth. They keep me so warm that I now wear them almost everywhere in the winter. I don't even own a big parka anymore.

As was seen in Chapter 1, vapor barriers work because they utilize rather than ignore the body's continual water vapor production. They aim to keep you warm and comfortably moist while your clothes and insulation remain dry, completely free of condensation. The warm water vapor generated by the body turns to water when it strikes a cold nylon parka. But if the same garment is kept warm, condensation does not occur. To keep the garment warm, it must be worn close to the body, not as an outer garment exposed to the cold.

The body works to maintain a relative humidity of 70–95% and a skin temperature of about 75°F. Allow the body to maintain a moist layer of warm air next to the skin and sweat production will be minimal. Remove that layer and the body will open sweat glands wide and strive to restore it, pumping greatly increased quantities of vapor through the skin. So, ironically, the way to avoid heavy sweating (with its excessive heat and water loss) is to conserve that layer of moist warm air against the skin. And that's exactly what vapor barrier clothing does. That's why a single thin layer of coated nylon can keep you 20°F warmer than you would otherwise be. And that's why vapor barrier clothing is the biggest technological advance in light weight warmth since the down sleeping bag. And it's dependable under virtually all outdoor conditions. I've bet my life on it innumerable times.

THREE VB TESTS

Readers still skeptical can easily conduct three impressive tests without spending a penny. All that's needed is cold and a little household plastic. Probably the easiest and most dramatic test, mentioned in Chapter 1, is to take an ordinary plastic bag and slip it over one bare foot when you get dressed in the morning. Then put on your normal shoes and socks and set forth into conditions that normally chill your feet. Not only should the foot in the bag stay dramatically warmer all day long, at night when you undress, instead of the bagful of sweat you expect there will only be faint warm dampness and your sock will be clean, warm, and dry. The other sock (and foot) will probably be just as damp, but it will also be cold and clammy.

Another easy test, this time for your torso, will crudely preview the virtues of the vapor barrier (VB) shirt. Take a clothing bag, the kind in which your clothes come back from the cleaners, or a big plastic trash or garbage bag, and cut holes for your arms and another for your head. What you want is a plastic vest. Put it on next to the skin (preferably) or over something snug and thin. Tuck it in your pants and then put on a relatively snug shirt or sweater that will bring the vest close against your body. Put on a light jacket if you wish, but don't bundle up, then go out in the coldest, windiest spot you can find and notice how amazingly warm you stay with low to moderate activity.

Jack Stephenson amuses himself, makes friends, and spreads the word about vapor barriers while downhill skiing. He carries a pocketful of polyethelene gloves, and he gives just one glove to people he meets on the slopes and lifts to wear under whatever ski glove or mittens they happen to be using, inviting them to see if they notice a difference. Invariably, they search him out later in the day to beg for another glove, amazed at how much warmer it kept their hand.

There you have three easy ways to test vapor barriers for yourself and discover how, properly used, they will increase body warmth by an extraordinary 20°F.

JACK'S "NO SWEAT" SHIRT

Assuming you've experimented and want something better than a garbage bag vest, it's time to look at commercially made vapor barrier shirts. Until vapor barriers "catch on," there's only one. Jack Stephenson's No Sweat shirt weighs 6 ounces and costs $30–35. The outside is a shiny wet-look urethane coating. The inside is a deliciously soft synthetic laminate he calls Fuzzy Stuff. It feels like cotton flannel and spreads sweat rapidly to promote faster drying. Because it feels so good, it's no longer necessary to wear a thin undershirt beneath it for comfort. The shirt can be vented at velcro adjustable cuffs, neck, front, and bottom.

Jack uses no underarm zippers in his shirt (although he pioneered the idea) because he believes they are unnecessary and defeat one of the basic purposes of the shirt: to prevent moisture loss. He recommends limiting ventilation to the clothing worn over the vapor barrier shirt. This should be easily removed or chimney vented to prevent overheating. The important ingredient in Jack's system is "wearer awareness." Most people, he finds, tend to overdress in winter. It is better to be comfortably cool than to overheat. The aim is to keep the skin pleasantly humid and warm, but never hot and wet, whatever the outside temperature or level of exertion.

Jack strongly believes (and I wholeheartedly concur) that gear should simplify life in the wilds, not make it more complex. Vapor barriers have a great deal to offer in this respect if one thinks of them simply as a thin substitute for one thick, bulky layer of insulation. They simplify outdoor cold weather living by reducing the wearer's water needs, reducing the weight and bulk of his clothing, eliminating the need for extra clothing by eliminating sweat in clothing, and eliminating the need for special clothing over your VB shirt. Just think of this new garment as a magic undershirt that lets you leave your heavy jacket home.

Under-arm zips help.

Jack's original VB shirt had underarm zippers (pit zips) for instant ventilation. I liked the greater comfort range they provided. VB shirts aren't foolproof. The biggest problem for new wearers is that they work *too* well—better than expected! One minute you're toasty warm and dry; the next minute you're overheated and sweating. Then you need ventilation, fast! VB shirts are not for mild weather. The colder it is the better they work. Below freezing you can forget about venting or overheating.

I like pit zips in my VB shirt because I can regulate ventilation without undressing or taking off my pack. I know the VB isn't working when the vents are open and I'm losing valuable water and heat, but when I need maximum warmth and efficiency, all I have to do is zip up. I rarely use the zips in the shirt itself, but it's nice to have them when they're needed.

For instance, when I'm cross-country skiing with a pack in bright spring sunlight across a frozen lake at the bottom of a snow-bowl, it can be unbearably hot, I need all the ventilation I can get. On the other hand, when I spent a week camped in snow in the bottom of a shady, windy canyon at 15,000 feet in the Bolivian Andes, I never thought of opening a zipper, much less taking off my VB shirt. I wore it day and night, with varying amounts of insulation on top, and never sweated. I stayed warm, my clothes stayed dry, and I was more comfortable with less clothing than any of my companions, some of whom were nearly hidden by the bulk of their expedition down parkas.

When it's really cold, as this application illustrates, ventilation is academic and zippers become superfluous. Sweating is unlikely and cold air inside the VB shirt itself would be painful. The question is simply how many layers of clothing over the shirt are necessary. It is only in marginally cold weather, with the likelihood of strenuous activity, that zippers have some utility—and then at the expense of body heat and humidity.

TRIPLE THREAT PROTECTION

When vapor barriers catch on, the big companies will offer them. In the meantime, buy Jack's excellent No Sweat, or take a hard look at your gear collection. You may already have one! If you have a light nylon rain shell or coated nylon wind shirt, you've already got a perfectly serviceable VB shirt.

As this suggests, the VB shirt can triple as both wind and rain protection. Weight and bulk conscious bicyclers love them. And there is no superior emergency survival garment. One is nearly always in the bottom of my daypack. I regularly dayhike into the wilderness in nothing but shorts and boots, confident that my VB shirt will bail me out if there's a sudden change in the weather. More than once I've been caught by snow or rain or high wind while following some ridge far from home. My flimsy little shirt stops heat loss instantly. When I cover it with a 6-ounce hooded nylon wind shell to protect it from chilling it immediately begins to function as a vapor barrier to keep me warm. With my torso toasty and protected I can then make my way home safely in comparative comfort. In fact I feel more secure with my two nylon shells (totaling 12 ounces) than I would with a bulky 3-pound down parka. You can carry the same sort of backup survival protection at no cost and less weight by simply stuffing a big plastic garbage or cleaning bag in the bottom of your pack.

Warmlite (Jack's firm) now also offers vapor barrier pants, custom made to fit for $100, from either Fuzzy Stuff or a smooth knit laminate without the flannel. But you can find adequate substitutes in the back of your closet, or at a fraction of the price in your sporting goods store. A pair of coated nylon rainpants work admirably, especially if they have zippers for ventilation control.

Two pairs, with fiberpile pants in between and long capilene underwear next to the skin, will almost keep you warm standing still in a blizzard! And a single pair, over the long johns or under the pile pants, are more than warm enough for cross-country skiing in the wind. Because your legs are generally moving, they are usually warm enough without VB trousers except in sub-freezing conditions. But VB pants are marvelous sitting around a chilly camp, and a VB suit is even better in bed than it is on the trail. Put plastic bags under wool socks on your feet and plastic gloves under mittens on your hands and, dressed head to toe in vapor barriers, you have added at least 20°F to the capability of your sleeping bag! (See Chapter 5, Beds.)

Finally, for those people who can't afford to buy vapor barrier clothing but don't want to settle for garbage bags, consider a plastic Storm Suit. It's a pullover shirt with snap-closing neck and simple pants with a drawstring waist, both of heavy-duty polyethelene. It comes compactly folded in a plastic pouch, altogether weighs 20 ounces and it's cheap. I often see them in surplus, sporting goods, and variety stores rather than backpacking shops. These cheap compact plastic garments are low on fashion and durability, but they're terrific as multipurpose emergency and survival gear.

Make a "magic" VB undershirt by snipping holes in a big trash bag and wearing it next to the skin ...tucked in.

I often throw one in my pack when I'm heading into the wilds and skimping on rain protection.

And worn against the skin they function admirably as vapor barriers. They're exceptionally good when sitting around a cold camp and as VB sleepwear, and of course they offer leakproof rain protection during an unexpected cloudburst. You can even carry two suits, one for vapor barrier warmth, the other for rain. Add plastic bag socks and throw-away plastic gloves and you're fully equipped for only pennies. The only thing cheaper is going naked!

NET SHIRTS

Net shirts are probably the only garments that deserve the term "breathable," but it isn't hard to get condensation in them, too, if conditions are right. They provide admirable ventilation, yet help maintain that layer of warm moist air on the skin that keeps the body content.

I used to wear heavy cotton Norwegian fishnet with quarter-inch holes when that's all there was. Nowadays I favor the open-weave T-shirts, polo shirts, and undershirts made of synthetic football jersey mesh or the tighter more stylish weaves worn for golf or tennis. I *never* wear cotton T-shirts, which soak up and hold sweat. Net/mesh shirts, because of their porosity, wick perspiration into a thin damp layer that gives the illusion of dryness and dries comparatively fast. My net shirts dry fast when washed in camp, serve as underwear in moderate temperatures, and triple as sleepwear.

UNDERWEAR

Warm weather underwear is mostly a matter of individual preference and habit. Some like it tight, others like it loose, but most people like it stretchy. Some demand full coverage while others insist on the barest briefs. And some of us prefer to wear nothing at all when it's warm. Nowadays there are dozens of different styles for both men and women. The essential qualities are stretchiness and flexibility to avoid chafing and rubbing, and lightness to avoid sweat-retention.

Cotton is therefore inferior to unsoakable synthetics, and open weaves (mesh, net, sheer fabrics) are preferable to tight weaves. Remember, it's no longer necessary to buy 100% cotton to get cotton's comfort against the skin. Some of the new synthetics can make you forget all about cotton. Warmth, ventilation, and protection are top considerations in choosing underwear. Take a hard look at what you customarily wear against your skin to be sure it will be suitable—before you take it backpacking.

Ladies' Underwear

Women will find a wide variety of sports bras offering firm support, flexibility, wicking fabrics, stretching mesh, and styling that permits use as outer sun and swimwear. And most large outdoor clothing makers now offer shorts, briefs, and trousers cut expressly for the female figure. Many have velcro fastened vents in the crotch for comfort and privacy when nature calls, plus excellent ventilation. If you can't find what you want in the stores, turn to the catalogs.

Long Johns

When you need underwear for warmth, you want complete coverage, usually in separates or a union suit. You'll find a bewildering array of designs and materials to choose from, never mind styles! There are suits of cotton, silk, polyester, wool, polypropylene, and the new hydrophilic polyesters, which wick and disperse moisture for rapid evaporative drying. Construction ranges from net to quilting to pile and fleece. Your choice will be determined by price, availability and your particular needs, but I recommend against the natural fibers (wool, silk, and cotton) because they absorb moisture.

For years I wore polypro because it didn't absorb water, but the new hydrophilic polyesters have left it far behind. Polypro doesn't wick well, pills, picks up odors, and feels scratchy, even though it's light, cheap, stretchy, and warm.

But the Patagonia Capilene I now prefer wicks wonderfully, rarely feels damp, is luxuriously comfortable, dries rapidly, and doesn't stink after being lived in around the clock for several days. Furthermore, its tops and bottoms conveniently come in four different weights, from sheer to Expedition. I wear the light tops on chilly summer evenings, and the heavy stuff under vapor barriers in deep cold, with vapor barrier combos in between. Pile and fleece pants and sweaters also make super underwear—and sleepwear—if it's cold enough.

I know people who like silk long underwear because it's light and smooth and slides nicely when worn as sleepwear in a nylon sleeping bag. But it absorbs water and fails to hold its shape, getting wrinkled and baggy.

FIBERPILE AND FLEECE

The newest backpacking garment in widespread use is the fiber-pile sweater, not to mention bibs and pile pants. Styles vary from baggy-looking sweatshirts to sleek models with underarm zippers (only Moonstone and Mark Pack Works). Most have crew or turtlenecks, zippers down the front, and elasticized cuffs and waistbands. They commonly weigh a pound and a half, which is heavy for only half-inch thick insulation, but worn between a VB shirt and a good shell parka they provide all the warmth most active outdoor people need, even in winter.

People accustomed to bulky down or polyester padded parkas will find the pile sweater startlingly different. Though it's comparatively thin, it won't compress very much and you'll find it harder to stuff in your pack than a down parka twice its size. There is no hood so you'll need a wool watch cap or balaclava for your head. Like all sweaters, it really isn't designed to be worn as an outer garment, except under mild conditions, because the wind blows right through. If it didn't, the snug waist and cuffs would seriously inhibit ventilation. But when you need heat retention the pile sweater can provide it. Zip it up tight, put a wind shell over it and a VB shirt under it and you begin to cook. It doesn't seem possible that only half an inch of insulation can keep you so warm—or provide such a wide comfort range.

Plush pile and fleece make attractive cozy sweaters that have become high fashion. Patagonia makes a wide range of classy-looking comfortable garments, but most of them never get near a trail much less a camp. They're worn for their style in the cities and ski lodges. Nevertheless, pile is popular in the wilds because of the toughness, durability, comfort, and dependability of this soft synthetic sheepskin. You can soak it in icewater, shake it dry in seconds, and put it on immediately without discomfort. Instead of babying it, as so often is necessary with fragile backpacking gear, you can treat it rough and count on its near fool-proof indestructability.

GORETEX UNFROCKED

Proving the success of heavy advertising, a large segment of the public naively believes it needs Goretex on its raingear for maximum waterproofing. Nothing could be farther from the truth. When it comes to waterproofing, Goretex is third rate at best! Urethane and PVC coatings are far better at sealing fabric against the elements, and they don't leak when soiled. The claim for Goretex is that it breathes, allowing the escape of body moisture while at the same time protecting you from rain. It doesn't. No fabric ever made does both adequately at the same time. Goretex is no exception.

Gore once published an analysis showing that 85% of body moisture was carried off by ventilation, while only 15% passed through his supposedly breathable fabric! No wonder most Goretex parkas nowadays are being designed for maximum chimney venting. So why pay for poorly breathing, third-rate waterproofing Goretex? Gore's imitators, if possible, are worse. In hopes of getting some of the gravy, several of them do a shoddy job of urethane coating and call the resulting coating breathable! Beware any manufacturer who uses some vague term to claim his waterproof fabric will pass body moisture. Only ventilation accomplishes that!

But Goretex has been sold so convincingly that it's hard sometimes to find shells coated with the far lighter and cheaper urethane, despite its superiority when ventilation is provided. One garment maker told me he reluctantly makes only Goretex parkas, despite their obvious shortcomings, because he can't afford to make an item that might not sell. Other manufacturers are ready to switch to urethane coatings when demand picks up, as it should when it's discovered that well vented sealed jackets don't have to get you wet.

In the meantime, garment makers are giving the customer what he asks for: Goretex-coated nylon jackets and parkas of every description. It seems only a matter of time before the word is out that you don't need Goretex and its extra weight and cost. Goretex in a parka adds $50 to the price and a pound to the weight, in return for which you hope your body vapor will somehow find its way out through the film's microscopic pores.

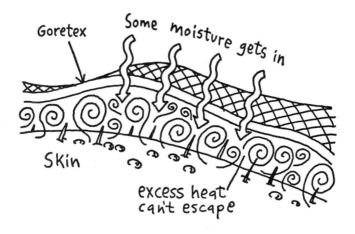

Unfortunately, Goretex's breathability is so negligible under critical field conditions that it can't prevent condensation. And when wet its pores are sealed and cannot breathe. Under ordinary conditions Goretex performs well, which impresses people who don't realize that under ordinary conditions *all* parkas perform well, provided there's reasonably good ventilation. As a waterproof covering for highly vulnerable down jackets and sleeping bags, Goretex makes slightly more sense, despite the considerable extra weight and cost. As a practical matter, truly adequate breathability in a waterproof garment under critical conditions is an impossible dream.

The bogus rationale for Goretex is that non-breathable parkas, coated to keep out rain, will drench the wearer with condensed body moisture. This fear ignores the fact that ventilation is far more effective than negligible breathability. It also conceals the equally bogus assumption that all parkas need to be waterproof. Sure, in many climates rain is so likely that it would be foolish to carry an uncoated parka. But in the summer Sierra and the deserts where I customarily hike, it seems equally foolish to carry unneeded rain protection when wind protection is all that's really needed.

In backpacking, "Better safe than sorry," doesn't always apply. It's true that lack of preparedness can ruin your trip. But if you try to prepare for all contingencies, to protect against all possibilities, you'll ruin your trip by overburdening yourself.

I like sheer unlined windshells, backed up by a vapor barrier shirt for warmth and rain, especially when dayhiking. A single layer of ripstop nylon or taffeta is all that's really needed. I have probably hiked more miles in the spring, summer, and fall Sierra in my old olive green 6-ounce hooded nylon taffeta shell than I have in all other garments combined. It shouldn't be assumed that all outerwear must be waterproof just because it could conceivably rain. One rain garment is ample in dry climates, and even that might be left home under certain circumstances.

PARKA INSULATION

Having considered all the fabrics of which parkas commonly are made, let's now consider the virtues and drawbacks of the various insulations with which they are stuffed. Down, long the standard, probably deserves first consideration. The attributes of any material, as we have seen, are neither good nor bad—until judged for a specific application.

expeditionary
parkas
are
rarely
needed.

Considered as parka insulation, the balance sheet looks like this. Down's chief virtue is lightness, followed by bulk (the way it snugs gently against the body), and compressibility (when being stuffed in your pack). But bulk also defeats ventilation, and excessive compressibility is a liability in clothing. Because of the fabric pressure in clothing, down must be packed so tightly that its weight advantage often disappears.

Down is the least uniform of insulators. Because of the fluidity of its unconnected pods, it must be contained in small pockets, usually formed by quilting with sewn-through seams. Insulation thickness is great in the middle but often non-existent near the seams. Because down pods are reluctant to work themselves into tight places, the gap in the insulating layer at the seams is far wider than the billowing quilt hints. Infrared cameras measuring heat escape have shown a shocking volume of loss through the grid of seams in many an impressively thick, expensive down parka. This great heat loss in so thick a garment is what makes fiberpile seem so remarkably warm for its half-inch loft.

Pile is pure, uniform, continuous insulation, while down is pockets of insulation with gaps in between. The rare and expensive exception is the expeditionary down parka engineered so that the pockets of down overlap and baffles over the seams. While these gigantic coats are warm, the vast quantities of nylon they contain (often four layers) make them heavy and incompressible.

But let me dispel a couple of myths. Down is *not* exceptionally vulnerable to wetting. The origin of that myth was the scare advertising of the people who want us to switch to synthetics. Down pods don't absorb water. Sure, down mats if you get it wet, so make reasonable efforts to keep it dry. But don't panic. Wearing (or sleeping in) down won't lead inexorably to hypothermia. Reject the mass hysteria created by the marketing hype of synthetic insulators. Down is not deadly dangerous near water or in the winter.

In fact, if the temperature is below freezing, there's little or no water to soak down garments from without—unless you fall through rotten ice while skiing across a supposedly frozen lake— which I once managed to accomplish. And don't believe the claim that polyester (or pile) is "warm when wet." It may not soak up water like cotton or wool, but it's dangerous to believe it can keep you from freezing if it's soaked.

Pile takes time to dry and polyester batting is hard to dry. I like the cozy bulk and quick warmth of down on cold winter days in the city, but I find myself increasingly reluctant to carry it on the trail. Having long since switched to vapor barrier warmth, I find I simply don't need it.

If I'm less than enthusiastic about carrying down clothing, it's not because I'm crazy about polyester. Far from it. There are dozens of trade names used by clothing manufacturers, but nearly all of them originate at Eastman (Kodasoft), DuPont (Hollofil), or Reliance-Celanese (Polarguard). Hollofil and Kodasoft are chopped fibers that rely on a silicone coating to make them repel one another and thus resist the matting that kills resilience and loft. Polarguard relies on the crimping of a continuous filament fiber to resist matting. The sad truth, however, is that these strategies don't work for long in the field.

After many years experience, gear makers have discovered that polyester batting "dies" in a comparatively short time. The fibers gradually interlock or align with the friction of use aggravated by compression and heat. Matting occurs, resilience disappears, and the loft that yielded insulation is permanently lost. Infrequently used parkas kept cool and never compressed may appear to last for years. Heavily used or abused garments can "go flat" (lose half their loft) in 6 months. Unlike down, polyester batting has a very short life.

Nevertheless it has virtues which make it worth considering, especially since it's become the favored insulator for many manufacturers. The batting is far more uniform, when used in garments, than down. It doesn't migrate so it doesn't need to be quilted into a series of small pockets. Not only are there fewer seams, the seams aren't as cold because the batting has far higher resistance to compression than down. Polyester is much cheaper than down and more cushioning, and it doesn't absorb water, which means garments soaked by rain or condensation retain usability and can be dried in the field. In this regard it lies about halfway in between hopeless down and easily dried fiberpile.

Unfortunately polyester has another drawback: weight. It takes two to four times the weight of polyester to achieve the same loft as down. In summary, parkas insulated with polyester batting may be worth buying when weight is less critical than the hazards of wetting and when the shorter life is reflected in the garment's lower price. Down parkas may be justified when weight and compressibility are vital, long life is essential, liability to wetting is minimal, and cost is not a limiting factor.

Down, polyester batting, and fiberpile account for probably 95% of outdoor garment insulation, but two others, foam and Thinsulate, though largely untried, show great potential. Urethane (open cell) foam offers unbeatable uniformity and resilience. It is cheap, competitively light, unaffected by wetting, and as easily dried in the field as fiberpile. Its short life is adequately offset by its cheapness. Foam's virtues outshine those of all three major insulators combined, but it has yet to enjoy success because of two problems. Despite its softness and stretchiness, foam has poor "drape," i.e., it stands out stiffly from the body instead of nestling cozily like down. Foam's other drawback is bulk, but in that respect it's no worse than fiberpile.

I have owned several foam parkas and find them exceptionally warm, if somewhat stiff. I also find the ease of ventilation an asset that greatly increases the garment's comfort range. Quarter-inch foam sandwiched between loose nylon facings performs insulating miracles in a well-cut jacket. Unfortunately, there no longer are any makers of foam parkas, not to mention foam sweaters, vests, and sleeping bags. Part of the problem is the weight, stiffness and bulk of foams that were used. Bulky bags aren't stylish. I'm convinced that a soft, large-cell, superlight, resilient, stretchy, uniform insulator would clearly excel all other materials in all vital respects. The reluctance stems largely from anxiety over public acceptance. See Chapter 5, Beds, for more on foam.

Closed-cell foam laminated between nylon skins is being used in skiwear as "wet suit foam" for racing suits. Like Thinsulate (see Chapter 1) its insulating qualities transcend mere thickness, utilizing a "vacuum bottle effect" to supply nearly twice the efficiency of the same thickness of down, pile, polyester batting, etc. Thicknesses employed are in the neighborhood of only one-eighth inch. As with any layer this thin, excess ventilation is a hazard. Closed-cell foam laminates are heavy, expensive, and a trifle stiff, despite their great virtues of uniformity and resilience. Thinsulate's prime qualities are super warmth, softness, and good drape. Its drawbacks are weight, expense, and the fact that its life and durability are unknown.

Fleece

One final material that shows promise is "fleece," another synthetic (acrylic and polyester) that resembles heavy flannel crossed with pile. This dense, woven material has a rich, warm soft feel with high style appeal because it's both warm and good looking, though heavy.

Insulated parkas, jackets, vests, and sweaters can be vital—if it's cold enough. By using vapor barriers, however, which add 20° of warmth, I often find it possible, even in winter, to leave home the insulation (or most of it) if I carry a well-designed lined parka. Two layers of fabric, thanks to the trapped air in between, offer more than twice the insulation of a single layer or shell. For years I wore a lined Synergy urethane-coated parka that was so warm when shut tight that I rarely wore anything heavier than a moleskin cotton shirt (and vapor barrier) beneath it.

SHIRTS

Let's leave parkas for the moment and return to shirts. As previously mentioned, when it isn't quite warm enough to go shirtless, I favor open-weave (net, mesh) nylon polo shirts with zip or button closable necks. For mosquito or sunburn protection in hot weather I like a light, long-sleeved button-up denim work shirt. For cool but active summer days I choose a heavier cotton pullover Ben Davis Hickory shirt. This, as all my friends know, is my favorite shirt, and I wear it alone, or over a mesh shirt or VB shirt, and sometimes under my 6-ounce nylon wind shell, or a urethane parka shell if rain is likely. I like the hickory shirt because the cotton feels so good and because the pullover design is warmer and more easily chimney vented than button-front models. If the weather gets too raw I wear an even softer cotton flannel moleskin or chamois shirt (from a variety of makers), over a VB shirt and under a good windshell. I realize that these cotton shirts are heavy and hold moisture.

There are probably superior synthetic pullover garments—lighter, unwettable, and just as comfortable—but I haven't yet discovered them.

I also break my own rules by sometimes carrying that car campers' favorite, the cotton/polyester hooded sweatshirt with hand-warmer front tunnel pocket. I take it (again) because I haven't found the same admirable design in pile or other inexpensive lightweight warm synthetic fabric.

As the weather gets colder I may wear a fleece shirt over the VB, but probably I will reach for a fiberpile sweater. I never wear wool pullover sweaters at all. They're too hard to take on and off and provide no ventilation control. Wool, once the essential insulator for backpackers, is now third or fourth rate. It provides an illusion of dry comfort as it soaks up sweat or rain, but when saturation is reached your wool garment has become a heavy sponge that is very slow to dry. Only soaked down is worse. There's no reason to wear wool when fiberpile is so cheap.

VESTS

Vests, usually down-filled, but increasingly available in polyester, pile, and even foam, can be highly versatile garments. Because they are open in the armpit, they permit ventilation while keeping the trunk warm. They likewise recognize a lesser need for insulation on the arms. Such a garment can be worn over (or under) a pile sweater in winter as an inexpensive and invulnerable alternative to carrying a heavy parka, if the sweater alone isn't quite warm enough. Vests, being a trifle old-fashioned and less than high fashion, are often overlooked in the search for backpacking clothing. But they offer an unbeatable combination of lightness, versatility, low bulk, and easy ventilation. And they concentrate insulation on the trunk where it's needed. A clue to their utility is that seasoned outdoor professionals regularly depend on them.

RAIN GEAR

When it comes to protection from heavy or continuous rain, a waterproof parka shell alone may be insufficient. The easiest improvement is the addition of rain chaps, 4–6 ounce tubes of coated nylon that are meant to be worn over regular pants and under a hip length parka. They begin at the crotch to provide maximum ventilation, tie at the waist and fasten under the instep.

The next step up in rain protection is the Anorak (the name given to a pullover, rather than a zip-up, unlined parka) that comes a little below the hip. I like anoraks for their warmth, wind resistance, and ease of chimney venting so I vastly prefer them to zip-front cardigans. My favorite in recent years has been the Sierra Designs Microlight because it only weighs half a pound and packs small, and I like the pocket arrangement. In addition to backpacking, I use it frequently for river running and dayhiking, even though its single polyurethane coating won't handle a downpour and its hood is skimpy.

If the weather is threatening I carry the 6-ounce companion Microlight pants, with ample pockets, elastic waist, and drawcord ankle cuffs. If it blows but doesn't rain, I can use them for windpants. If the day grows cold I can wear them under trousers as VB pants. On a cool rainy day I might wear them over trousers and Capilene long underwear. For maximum warmth I reverse the order, wearing them as VB pants against the skin, with the Capilene over them and trousers on the outside. The layering versatility of these three garments is hard to beat. For ultimate protection you can add a second pair of rain pants (in plastic or coated nylon), using one as a vapor barrier and the second as rain protection. What you choose depends on whether you expect to live and travel in it under dependably cold wet conditions, or whether you want temporary backup or emergency protection for unexpected bad weather. In either situation, I do not recommend Goretex.

Ponchos and Cagoules

The other garments for rain protection are the poncho and the cagoule. Ponchos tend to offer more ventilation but are so vulnerable to wind that they become virtually useless in anything but the quietest drizzle. Their advantages: they can double as ground cloths or emergency sleeping bag shelter. The cheapest are heavy army surplus, or superlight but short-lived plastic. Most come with snaps on the side. Adjustable ventilation at the neck is vital.

In a steady drizzle without wind you can hold out the poncho to keep your trousers dry. If it's windy or raining hard, you'll need rain pants or chaps. If it's howling sit down and spread your poncho to make a mini-tent, and wait it out.

The garment most likely to keep you dry in wind-driven rain is a cagoule, a cross between a poncho and an anorak, with a full skirt that comes below your knees. Usually there's a drawstring at the hem so you can retract your feet and bivouac inside in an emergency. And there ought to be hand-warmer pockets. Neck ventilation should be better than in a poncho, and cagoule hoods are better cut and more adjustable. The great drawback in cagoules is that condensation is often massive if you exercise at all because ventilation usually is poor. Underarm zippers could transform this sweatbox into a valuable garment, but so far there are none on the market. And rain chaps or pants will still be needed if you expect your trousers and socks to stay dry.

Gaiters

The alternative to rain pants or chaps is gaiters. These coated nylon leggings, which fasten under the instep, come in two sizes: shorties with elastic tops designed to cover only ankles, boot tops and socks, and high gaiters, which zip and snap up to a drawstring or elastic band that fastens just below the knee. Once used exclusively by climbers and skiers, gaiters are increasingly being used by backpackers who find them invaluable in spring snow and slush or as a substitute for rain pants or chaps in mild summer storms. I rely on Sierra Design shorties to keep my feet dry as long as puddles and snow last in the Sierra, even though I'm wearing shorts. Gaiters offer a legitimate application of Goretex to keep down condensation while keeping out mud and snowmelt.

Trousers

The trouble with most trousers made for backpacking is that conventional belts and buckles, beneath a tightly cinched hipbelt, not only serve no purpose, they dig into the body. Even belt loops and buttons may mark the skin uncomfortably. Suspenders, which compete with pack shoulder straps, are no better. Another problem is the lack of ventilation in the crotch.

After skiing one bright spring day across a frozen lake in re-flected heat so great that my crotch was soaked, I prevailed upon friends to alter a pair of loose cotton work pants for me. They removed the zipper fly and replaced it with a double opening coil zipper that ran all the way from my navel through the crotch and up the back to my waist. And they removed belt loops and but-ton and installed an elasticized waistband of the sort found on golf slacks, with an adjustable velcro-closed tongue.

The trousers have proved entirely successful. The waist is so adjustable that I can tuck in several bulky layers for ventilation control without discomfort. I save the weight and bulk of a belt and buckle, and when I cinch my hipbelt tight there is nothing beneath it to dig in. Perhaps best of all is my ability to open both zippers wide and let the cool breeze blow through instead of overheating and sweating in the crotch. And it's amusing to see the puzzled look on people's faces when they see that zipper in the rear—especially if it's open! They tend to think they've met a man who's put his pants on backwards!

Stephenson's
"Converta Pants"

At about the same time, Jack Stephenson put on the market a version of the pants he's been personally testing for the last 8 years. Called Converta Pants, they are designed for maximum versatility and ven-tilation. Full-length coil zippers in the inseam permit varying degrees of ventilation. Zipped all the way open the pants can be tucked into the waistband to form adequate shorts. A stem to stern zipper, as in my pants, permits crotch ventilation. The waist is fastened shut by a vel-cro tab and a separate velcro half belt is adjustable. Adjustable velcro-closed cuffs permit snug closure around the ankle for added warmth. The fabric is a synthetic with the feel of cotton and the toughness and windproofness of nylon.

Nowadays it isn't necessary to customize your pants. Compa-nies like Sportif, Woolrich, and Columbia offer cunningly designed trousers for both men and women that provide all the needed fea-tures, like adjustable elasticized waistbands that require no belts, sizable well-arranged pockets, roomy cut and construction from featherweight, non-absorbent synthetic fabrics. They cost more than jeans or work pants, but they're well worth the extra money.

My current favorites are Supplex (nylon) Regatta pants from Sportif that weigh a mere 6 ounces, take no room in my pack, resist wetting, dry quickly, feel like cotton, and are windproof. The six pockets are well located and the pants are so light and roomy that I hardly know I have them on. A number of makers now offer clever trousers that convert to shorts in warm weather. You simply unzip (or open velcro) to remove the legs and stick them in your pack. Other features to look for are elastic cuffs to keep out wind and snaps or zippers to get them over your boots.

As previously mentioned, pile pants are a hundred times preferable to wool if you need the extra warmth, but I much prefer to employ 2–3 thin layers, starting with either VB pants or hydrophobic long underwear, covered with windproof nylon and rain pants if needed. Layering adds great versatility, cuts weight and bulk, and avoids overheating. Nowadays there are all kinds of cleverly designed trousers waiting to be discovered. Whatever you do...

DON'T WEAR JEANS!

A majority of backpackers probably still wear jeans, despite the fact that they are uncomfortably tight, heavy, hot, and water absorbent. Back when I wore them regularly I overcame their tendency to soak up rain by rubbing the front of the thigh and the back of the calf with the cake of wax in my fly tying kit. The surfaces most exposed to wetting were thus effectively waterproofed while most of the fabric remained free to breathe, thus preventing

wax
rubbed on
where
the rain hits
keeps
legs dry
without
sweating.

condensation. Though few will admit it, most backpackers wear jeans because they're in style, not because they are comfortable.

When it comes to choosing clothing, wilderness travelers who want to maximize comfort and hold down cost should not limit themselves to the stylish offerings of backpacking shops and catalogs. Work clothes and skiwear are worth considering, too. And a lot can be learned from our cousins, the climbers. For mountaineers the priorities are different. Dependability and ruggedness are vital when you're counting on your gear to help keep you alive. Weight and even fashion become secondary.

WALKING SHORTS

Except in mid-winter I do almost all my hiking in shorts. I like the feeling of freedom, the breeze on my legs, the ventilation in the crotch. As a consequence I wear shorts when almost no one else does: in rain, snow, wind, brush, and mosquitos—because I'm happier that way, thanks partly, I'm sure, to the fur on my legs. But I've got lots of company, worldwide. The Swiss hike in shorts if they possibly can. In Switzerland I learned that if you are careful to keep the torso warmed, you can hike all day on snow or ice without chilling your legs. In New Zealand's rainforests it was explained to me that shorts are best in the rain because it rains every day and legs dry more quickly than trousers. I was also right at home in Australia where everyone wore shorts to combat the heat and humidity.

But the culture may be more important than the climate. In South America the custom is long trousers, even when it's sweltering. In hot, humid Buenos Aires, people gaped at my shorts and sandals as though I'd come from outer space. Here in America many people wear heavy, hot long pants for no reason beyond habit, or a vague anxiety about exposing their legs to bugs and scratching. While I rarely go day hiking in anything but shorts, when I backpack I always carry the appropriate long trousers needed for protection against the cool of evening in camp.

It used to be hard to find good hiking shorts. Now the selection is overwhelming. Tastes differ but beware a snug fit. It's always better to be baggy and comfortable. I like mine short with a conventional pocket arrangement. When trying on shorts be sure seams and hems in the crotch are not bulky enough to cause chafing or you'll be painfully raw in a couple of miles. A slit up the outer seam can further increase comfort. Good shorts are where you find them, and most of mine do not come from mountain

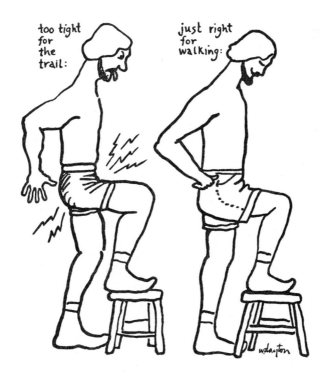

shops. Because I don't like belts or belt loops, I look for elasti-cized waists. As a consequence I often set forth into the wilderness in 2-ounce running shorts of parachute cloth or boxer-style swim trunks with pockets. Their lightness, freedom, and comfort make for great ventilation, and they're increasingly available with trouser pockets. I like mine with a liner of net or mesh and an elasticized waist backed by a drawstring. I used to wear 100% cotton for the comfort, but now I insist on lighter, tougher, faster-drying synthetics.

As backup, I usually carry a 2-ounce pair of nylon sheer run-ning shorts for a clothing change while I'm washing the others. They're also great as underwear if it turns chilly and as sleepwear and swim suits.

HEADGEAR

Veteran outdoor travelers know the value of headgear, even if, like me, they don't particularly like hats. When it's cold or windy, head coverings are vital for the simple reason that since capillaries in the head and neck don't contract when chilled, heat loss can be enormous. Protecting the head's warmth can make the difference between overall comfort and dangerous chilling. Remember the old axiom: if your feet get cold, put on a hat. The best all-purpose hats for warmth are thick synthetic watch caps or Balaclavas, widely available at ski and mountain shops and clothing stores. One or the other will be indispensable as sleepgear in all but the mildest summer nights. The warmest weigh 4–6 ounces, while light knitted stockingcaps for summer use may weigh as little as 2–3 ounces. And 1-ounce nylon or silk balaclavas are ideal for anti-hypothermia emergency gear, dayhiking, or sleeping.

For really harsh weather, like ski touring in the wind, I have devised a sort of crude helmet out of half-inch open-celled foam which I call the "Wood Hood." Anyone can make one by draping a square yard of foam over the head from shoulder to shoulder so that you're looking out a tunnel that extends slightly beyond the nose. Have a friend mark the back appropriately for cutting. Cut with scissors and glue together with rubber cement. Glue a scrap across the front to bridge the tunnel somewhere between chin and nose. Be sure foam extends down onto the torso on all sides. Although my design impairs lateral vision, the increased protection from raw winds more than compensates, and in lighter air the tunnel can be folded back for better vision. The Wood Hood converts a shell and sweater or jacket into an insulated parka. Weight is negligible, compressibility is great when not in use and cost is so low that experimentation is cheap. The tunnel will keep your face surprisingly warm in deep cold. It is even more impressive in your sleeping bag at night.

Hats are also worn for protection against sunburn, glare, light rain, wind, and bugs. Probably the most popular summer trail hat is the 3-ounce hobo or rollercrusher with 3-inch brim. The back of the brim needs to be turned up, perhaps fastened with a safety pin, to avoid constant rubbing when a pack is worn. These felt hats become cooler and lighter when scissors are used judiciously to cut holes for ventilation. Since there is no perfect hat, most people carry what they like. Some of my hiking partners stubbornly wear baseball caps, others insist on tennis hats, hunters caps, straw hats, and wool berets. All but the snuggest fitting hats should be equipped with nylon cords that can be tied beneath the chin on windy days.

Since I dislike the restrictive feel of a snug hat when all I need is sun and glare protection, I generally wear one of my collection of sunshades, usually one of straw. I also like a tennis visor which

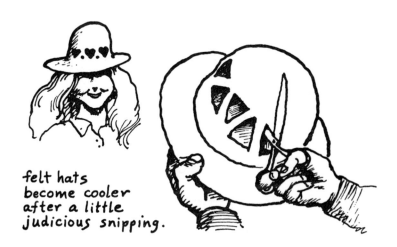

felt hats
become cooler
after a little
judicious snipping.

incorporates a useful and cushiony sweatband. My latest favorite, however, is a white lined guide's cap. Noticing that it had several grommeted airholes around the headband, I wondered if I could make it cooler by employing chimney ventilation. I got my wife Deanne to punch an equal number of grommeted holes in the top of the crown, to let out heated air. Sure enough, the hat became 50% cooler.

But the coolest hat I own is a woven Panama hat with a solid brim and quarter-inch apertures in the crown. My grandmother brought it back from Panama in 1922, so I don't know if they're still available. It folds perfectly flat, and I've fitted it with nylon ties that knot beneath my chin when I'm wearing it in wind or on a river, a necessity with all loose fitting hats you don't want to lose. And ties make it easy to tie your hat on your pack when it's not needed.

HANDGEAR

My rule of thumb says, "If it's cold enough to carry a watch cap, I'd better take mittens." Non-absorbent acrylic has replaced heavy wettable wool as the premier fabric. There are a great many weights, styles, and cuff lengths to choose from, ranging from sheer gloves to thick bulky mitts.

THREE

Footgear

*Composite Boots ... Cement Boots ... Composites **Will**
Leak ... One Width Fits All ... Low Cut versus High Top ...
Leather — Top Grain versus Splits ... Beware Mail-Order Boots ...
Major Bootmakers ... Fit Comes First ... Walking Tests ...
Quest for the Perfect Sock*

Backpacking boots are steadily getting lighter and more sophisticated, thanks to space age materials and new construction techniques. A revolution in footwear began in the late seventies when the featherweight running shoe was born. In 1979, the first bootmaker audaciously offered lightweight hiking boots modeled after running shoes, featuring fabric and plastic instead of stiff, heavy leather. The hiking boot market hasn't been the same since.

Backpackers heaved a giant sigh of relief and revolted against stiff, heavy boots. Having tasted the freedom of magic running slippers, the public refused to buy anything else. Well, almost.

Conservative, safety-oriented boot buyers and hard-core backpackers who carry heavy loads on difficult terrain still willingly bought the big clodhoppers ... and endured the endless torture of break-in. But dayhikers, weekend and trailhiking backpackers, and style-conscious street hikers merely making a fashion statement — making up 95% of the market — fell in love with the sophisticated, colorful, decorator sneakers that masquerade nowadays as backpacking boots.

But now there's a middle ground: boots that look traditional, thanks to all top-grain leather uppers that are surprisingly light and flexible. They're probably the best choice for people who are serious about backpacking and do a good deal of it.

Featherweight footwear has been transformed by some into "disposable" boots. Boot buyers willingly risk their feet for light weight. They knowingly "under boot" to escape what they imagine are stiff heavy boots. They prove the old adage that "one pound on the feet is worth 5—maybe even 10—on the back." Some comfort-oriented backpackers will even buy lightweight boots for a forthcoming trip, knowing they won't last, planning to throw them away when they return! A majority of walkers just *won't* go back to heavy boots, no matter what! They'd rather risk their feet and make lousy investments. Some end up injuring their feet and ruining their trips.

COMPOSITE BOOTS

Bootmakers have responded to this nationwide revolt in several ways. They've made more "composite" boots, i.e., running shoe/boots with fabric and split leather uppers. And they've used new methods and lighter materials to bring down the weight and stiffness of top-grain leather boots.

The industry emphasis has understandably been on composite boots that barely touch the ground, but there's been a quieter revolution in boots with leather uppers. Thanks to improved technology and synthetic midsoles, they've become amazingly

light (often under 3 pounds) and much more supple. Break-in time has dropped in some lines from a grueling year to a breezy week.

Boot buyers planning long trips, heavy loads, or heading for rough country shouldn't pass over leather boots just because they look old-fashioned (no orange flames leaping from the soles!) and carry high ($150) price tags. They're easier on your feet and lighter than they look and a sound investment for serious backpacking.

Nowadays, hiking boots can be divided into footgear for (1) dayhiking and weekend trailbackpacking, (2) longer backpacks with some cross-country with larger loads, and (3) heavy-duty rough country mountaineering boots capable of handling crampons.

Boot construction, on the other hand, is divided into those that employ EVA (Ethyl Vinyl Acetate) foam midsoles, those that use a fiberglass or plastic midsole and those few that still rely on leather. EVA is further subdivided into low density (spongy) for aerobics, medium stiff for basketball and running, and (3) super stiff for hiking and backpacking.

EVA-based boots and shoes offer maximum lightness, but the lighter density the foam, the sooner it's likely to collapse (go flat). But while they last they're winged slippers that let you fly! All the major running shoe companies now offer some kind of hiking boot—some much better than others! And new companies are constantly entering the market. There is now a wider selection to choose from than ever before. And boots are becoming more specialized all the time. There's a boot for every conceivable use. One serious outdoorsman told me he owns 12 pairs of boots, each for a slightly different purpose.

As it happens, most heavy-duty, all top-grain leather serious backpacking and mountaineering boots are made in Europe, while most of the featherweight composites are made in the Orient—because that's where the expensive manufacturing machinery (and low-cost labor) is located. But there are noteworthy American-made boots, too. For instance the Danner Sundowner, with steel shank, fiberglass midsole, glued construction, and top grain leather upper, weighs a mere 3 pounds and makes a durable, re-solable mid-weight backpacking boot that's extremely popular, because it combines support, protection, long life, and light weight.

CEMENT BOOTS

A decade ago, glued (or cemented) boots meant cheap, undependable construction. But new gluing techniques have changed that, and cement boots are now highly respectable. There are two types. The higher quality "board last" hiking boots are built around the synthetic midsole, while in cheaper "slip last" athletic shoes and day-hiking boots the upper is made first, then slipped over the midsole.

The old cement boots weren't resolable. When the soles wore out, you threw them away. But the new ones can be resoled. The boot is simply heated until the glue melts, allowing the sole to be neatly peeled off and a new one glued on. But re-soling is rarely practical in composite boots because the life of the uppers is so limited. It would be foolish to spend $30 to resole a pair of boots whose uppers are worn, when you could buy a brand new pair for only $50–60.

Since the glues in cemented boots are susceptible to melting, beware leaving your boots in the trunk of your car, where temperatures can reach 150 degrees. Bootsellers report a substantial number of complaints that glued boots delaminate when accidentally overheated. Be warned that the bootmaker regards this catastrophe as "mistreatment," not "defective manufacture." Warranties don't cover delamination.

In recent years, bootmakers have increasingly employed a rubber gusset called a "rand" to add waterproofing at the seam where the upper meets the sole, and to add lateral stability. Rands take different shapes, ranging from skinny sawtooth to uniform, and in widths from $\frac{1}{8}$ inch to $\frac{3}{4}$ inch. Some are structural, some aren't. They're valuable when they cover the stitching on an all-leather mountaineering boot, but they also add weight and cost, and don't forget that rubber on an upper holds heat.

COMPOSITES *WILL* LEAK

The biggest drawback to featherweight composite boots is that it's impossible to waterproof the uppers above the rand. No amount

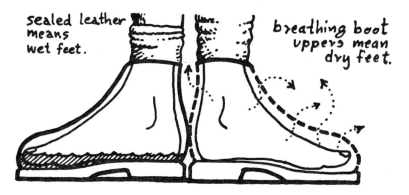

sealed leather means wet feet.

breathing boot uppers mean dry feet.

of Snowseal, oil, Goretex, beeswax, or seam sealer will stop water from penetrating any kind of flexing fabric, and the same is true for spongelike split leather scuff protectors. Therefore the addition of expensive—$30 per pair—Goretex isn't justified on composite boots, since it won't keep them dry, leaks when soiled, and its breathability is inconsequential. And Goretex in a low-top boot or shoe is even more ridiculous, since your sock is so vulnerable to wetting.

Upper fabric weaves range from open mesh for maximum ventilation—which also passes dirt and water—to tight weaves that keep out more water. Most are some species of nylon Cordura.

An unofficial boot category is the "city boot," or "street hiker," a fashion statement implying the wearer is an outdoorsman or woman. Since they never leave the city sidewalks or encounter more than slush or rain, these often poorly made boots tend to push appearance over function. Beware taking these stylish discount store, make-believe boots into the wilds! They can self-destruct with amazing suddenness, leaving you dangerously stranded!

ONE WIDTH FITS ALL

While all boots are now built around American lasts (wooden models of the typical American foot), fewer and fewer bootmakers offer a selection of widths, relying on layered socks and insoles to somehow make the boot fit. Because composite boots are so flexible and require no break-in, bootmakers can get away with making just one width: medium. In boots with stiff leather uppers, it's harder to get a good fit. Vasque boots, long made for Redwing in Italy, solves the problem by offering a choice of three thicknesses of removable insoles, lifting the foot into the upper to achieve a good fit.

Savvy bootsellers cite certain idiosyncrasies of fit peculiar to individual makers. For instance, Hi-Techs run wide. Nikes tend to be narrow. Merrells have a roomy toe box, while Asolos have a narrow one.

There's greater variety nowadays in outer soles, too. Vibram is still the leader, but the selection of rubbers and tread patterns is growing larger. And many bootmakers have their own patented rubbers and unique gripping configurations.

Midsoles, once made of nothing but leather, are increasingly made of stiff but light and inexpensive synthetics, chiefly fiberglass and a spectrum of space age plastics. EVA is the leader, being light and stiff. It is found in nearly all composite boots, a major contributor to boot weights of less than $2\frac{1}{2}$ pounds.

Shanks, too, are no longer made solely of steel. Stiff plastics and fiberglass are lighter, cheaper, and don't rust.

Getting back to the adage that a pound on the feet is equivalent to five on the back, just think what that means on a 10-mile walk. If you take an average 2000 steps per mile, it means you lift 5 tons in 10 miles for every pound of boot on your feet! So every pound you save—going from 4- to 3-pound boots, or 3-pound boots to the new 2 pounders—saves the energy needed to lift 5 tons. Think what that energy saving could mean to your enjoyment of a trip, or how it might extend your range! Instead of collapsing in camp to soak and patch your swollen red feet you might actually enjoy a stroll after supper.

LOW CUT VERSUS HIGH TOP

The notion that a high top provides ankle support is a myth, despite appearances to the contrary. The vast majority of sprains, twists and related injuries occur well below the ankle bone in the subtalar region of the heel. Even the most rigid high-top boots do not always provide protection against such hazards. Strong, durable, tight-fitting heel counters offer the best security. As evidence of the fact, many professional athletes now wear low-cut shoes.

Leather may be classed as "top grain" or "split." Top grain refers to the layer on the outside or hair side of the hide and is naturally water-repellent and easily sealed. Splits are layers from any other part of the hide. They are not waterproof and cannot be made so by any kind of dressing. Needless to say, top-grain leather is needed and used in good (and better) boots while splits, though common and much cheaper, are decidedly inferior and only suitable for dry trail use. Top-grain leather may be smooth (hair side) out or rough-out, while splits are always rough-out. But beware imitation smooth-outs. Unless the maker's catalog clearly states "top grain" leather, the buyer must assume that a split has been used. Hides are tanned by one of two means, or a combination. Chrome tanning gives the leather heat and abrasion resistance, while vegetable tanning provides moisture resistance.

LEATHER—TOP GRAIN VERSUS SPLITS

Leather boots need strong, long-lasting heel counters that grip and socket the heel firmly, and hard toe boxes that will not soften or collapse. Theories of tongue design are endless, but the chief aims are comfort and protection from water and dust. Although interior padding often causes problems when it wears out or becomes tattered prematurely, its absence makes still more trouble because unpadded leather boots tend to brutalize the feet. And padding can be essential where the foot is hard to fit. The scree collar design is important: it needs to be flexible and snug without abrading the foot, but the collar itself must be protected by the upper from outside abrasion and from excess rubbing from within. The top of the boot should never be rigid or the wearer will suffer unduly.

BEWARE MAIL-ORDER BOOTS

While some people have successfully bought boots by mail for years, the practice is more often unsatisfactory. The buyer usually needs more help than he can get from a catalog in choosing the right model and getting a good fit. Drawn patterns and shoe sizes are not really reliable; buyers often fail to discover the poor fit until too late, and exchanging boots for "the next size larger" does not always solve the problem. As a consequence, I strongly urge against buying boots by mail. Most people are better off with the best model and the best fit that a competent salesman can provide than they are ordering a perfect-sounding boot by mail.

MAJOR BOOTMAKERS

The manufacturers that follow have been chosen on the basis of size (assuring wide distribution and availability) and decent reputation.

mail-order boots

rarely fit the way

they should.

ASOLOs, made in Italy, are relatively new in America, but they have earned a considerable following for fit, comfort, and durability in a wide selection of boots. Known for sturdy leather boots, they now make a variety of composite creations. They aren't the lightest or cheapest boots available, but they're comfortable and they last.

FABIANOs, also from Italy, offer an equally wide range of lightweight full-grain leather boots for backpacking.

HI-TEC SPORTS is best known for its large line of ultra light, inexpensive, widely available composite boots, though it offers leather boots, too. Though viewed by some as "disposable" boots, several pairs of Hi-Tecs have given me hundreds of miles of good service, used for dayhiking and light backpacking. And when my Sierras came apart prematurely, Hi-Tec willingly credited me with their purchase price on my choice of a new pair at REI.

MERRELL makes an extremely wide assortment of boots, 45 models in 10 categories, mostly composites but with a few leather boots too, at moderate prices. Toes have front bumpers and heels offer Air Cushion shock absorbers, plus moisture-absorbing Quick Dry lining.

RAICHLE boots, made in Switzerland, are known for their traditional full-grain leather uppers, though they have reduced boot weight by employing nylon midsoles and cemented construction.

VASQUE, made in Italy for Redwing, has been making good lightweight leather boots for 25 years. I've worn out a number of pairs. The uppers lasted through several resolings. Today Vasque offers mostly leather-topped boots that start at less than 2 pounds and a Variable Fit System of footbeds that works—and can be bought separately for use in other makes of boots.

There are doubtless other fine bootmakers whose products I don't know personally.

. FIT COMES FIRST

It's impossible to overemphasize the importance of fit. The greatest boot ever built will be useless if it doesn't comfortably fit your foot. Badly fitting boots are still the greatest source of misery in the field. And the greatest potential mistake is being in too much of a hurry to buy them—or letting the sales clerk hurry you or assure you that the boots you're undecided about "fit perfectly." No one is immune from the danger.

Only three years ago I allowed myself only 20 minutes to buy a pair of low-cuts at REI. None of them seemed to fit—they were too long, too short, or too wide in the heel—but I made my purchase anyway. In the weeks that followed, I limped home from half a dozen painful dayhikes before I was ready to admit to myself that the shoes were too short. I tried to stretch them with shoe trees and soaking to no avail. Finally I had to concede defeat and give them away.

Today's pliable synthetics make fitting boots less crucial than it used to be in the bad old days. With the rigid all-leather boots of yesteryear, you either got a good fit or you ended up breaking down your feet instead of breaking in your boots. Nowadays, all-leather uppers don't have to mean painful break-in if you fail to find the elusive perfect fit. Leather boots now are cunningly padded, come with replaceable footbeds, removable liners, booties, shock absorbers, and optional insoles. And composite boots are so flexible, stretchy, and pliable that they're no harder to fit than running shoes—because they're made from the same materials.

when the boot is firmly anchored the fit is easily checked.

Boots should be fitted over whatever sock(s) the buyer expects to wear, or, if there is doubt, over a single heavy rag sock. In general, a hiking boot should be a little less roomy than a street shoe—comfortable, but snug. It should be remembered during fitting that the weight of a pack causes feet to flatten out, and vigorous hiking causes the feet to fill with blood and expand. At the same time, it must be remembered that loosely fitting boots will generate painful friction and lessen badly needed support.

Boots being fitted should be firmly laced, especially across the instep. Since leather is certain to stretch, one must be sure that the bands holding the laces remain half an inch apart when the boots are firmly laced or it may be impossible to lace them snugly once they are broken-in. With the boots firmly laced, the toes should have room to wiggle, but neither the ball of the foot nor the heel should move perceptibly when the salesman anchors the boot rigidly and the buyer tries vigorously to twist the foot.

Generally speaking, boots should be snug in width and generous in length. It is vital that the heel be socketed down within the cup formed by the heel counters so that it lifts no more than an eighth of an inch off the innersole when the heel is raised at the end of a step. A small allowance can be made for the stiffness of new boots, but the buyer should be convinced that the boot will fit snugly enough to keep his heel from lifting. Misery and blisters are the alternative. Foam padding around the ankle helps somewhat to socket down the heel. So does an inward taper of the boot's heel profile, but the principal grip comes from the construction and stiffness of the heel counter.

WALKING TESTS

If the boot passes stationary tests satisfactorily, it is time to take it walking. (Any reputable boot salesman will be agreeable—providing his boots come back promptly, clean and unscuffed.) If the heel remains socketed on the level, one should walk briskly uphill or climb stairs. If the heel lifts more than a little, the boot is too large, at least in the heel. Next, one should walk briskly downhill for at least fifty yards. If the foot slips forward far enough for the toes to hit the front of the boot, it means the boot is too wide or too short, or not laced tightly enough. Patience and thoroughness during the fitting will reward the buyer with many miles of comfortable walking.

QUEST FOR THE PERFECT SOCK

A great many hikers pay far too little attention to their socks. People who will spend a fortune on the finest gear will perversely refuse to spend $5–8 on the best in boot socks, preferring to take old or cheap cotton work socks camping. Seasoned hikers don't cheat their feet. They know the right socks can make the difference between comfort and misery on the trail.

Socks serve four vital functions: (1) they cushion the feet against the shock of each step; (2) they absorb perspiration from the

more than 1/8 IN. Lift means trouble in the heel.

feet; (3) they absorb friction between boots and feet; and (4) they insulate the feet from extremes of heat and cold. Socks that can do all four jobs well tend to justify their immodest price tags.

There is no single best sock or sock combination. Too much depends on the fit of the boot, the temperatures expected, the terrain, the tendency of the feet to sweat, skin sensitivity, etc. But it is generally true that too many pairs (too thick a layer) of socks reduces boot support and increases friction, and too thin a layer diminishes all four of the above vital functions. For trail backpacking in the summer Sierra the choice is generally between a single heavy sock by itself and the same sock worn over a light inner sock.

Generally, less sock is needed on easy terrain in well broken-in boots. Two heavy pairs of socks may be advisable for stiff boots or cross-country hiking likely to be hard on the feet.

As the realization of the importance of socks grows, so does the selection and sophistication—and price. Once dismissed as unimportant, hiking socks now come in a variety of shapes, fabrics, and endless combinations. While it's difficult to test a variety of boots, it's easy to try all the various socks on the market. I've got a drawerful to prove it. When it comes to fabrics, I'm dead against cotton and prejudiced against wool for the simple reason that synthetic fibers have been developed that are better in all respects than natural fibers.

But I have to admit that wool is still a useful component in a synthetic sock for the stiffness it provides—even if all wool socks are now decidedly second rate because they absorb *too* much water and hold it too tenaciously. After years of experimentation, I had just about given up hope of finding the perfect sock. Then my wife began to rave about the Thor-Lo Hiking Socks she had bought at the recommendation of a friend.

I took a look at them. They reminded me of the wool green army Cushion Soles I used to buy by the dozen at War Surplus stores. I resisted a little longer because it hurt me to pay $11 for a pair of socks that looked so much like the ones that used to cost 79¢ a pair! Finally I bit the bullet and bought a pair of Thor-Lo Trekking Socks. (Thor-Lo is serious about socks and builds them a little differently for every outdoor—and indoor—occasion.) My Trekkers were so bulky in the heel and toe that I feared I wouldn't be able to stuff them into my boots—or the boots would feel painfully short on the afternoon downhill trail—again!

I needn't have worried. At the end of that first day, my Thor-Los still felt as snug, dry, flexible, and luxuriously cushiony as they had when I put them on, seven hours earlier. To quote Thor-Lo, "High density pads under the ball and heel protect the foot against shock, concussion, abrasion, and blisters." It's true. And medium-density pads in the arch, instep, and overtoe cushion support and protect the toes. My Trekkers are 45% acrylic, 38% wool, 9% stretch nylon, 6% Holofil, and 2% Spandex, while my wife's less-bulky Hikers have a less sophisticated mix of 85% acrylic and 15% stretch nylon. They also cost $4 less. Take your pick. You won't regret it.

Inner/Liner Socks

Inner or liner socks are popular with many walkers, for a variety of reasons. With new stiff boots or difficult-to-fit feet, a second layer of sock may be the answer to your prayers, reducing painful friction. Other people find heavy socks too coarse and want something smooth and soft underneath. Non-absorbent synthetic liners keep the foot drier because they wick moisture to the outer sock, away from the skin. Inner socks need to be snug or stretchy to make sure there are no bags or wrinkles to generate blisters.

If all else fails to bring you comfort, give liner socks a try. Or add Spenco insoles of cushiony, cooling, closed-cell foam or Vasque footbeds. As a last resort, soak your leather—not fabric—boots and walk them dry for a custom fit. It isn't guaranteed and may harm the leather, but it's a strategy that's worked for a lot of us.

The important thing is to be kind to your feet by taking pains to obtain good, strong, cushioning socks that fit without wrinkles. Brand, number of layers, and even fabric (avoiding cotton) will not matter if your socks are comfortable and protect your feet.

For many of us, machine washability without shrinkage is vital. We just can't be bothered to remember the special washing instructions for every pair of socks. My synthetic socks survive the washer/dryer nicely, while wool socks, even those advertised as pre-shrunk or shrink-resistant, have often been a total loss.

And once you've found the socks that suit you, don't forget to take them along when you go shopping for boots—or you may be forced to switch in order to make those new boots fit!

Magic Vapor Barrier Socks

When it comes to really cold weather, nothing will keep your feet warmer than vapor barrier socks. The colder it is the better they work. Since they take up no room you can wear them beneath your favorite socks without tightening your boots. Since they protect your socks from moisture, they never get damp or dirty and a change of socks becomes unnecessary. What's even nicer is that they're weightless and virtually free (if you use bread or produce bags).

If you want real quality and durability, you can order nylon VB booties from Warmlite. For only $7 you get carefully shaped and sewn ankle-length waterproof white socks that are far more comfortable against the skin than plastic bags, with a vastly greater life. Just send Jack your shoe size. After wearing his VB socks once, I gratefully threw away my stash of produce bags.

If you're going to start with (or stick to) baggies, take along plenty. It's easy to wear out a couple of sets a day. Some people put on two, three, or even four bags in the morning during the winter, so they don't have to stop in the snow and take off boots to replace a popped bag, signaled by a sudden cold spot—usually the big toe. Of course the more bags you wear, the more your foot is liable to slip/slide excessively in your boot.

Baggies work best over your bare foot, but if you can't bear the thought of plastic on your skin it's perfectly okay to wear it over a thin inner sock, which will probably grow no damper than it would if you weren't using a vapor barrier. The only way to discover that a baggie on your foot will keep it unbelievably warm and not fill up with sweat is to try it—on just one foot—and compare. The price is right!

As the revolution in footwear gathers momentum, there are sure to be exciting designs in store for us—light comfortable footwear with unbelievable durability, and some of it may even be cheap!

Packs

Today's vast array of backpacks offers more variety and comfort than ever before. Space age design and materials, coupled with Yankee ingenuity, have produced a broad spectrum of clever, sophisticated ways for hikers to carry their homes on their backs. It has also left them scratching their heads, wondering which of these ingenious creations they should buy. The choice used to be simple. For trail backpacking you want an external frame pack; for cross-country, climbing and snow camping you need a body hugging internal frame.

But nowadays the dividing line is getting blurred. The two types are beginning to merge; there are various hybrids and combinations available: frameless packs are getting more sophisticated and daypacks and fannypacks are getting bigger. There are hundreds of packs to choose from. It's no longer possible to pick the best pack, much less test them all. You have to rely on guidelines to choose the best alternative from the packs available where you decide to shop.

Of course some people stagger into the wilderness bizarrely burdened with duffel bags, suitcases, pillow slips, satchels, baskets, cardboard cartons, hampers, and ice chests. On the heavily traveled trail that passes near my cabin I have seen families pushing wheelbarrows, ladies dragging shopping carts, Boy Scouts toting laden stretchers. And hikers still load themselves down in strange ways—often because they simply don't know what they need. The array of available packs is bewildering, even intimidating.

There are wraparounds, terraplanes, a huge selection of frame packs, a wild assortment of internal frame packs, fanny packs, daypacks, rucksacks, softpacks, kid packs, and dog packs. To further complicate matters there are all sorts of special features, options, extras, innovations, and departures. The prospective buyer is often buried under an avalanche of new terms: compression straps, stays, struts, quick-release buckles, ski sleeves, detachable pockets, crampon patches, telescoping frames, double bottoms, hold-open bars, zip-out dividers, sternum straps, leather lash points, stabilizers, shoulder yokes, framesheets, detachable this and convertible that.

PACK CLASSIFICATION

To escape the maze and sort out all these offerings requires some organization and classification. First of all, I divide packs into (1) overnight and (2) daypacks and specialty packs. Overnighters are further divided into (a) external frame, (b) internal frame packs, and (c) frameless softpacks. Though there are notable exceptions, external frame backpacks are still the best choice for trail travel. Carrying capacity and comfort are maximum because the frame is unlimited in size and holds the load away from the back, permitting welcome air circulation. Where the terrain is difficult or the footing tricky, the size and high center of gravity of an external frame becomes a liability. In dense vegetation the pack rails catch on brush and limbs and the hiker is easily thrown off balance. Similar difficulties are found in skiing, snowshoeing, and climbing.

For all these rigorous activities, where the body must twist and turn and balance is vital, it is generally agreed that internal frame packs are superior and safer, even though they may be sweatier because the load is carried tight against the back. Thanks to flexible, form-fitting frames, internals become an extended part of the body, greatly improving balance. An intricate and sometimes bewildering array of straps produces almost infinitely adjustable suspension, leading to unparalleled load control and carrying comfort.

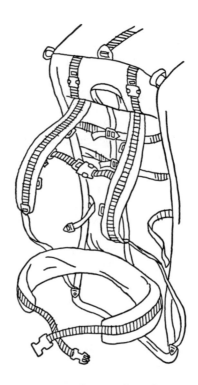

Frameless Softpacks

Frameless softpacks have evolved in recent years from the most primitive category to perhaps the most sophisticated. Once merely large bags hung on the shoulders, they have taken up the no man's land between frame packs and daypacks. Often known as "shoulder-carry" or "day-and-a-halfs," they serve climbers, photographers, ski tourists, canoeists, overburdened dayhikers, ultralight overnighters, and speed hikers—anybody who's got too much for a daypack but not enough for a framed backpack.

Generally they offer under 2000 cubic inches of storage and carry about 25 pounds. Though cunningly designed for flat, body-hugging comfort (aided by a slim profile and compression straps), they aren't tall enough to justify a frame. A frame only works when the pack extends well above the shoulders, making it possible to transfer the load back and forth between the shoulder straps and the hipbelt.

Internal Frame Packs

In recent years, thanks to cunning new designs, internal frames have enjoyed a surge of popularity that has in many cases propelled them ahead of conventional external frame packs for climbers, winter campers, cross-country trampers, and experienced backpackers. The appeal: generally lighter weight, lower price, all-terrain capability, flexibility, simplicity, versatility, and much improved comfort and freedom of movement.

Structurally, the internal frame consists of two vertical aluminum stays, usually connected by one or two horizontal braces, or two stays in the form of an "X." Either way, the stays run to the pack's four corners. Shoulder straps attach to the bag at the top two, while the hipbelt is hung from the bottom two. The stays, usually of low-temper soft aluminum that can be bent to custom fit the individual spine, permit the wearer to transfer pack weight back and forth between the hips and the shoulders at will, as with a good external frame pack. There are still internal frame packs on the market that cause supreme discomfort, but the best of the new offerings are marvels that deserve consideration for use in all seasons.

Much of the appeal of internal frame packs stems from the fact that the stays tend to flex and move independently, minimizing transference of shoulder torque to the hips and vice versa, as encountered in most rigid external frame packs. The lack of jarring means added comfort. Being on the inside, the frame takes up space and gets in the way somewhat, but internal frame packs are low on bulk, and many of them collapse nicely for storage or transport.

In use, the bags tend to be a bit floppy, lacking hold-open bars and the neat compartmentalization found in their external-framed brothers. Ideally, stays are encased in sleeves (although this increases price and weight), and the bag must be heavily reinforced at the four points where stays end and hipbelt or shoulder straps attach. Armoring leather or fabric patches and the sewing at these critical wear points are the chief index (along with fit) of pack quality.

The best shoulder suspension on an internal frame pack involves straps that come up from the back in a harness arrangement and wrap around the shoulders. Adjustable lift straps attached to the tops of the stays actually support the load and permit cinching the load snugly against the back. A back band or mesh panel attached to the pack's four corners can likewise be cinched tight like the string of a bow to keep most of the pack away from the back and permit badly needed air circulation. Other strategies include closed-cell foam over hard plastic framesheets, mesh over open-cell foam, and vertical tunnels to aid chimney ventilation, but there

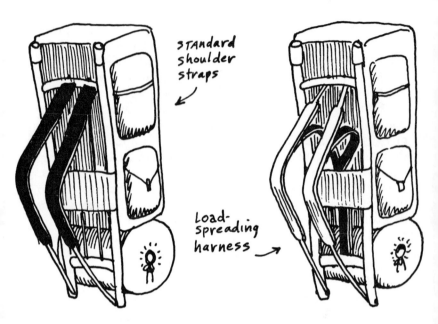

Standard shoulder straps

Load-spreading harness →

is no escaping the fact that a pack against your back makes for a sweaty shirt. To yield the stiffness that provides stability, the internal frame must be stuffed as tightly as sausage. Most proponents put their gear in a series of color-coded small stuffsacks. These are tightly crammed in, then the compression straps are cinched to tighten the skin on the sausage. Framesheets protect you from a poke in the back from a stove leg. Internals are quieter, with less shoulder slap than externals, because they move with you, not against you.

The best new internal frames are designed with belts that ride significantly higher than do the belts on any external frame packs. Snugging down around the waist and the tops of the hips, instead of hanging low on the hips, they permit the wearer greater freedom to twist and bend without being thrown off balance. And the higher ride offers more support by bone and less from working muscle, which more than offsets the slight curtailment of deep breathing—especially with big loads or in dangerous terrain.

Some of my friends who are expert four-season campers insist that the very best 3–4 internal frame packs make external frames obsolete. They claim (1) greater comfort with large (50 pounds plus) loads, (2) better balance with any load, (3) vastly superior versatility (ski-touring, climbing and cross-country capability), (4) far greater durability in the face of rough handling, (5) the pack's lower and closer center of gravity fits the body better, (6) far greater adjustability (because the stays can be bent) means a custom fit for every wearer, and, finally, (7) greater safety in difficult terrain, on skis or snowshoes or where the footing is poor or dangerous.

I cannot disagree. People who plan to use a pack more off the trail than on and spend much of their time on truly difficult terrain are probably better off with a superb internal frame—especially if they can afford only one pack. As internal frames become more sophisticated and comfortable and more and more people go camping in the snow, there is a definite trend toward these new creations.

External Frame Packs

Meanwhile, external frame packs are evolving too, moving in the direction of internal frames. Some frames are growing less angular and bringing loads closer to the back, trying to regain their lost popularity. Others are merely refining the basic design. While internal frames are now high fashion, externals are still superior in many respects for many applications.

They're making a comeback because they're much easier to use, lighter, and cheaper. And they're all that most backpackers really need. For instance, external frames average 1–2 pounds lighter and cost an average $100 less than internal frames. So why carry more and pay more just to be in fashion with an internal frame, if an external frame will do as well—or better?

Expeditionary capability is a foolish, pretentious investment just to look cool if, like most people, your backpacking is primarily weekend trips on trails. The people who brag loudest about their expeditionary packs are usually the ones who never step off the trail on weekend trips. They think a big pack provides status, but it's the other way around.

Veterans don't carry the kitchen sink; they've learned to pare their loads by making each item do double duty and they take intelligent risks in order to go light. So don't dismiss the external frame pack because it's not currently in vogue. That giant internal frame pack may well mark you as an amateur, not a pro.

Hipcarrys—A Blind Alley?

Makers of both internal and external frames have long sought ways to better support pack weight on the hipbelt, trying to avoid the pull down in back and the lifting tightness across the belly. They thought they had the answer in the Wraparound or Hipcarry pack, in which the belt was hung from semi-rigid arms extending

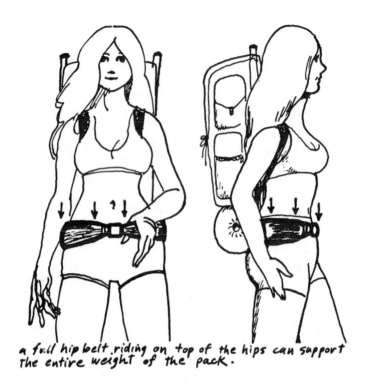

a full hip belt riding on top of the hips can support the entire weight of the pack.

from the frame around the waist to the top of the hips. The intent of this design was to put the weight of the pack squarely over the legs, in direct line with the body's center of gravity, hopefully increasing comfort and carrying capacity by spreading the weight more evenly. I field tested these frames extensively and found they didn't work. When my findings were published they polarized the pack industry and killed the Hipcarry pack. Only Jansport continues to make a modified model.

In summary, I discovered that putting the weight of the pack in line with the *body's* center of gravity rather than the *pack's* center of gravity caused the pack to pull backward on the shoulders and push forward on the hips with something like three times as much force as when the hipbelt was fastened in the traditional manner. To neutralize this push–pull it became necessary to lean about 30 degrees forward while walking! But this push–pull was only half the problem. The other half was bruised hips. On the conventionally hung hipbelt, weight is concentrated on the outward swell of the sacral promontory, a broad shelf of bone at the base of the spine that is admirably suited to bearing weight.

External Frame Advances

The principal refinements of the external frame pack are to be found in its suspension. Packmakers have embraced the yoke and harness shoulder suspension that originated on external frames, in which shoulder straps are joined in the back of the pack (the yoke) and made adjustable by the addition of stabilizer straps that come down at a 45° angle from the frame to the top of the straps. These adjustable straps not only "stabilize" your load, they cut down on swing and sway and make possible the more effective transfer of weight from the hipbelt to the shoulders—and vice versa.

The other suspension advance is the cut of the hipbelt. Endless experimentation has taught that a conical configuration of the belt minimizes the unwanted push-pull described above. Flexing stiffeners in the belt gain some of the advantages hoped for in the Hipcarry without the pullback and bruising. And hipbelt construction has grown more sophisticated as manufacturers sandwich together different materials, aiming at more comfort without the loss of support. Belts gradually grow thicker and firmer and softer on the inside. Belt stabilizer straps on some packs add adjustment capability.

Hipbelts continue to be attached to the frame in two ways: hung loosely or rigidly attached. Both have their adherents, but the trend is toward rigidity because it offers more support and less wobble and sway. Both hipbelts and shoulder straps in a well-made pack are differentially cut, meaning they're smaller on the inside of the arc to avoid wrinkling. Differentially cut belts and straps have reduced the bunching of fabric that often led to chafing, and contouring hipbelt shape to match the curves of the body has permitted belts to be worn a shade looser without slipping down. These decided improvements are increasingly found in high-quality packs.

The other chief area of external frame advance can be found in packbag design. One of the external frame's biggest advantages over the internal is ease of packing and its profusion of pockets. Designers are making the most of it by dreaming up cunning new ways to emphasize the fact that you can literally throw your gear in an external frame and take off. Just toss the big things in the main compartments, the little things in the endless pockets, zip the zippers, close the lid—and go.

USE DETERMINES CHOICE

The trends in pack design may or may not be helpful when it comes to choosing what pack to buy. As with all other gear, what you need depends on how you expect to use it. And as with choosing boots, nothing is more important than fit. The best available pack that suits your purposes will be superior to the world's greatest pack that just isn't comfortable. People are built differently and they walk differently. What's comfortable for you may not suit your twin brother. Don't buy a mail-order pack unless you (and the manufacturer) are prepared for you to ship it back for a refund.

Keeping availability and fit in mind, the field can be narrowed by considering intended use, size (capacity), weight, durability, price, and cosmetic appeal. (Packs are impressively styled and, unfortunately, many people buy on the basis of name, fashionable profile, or the profusion of clever compartments.)

In terms of use, external aluminum frames carry the largest loads, provide the most comfortable ride (in terms of ventilation) on trails, cost most, weigh most, and usually provide the most accessories and conveniences—generally speaking. Internal frame packs are second in comfort, capacity, cost, and weight. They bring the load closer (partially against the body), flex with the body to some extent and are therefore less apt to throw the wearer off balance as he climbs, skis, bushwacks, or boulder hops. They are hotter and usually carry less, but they're decidedly cheaper, lighter, and safer when balance or

As both internal and external frames are refined, the area of overlap between them grows, so that many snow campers are happy with huge capacity external frame packs, and an increasing number of clever internal frame packs are being successfully used for summer backpacking, even on trails. Of course not everyone who packs under a wide range of conditions can afford two packs! Once the choice is made between internal or external frame, pack capacity should be considered.

There has been a tendency in recent years, with the influx of newcomers, for packs to get larger and larger—because people buy them. They then proceed to fill them up with gadgets, extra protection, spare this and essential that, no matter how far they're going or how long they stay out. Not surprisingly, they feel like pack mules on the trail. I can't tell you exactly what to take, but most people could get along with less. And many would enjoy their trips more if they simplified their wilderness lifestyle. Just because you admire a devilishly clever design doesn't mean you need it. Unless you plan long distance trekking or expedition travel, you may be better off if you're limited financially. The simpler packs also weigh less. Packs have gotten steadily heavier because very few manufacturers worry much about weight—chiefly because their customers don't.

TEST THAT PACK

Pack-frame joints:

Brazed is poor

arc welded is better.

When you've made the appropriate decisions on use, size, weight, and cost and are ready to scrutinize the models actually available, there are a number of ways you can evaluate quality, durability, features, and other attributes. With an external frame pack, the place to begin is with the frame itself, especially the joints.

Joints have always been the weakest, most vulnerable parts of aluminum frames. Some makers have chosen to bolt or clamp their frames together, but most represent their frames as "welded." Other methods of securing joints can be as strong as good welds, when done properly, like nuts and bolts and adhesive bonding.

To test joint and frame strength, tilt the frame to one side so just one rail is on the floor, then push down. The salesman may turn pale but you'll get a real sense of the strength and rigidity of the tubing and connections. Another useful test involves setting the bottom ends of both rails on the floor and holding them rigidly in place with your feet while attempting to twist the top ends of the rails. Of course some frames are meant to flex.

Next in importance is the frame's suspension system: shoulder straps and hipbelt. Shoulder straps on good packs are fairly standard: about two inches wide, padded with ensolite or other closed-cell foam, encased in differentially-cut rough-finish nylon duck or Cordura. Avoid slippery finish nylon that will slip with every step. Straps should be one-hand adjustable for length as you walk, so weight can be shifted easily from shoulders to hipbelt without breaking stride. On most good frames the attachment points at one or both ends of the straps are adjustable so the spread between them can be changed and also raised or lowered for an ideal fit.

More and more packmakers offer a harness arrangement wherein the straps continue down the back of the shoulders and meet in a yoke above the middle of the back. A short adjustable strap joins the strap to the upper crossbar. The harness, designed by Trailwise and later copied widely, effectively spreads pack weight over the entire shoulder instead of concentrating it on a comparatively small area.

BACKBANDS AND HIPBELTS

To distribute pack weight against your back and provide ventilation, there are four main kinds of backbands. Best for warm weather are the full-frame mesh panel or the mesh backband. The old standby is one or two 6-inch nylon back bands, and a few makers pad them with foam. Beware the suspension system in which a low padded backband doubles as the back section of the hipbelt.

The hipbelt, the biggest boon to carrying comfort since the invention of the aluminum frame, is now standard equipment on all decent overnight framed packs. But there is considerable variety as pack makers experiment and refine. They range from two web straps from the lower pack rails (primitive) to gigantic floating belts of complex construction. Functionally, the aim of all belts is to allow all or part of the load to be transferred from the shoulders to the buttocks, pelvis, and legs.

As mentioned earlier, there are two schools of thought on mounting conventional hipbelts. Free-floating belts are most common, but the newer rigidly attached belts have considerable appeal. The former may be more comfortable; the latter provide more control and support. Any hipbelt, however hung, should offer a velcro closure (increasingly popular) or quick-release buckle that allows the pack to be instantly jettisoned with one hand during a fall to minimize the chance of injury. Belt tightness must be easily adjustable as you walk to facilitate the weight shift between hips and shoulders that prevents premature tiring. Hipbelt padding, once a luxury, should be regarded as essential for carrying comfort.

GETTING A PROPER FIT

Nothing is more crucial to pack selection than fit. When you go shopping for a pack, wear the trousers you'll use on the trail—for the same reason you wore trail socks when shopping for boots. The waist needs to be snug, without a bulky belt (beltless is best, providing the working of the hipbelt won't gradually pull your pants off). You might also bring along your favorite hat, to make sure the pack won't prevent you from wearing it. If you have a choice, favor establishments that offer more than one brand and that provide experienced, patient salesmen who feel a responsibility to see that you get a good fit. Don't be bashful about asking for help. You need it and you're paying for it! Beware a pack seller who doesn't have a supply of sandbags with which to load his test packs. He also needs rocks, slopes, or stairways or the like to simulate going up and down hill.

In a properly fitting loaded external frame pack, the shoulder straps should meet the frame on a level with the shoulder top or slightly above it, and you should be able to hunch your shoulders high enough to lift the unfastened hipbelt easily into the ideal position for tightening. Conversely, when the hipbelt is snugged moderately tight it should accept the full weight of the loaded pack when all weight is taken from the shoulders. Bend over as you lift one knee toward your forehead to test for hipbelt pinch on your stomach.

If the frame is too short, it will either be impossible to get all of the weight off the shoulders, or to do so will drop the crossbar well below the shoulders, causing the pack to ride low and away from the back. The pack may bang the back of your head, and you can't get the shoulder straps and hipbelt far enough apart to transfer weight. Or the shoulder straps are too short, even when let out all the way.

If the frame is too long it will be impossible to fasten the hipbelt high enough to support weight unless the shoulder straps are abnormally tight. The top flops around on the shoulders or the shoulder straps bottom out uselessly. Straps should be set wide enough so they don't pinch, but not so wide that they slide off the shoulders. Mounted too high, they pull back hard on the front of your shoulders.

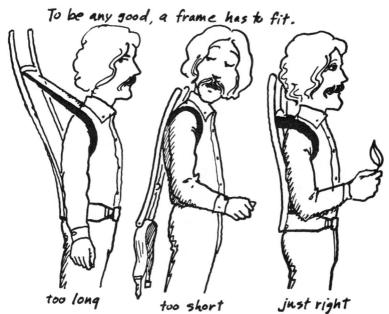

To be any good, a frame has to fit.

too long   too short   just right

Mounted too low, they won't release enough to transfer pack weight to the hipbelt. Fine tune with stabilizers (load lifters). Tighten them to take more weight on your shoulders; loosen them to drop it onto your hips.

Fortunately, most manufacturers make their frames in three or four sizes, and one of them can probably be adjusted to fit.

Internal frames are fitted much the same way because the hip and shoulder belts and straps are similar, with the same adjustments. But fit is more critical and often more difficult to obtain. Wayne Gregory, builder of Gregory packs, feels strongly about the procedure for fitting one of his sophisticated internals. He advises first hunching your shoulders to lift the loaded pack, then tightening the shoulder straps and hipbelt. Now relax your shoulders and readjust the straps for maximum comfort.

Finally, connect and adjust the sternum strap, and tighten both hip and shoulder stabilizer straps for snug comfort. The sternum strap should ride just above the part of your chest that expands the most when you inhale. Now you're ready to walk, but don't entirely forget about your pack. After a couple hundred yards you may need to fine tune the fit.

While wearing the loaded pack (try several different weights) test every adjustment and all sorts of positions. Does the frame gouge your back when you bend double? Try long strides and short, uphill and down. The pack should move with you, with your rhythm, not its own. Internal frame packs should snug against you and become part of you, but are you satisfied with the comfort, and will the ventilation be adequate?

Compared to pack frame selection, choosing a pack bag is almost inconsequential. The fit, strength, and suspension of the frame are vital. The selection of the bag has far less bearing on

— how to put on a heavy pack —

carrying comfort, even though the best bags cost as much or more than the best frames. Backpackers on a tight budget are advised to put their money in a really good frame and buy a cheap bag or improvise with a tarp.

When I first went backpacking, I owned an excellent frame (for those days) but no pack bag. Keeping weight distribution in mind, I positioned all my gear in a rectangle in the middle of my waterproof nylon ground cloth, folded over the edges to form a neat package, then lashed it to the frame. The resulting pack was as neat, compressed, compact, and well centered as any that can be loaded in today's fancy bags.

Do not imagine that I scorn the modern pack bag. I don't. I'm as much a slave to their endless conveniences as anyone. But don't be so dazzled that you forget your rational criteria for choosing a pack. There are basically two bag styles: the full-frame bag, which is a single compartment of maximum size, and the three quarter bag, which leaves room at the bottom of the frame for your sleeping bag. In external frame packs nearly all are three-quarters length, and most are divided horizontally into two separate compartments, often with tunnels down the sides for tent poles, tripods, and fishing rods. Dividers are often removable. And there are 2–6 side pockets.

Internal frames are dependent on tight and careful packing to achieve pack rigidity and stability. If the pack isn't sausage tight with gear, it must be made tight by cinching down on compression straps. First you cram your sleeping bag into the bottom compartment designed for it, working it into the corners. Zip it shut and cinch it tight with compression straps to form the foundation of your load. Now load the rest of your gear, with the heaviest items high and close against your back. Finally, tighten compression straps as needed to make the pack rigid and ready for the trail.

PACKBAGS

Packbags are either top loading or panel loading. On external frames the lower compartment is front loading of necessity. The most important bag design consideration is its depth. The best bags keep the load as close as possible to the body. My rule of thumb is that, to keep the center of gravity close, the bag should be no more than 9 inches thick at any point. Higher and wider is far better than thicker. I therefore take a dim view of packs with large pockets on the back because they tend to pull the pack backward. In this case, the fashionably slim profile makes perfect sense.

The other important feature in top-loading packs is a large storm flap that will cover everything you could ever stack on top of the already stuffed pack. The buyer will have to make up his own mind about the value—in ounces and dollars—of such myriad accessories as pockets, hold-open bars, lash points, leather-reinforced bottoms, ski sleeves, hauling loops, compression straps, sternum straps, camera rings and the like. Like the blades on a Swiss Army knife, a few are handy, but most are unnecessary. Aside from sleeping bag straps, laces or shock cord, little is really essential.

Despite all the clever features built into packs, sometimes it will be necessary for the buyer to improvise his own innovations, perhaps to carry a coat that won't fit inside, to dry wet socks while you walk, hang a camera, keep a map handy, carry an oversize foam mattress, etc. I generally carry a two- or three-piece fly rod with the reel attached and the line and leader threaded through the guides to my fly. The best method I have found for attaching this rig to my pack is an aluminum film can taped flush with the bottom of the right hand rail, into which the rod butt and additional section(s) fit snugly. At the top crossbar a piece of nylon line is secured to lash the rod sections against the rail. The rod, of course, is somewhat vulnerable in this position, but I have never broken or damaged a section, even during the many years that I carried split bamboo. And the danger, for me at least, is more than offset by the fact that I can be ready to fish within 30 seconds of stopping.

CHECK PACKBAG QUALITY

Nearly all good packbags are made of coated nylon (usually Cordura). To check bag quality be sure to examine such stress points as seams, corners, attachment and lash points. Stitching should be 5–10 to the inch and reinforcement should be impressively evident. Zippers should be nylon coil or plastic tooth and covered with tight-fitting storm flaps. Be sure there is no pucker in hipbelt or shoulder straps. Examine how floating hipbelts are fastened to the frame because this area gets maximum continuous stress.

Closely check all moving parts because these wear fastest, along with the points where body meets pack. Bag mounting is a good index to quality. Clevis pins are most common and dependable. Individual pins are far superior to the long wire cotter pins that rattle, bend, and get caught on things. Snaps need to be tested because some are undependable. Straps and lashings are effective but sometimes cumbersome and heavy. Sleeves are generally cheap and flimsy and deserve a skeptical appraisal.

I am a little dismayed at the way packs have been growing in both weight and size—not to mention price, because the growth seems based on fashion (demand) rather than genuine need. While 2500 cubic inches should be enough volume for 90% of the trips taken by recreational backpackers (averaging 2–3 nights), bags of 5–6000 are being made because they sell. Not surprisingly, average pack weight has crept up to 4–5 pounds for externals and over 6 pounds for internals. A few weight-conscious packmakers, however, can save you 1–2 pounds with ultralight models that aren't bombproof. Thanks to growing pack size and inflation, decent packs for under $100 are distinctly scarce. The average good external frame now runs $125–175, while good internals cost $100 more.

INDIVIDUAL PACKMAKERS

With this general background, the shopper should be able to fairly evaluate what he or she finds for sale. It's difficult to recommend individual packs or even companies, because models are always changing and companies come and go with regularity. The packmakers listed below have stood the test of time and built decent to excellent reputations. There are doubtless others offering good to exceptional packs, but will they be here next year? The backpack that exactly fits your needs, your back, and your pocketbook is where you're lucky enough to find it.

CAMP TRAILS offers an unusually large selection of inexpensively priced, durable internal and external frame packs, and they have continued to refine their designs over the years without getting radical. For decades I have been pointing newcomers (as well as women and children) who want a dependable first pack to Camp Trails, with no complaints. Best known for its tough, no-frills externals, it now offers a full line of internals as well.

KELTY has long been justly famous for rugged, well-engineered dependable external frame packs. They now offer a full line of light, strong internals, too. Once expensive, they've become competitive and offer a wide range of sizes, including packs specifically for women.

JANSPORT is a major supplier of external frames, a tireless innovator who pioneered flexing frames, questionable hipcarries,

Backpacking -
the hard way.

and plastic lightweight frame construction. But Jansport durability remains suspect.

GREGORY MOUNTAIN SPORTS makes probably the finest internal frame packs on the market. Continuing experimentation has led to steadily improving comfort through greater adjustability, design innovation, and top workmanship. My 4800-cubic inch Polaris is unusually comfortable with a 40-pound load and amazingly stable with my 110-pound daughter on my back, thanks in part to a new molded foam-cupped hipbelt. It's not cheap or light but it's a dream to carry, a snap to adjust, and cooler on my back than most internals. Nowadays, internal stays are pre-bent to fit 95% of buyers, not custom bent in the store by a salesman.

DANA DESIGNS, like Gregory, makes only internal frame packs. Instead of two stays, Dana employs one and a plastic or aluminum framesheet to positively protect the wearer's back from being poked by a stove leg. Otherwise designs are similar to Gregory's, reflecting the fact that the two owners are longtime friends as well as competitors. Everywhere I go I meet people who rave about Dana internals, and some of them are pros.

LOWE ALPINE SYSTEMS completes the big three of internal frame packs. Lowe pioneered many of today's standard features, and it continues to contribute innovation, not gimmicks. Adjustability, wide selection, workmanship, and dependability are excellent. My wife and I have long been delighted with our capacious Lowe fannypacks, and she loves her frameless Walkabout for extended dayhikes.

MOUNTAINSMITH is the newest contributor of quality internal frames, stressing comfort, fit, stability, and utility.

Good internal frames are also made by NORTH FACE, OSPREY, MILLET, REI, and McHALE. And Coleman packs have improved mightily. There are doubtless other makers of decent—even excellent—packs of all kinds.

DAYPACKS

Packs designed for dayhiking—often as extensions of a backpacking trip—are so numerous and similar that no one has ever cataloged them all. The tear-dropped shape has for years been most popular because it keeps the load close to the back and provides decent ventilation, but there are excellent rectangular designs, too, which offer more capacity. The things to look for in a daypack are padded, adjustable shoulder straps, quality sewing, reinforcement of stress points, effective zipper covers, and coated nylon fabric. As with overnight packs, a flat profile is greatly to be preferred to a deep pack which will tend to pull you backward. There are a variety of ways the bag may be divided and zippers placed, none of which is best for all occasions, although two compartment bags are preferred by most hikers.

Because I sometimes need to hang a bulky jacket on my pack, I find an attachment point on top essential. And a carrying loop is useful for times when I want to dry off my sweaty back and pack but keep on moving. Most important of all, of course, is a comfortable fit. Don't buy a daypack without trying it, loaded. Because some have poorly designed shoulder straps, even a lightly loaded daypack can be irritatingly uncomfortable. If you want those dayhiking miles to be pleasant, you'll have to exercise some care in making your choice. Another source of daypacks on backpacking trips is the removable/convertible top pocket increasingly found on the fancier internal frame packs. You'll have to exercise some care in making a choice.

Don't buy a daypack if what you need is a child's pack for overnight travel. If you want your children to enjoy the trip, you have to make them comfortable on the trail. Kelty, Jansport, and Camp Trails all make good child-sized frames and softpacks with varying capacities for different age ranges. Fit and comfort are even more important in kid's packs. Take the trouble to make sure that shoulder straps don't rub or chafe and that hipbelts will stay up and support. Adjustability may be important for a good fit. A decent pack can make the difference between your child's loving the trip and wanting more, and hating the outdoors. Decent packs that fit well cost no more than good daypacks and may be an even better investment.

In recent years I have developed an affection for fannypacks because they sit closer to the body, do not swing like a daypack, leave my shoulders free, and my back sweat-free. The pack's center of gravity is lower and the minimal weight is so easily supported by the sacral promontory that I'm scarcely aware I'm wearing a pack at all. Another plus is that I can lift the pack until the belt is loose and slip it around to the front to get at whatever I need without taking it off or even loosening the belt.

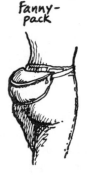

Fanny-pack

In fact it's perfectly feasible to wear two fannypacks, one in front and one in back to increase capacity, or one or two belt packs or pouches can be worn in front. Since fannypacks have been growing in popularity, the selection has been increasing, designs are being refined, and larger volume models are now available. Especially if it's warm enough to go shirtless, I enjoy a day outing far more with a compact fannypack that I do with a pack I wear on my shoulders.

Belt-pack

In winter or for a week's extended day-hikes, I'm happy with a teardrop daypack. Fannypacks are no fun when they're overloaded. My big Lowe fannypack has a capacity of almost two thousand cubic inches, enough for a spartan overnight trip, but if I'm carrying more than about 5 pounds, it bobs up and down with every step, destroying my rhythm.

A lightly loaded fannypack lets you float up the trail without a care. I can even run if I want to. If I need to get into it, I just lift it to loosen the belt up and swivel it around to the front. Some people wear two of them, one in front and one in back, rather than submit to shoulder straps. But if I have to carry more than a single quart of water, I either hang it on my belt or reluctantly decide to take a daypack instead. Two quarts is just too heavy for any fannypack.

Like most other packs, fannypacks should be loaded with the heavy, dense items up against the body to keep them from bobbing. The best designs hug the back and are vertically, not horizontally, deep. Teardrop daypacks should also be flat against the back and no more than 3 or 4 inches thick, to keep the weight close to the body. Beware large back pockets, which, when loaded, pull you backward. If you need more capacity, consider a rectangular knapsack design or climber's pack that covers more of your back rather than a thicker daypack. A flat profile is always best.

Daypacks can be extremely uncomfortable if they hit you wrong. Try them loaded in the store before you buy, checking sway, swing, pullback, buckle release, and strap adjustability. I want well-padded shoulder straps, a carrying loop, top outside attachment points, reinforced stress points, quality sewing, and well-covered zippers—features you may not find in supermarket offerings. A rugged daypack of coated nylon should last you half a lifetime, so be sure it suits your purpose and fits. My North Face teardrop pack is still going strong after more than 20 years.

Beltpacks come in two distinct styles. There are coated nylon pouches that you thread onto a conventional belt and miniature fannypacks with integral belts that you wear in front or back. The largest of the latter are built for camera gear and may also be supported by a strap around the neck. But they're good for a lot more than cameras. The smallest are oversize money-belts, or wallets or purses with built-in belts. All can be extremely useful to the dayhiker. Aerobic walkers and runners like the small ones because, when lightly loaded, they move with the body instead of bouncing, even when you're running.

I have a pair of individual pouches that I can mount on the front of any fannypack, giving it added capacity for small items, placing them where I can reach them in a hurry, and freeing up the fannypack for bulkier, heavier items such as water, lunch, and clothing. I use the pouches for carrying a small camera when I'm looking for pictures; lip ice; a map and compass if I'm groping my way through new country; a notebook and pencil if I've things to write down; a knife to sharpen the pencil; snack food if I'm hungry; a handkerchief if the cold is making my eyes water; money; ID— anything small that I may need fairly often but don't want to put in my trouser pockets.

PACKS FOR WOMEN AND CHILDREN

To my knowledge no sizeable firm makes packs exclusively for women (or children). But the larger producers are gradually expanding lines designed expressly for them, in recognition of the steadily growing numbers of women on the trail. Unfortunately, the ladies' models haven't always been successful. The women who have tested them often complain that they can get a better fit—and better quality and variety—by doing their shopping in the men's (and boy's) department, just as they do for their clothing.

SPECIALTY PACKS

If you want or need to carry a baby on the trail, you need a Kiddie Carrier. Tough Traveler of Schenectady, New York offers five models to accommodate everyone from brief casual strollers to strenuous all-day trekkers.

If you're off to Europe or hitchhiking around New Zealand, you should investigate the wildly proliferating assortment of backpacking luggage, framed and softpacks designed for use on airplanes and buses. Companions to these are duffels equipped for carrying. These Travel Packs constitute the fastest growing category of packs.

Combination backpack/suitcases are the answer for travelers tired of seeing their pack frames—especially external—mauled by sadistic baggage handlers. Many Travel Packs provide the maximum allowable size for airline carry-on luggage. Features include padded removable shoulder straps, hipbelts and back panels, sternum straps, zippered pockets, compression straps, divided lockable compartments, hand carry straps, and detachable daypacks.

Pack accessories are also proliferating. The stores and catalogs offer myriad shoulder bags, pouches, envelopes, stuffsacks, duffels, wallets, organizers, bags, insulators, cases, beltpacks, boxes, kits, satchels, money belts, cargo bags, briefcases, daypacks, dog packs, fannypacks, etc., etc.

I can't resist clever specialties like the fannypack from Outdoor Products that carries an add-on daypack in its top pocket if you need more capacity. Or the Alpenlite fannypack with a compression strap to keep it tight and holsters that hold two 22-ounce water bottles. There's the Mountainsmith Lumbar high-riding fannypack. And what about the water belts made for skiers to stave off dehydration. We use the 2-liter Fanny Flasque for hiking Hawaii and the desert because the water supply hugs your waist instead of bouncing in hanging water bottles.

LOAD UP YOUR DOG

Load
up
the
dog.

As dogs become less welcome in the cities, more people take theirs backpacking. When I first took our St. Bernard, Rafferty, backpacking, I had to make, by trial and error, a pack in which he could carry the considerable quantity of food he required. Nowadays there are probably half a dozen commercial dog packs on the market that do a considerably better job than the primitive rig of harness, old towel, and handsewn saddlebags that I devised. Most dogs love to go backpacking and well-trained animals that don't chase wildlife, disturb others, or raid the larder are a joy to take along.

An effort should be made not to change a dog's diet on the trip, unless he is used to fresh meat. I once packed two half-gallon bottles full of fresh cooked meat for a 10-day trip for Raff, but after five days it began to ripen and after seven it was all I could do to empty the containers in a hole without gagging. The rest of the trip Raff shared our food; he even came to enjoy small overcooked trout. Dry kibbles and canned meat make the easiest combination; and dogs do not mind carrying out the flattened cans. In fact, Raff regularly carried home a good deal of my more indestructible gear.

If you want to go one step further, get a llama! These docile, friendly, amusing animals can be led like a dog and will cheerfully carry a hundred pounds while you swing along whistling, unencumbered. We enjoyed using them in Bolivia and now they're widely available in the West.

Whether you get help from your pets or go it alone, you can hardly go wrong if you put function and fit ahead of fashion and fancy features.

FIVE

Beds

*Needed: A Better Mousetrap... Sleeping Comfort Varies...
Choosing the Right Bag... Down versus Synthetics... Exploding
Some Myths... Fiberfills You'll Encounter... How Synthetics Die...
Vapor Barrier Liners—They Work!... Three Bags in One... The
VBL Experience... The DeWolf Sleeping System... The "Down
Home" Approach... What to Look for in a Bag... The New
Inflatable "Cocoon"... Polyester Versus Foam... Cleaning and
Storing Bags... Protect Your Bed... Pillows... Mattresses*

Beds for backpackers slowly improve as materials are refined and traditional designs slowly evolve, but basically the mass-production sleeping bag industry is sluggish. It steadfastly ignores the workings of the human body and turns its back on both the best designs and the best materials. It cautiously cranks out dinosaurs instead of innovating.

Nowadays new models differ only in detail from the bags of 10–20 years ago. In fact, the industry may be going backward. Ten years ago vapor barrier liners were offered by a number of enlightened makers, but demand never materialized and now there are only two (Warmlite and Down Home). Ten years ago you could buy a sleeping bag made of the premier insulator, polyurethane foam. Now you have to make your own.

An exciting new design, an inflatable down-filled bag, may be destined for the same trash heap, not because it doesn't work—though it badly needs refinement—but because it's different and primitive, heavy and expensive.

Production bag makers haven't even been smart (or daring) enough to copy the advanced design of the Warmlite bag with its bottom of air or foam, or the refinements of Down Home's advanced bags. Instead, the backpacking public is offered a monotonous diet of uniform nylon sacks stuffed with polyester or down. That's about it.

NEEDED: A BETTER MOUSETRAP

There's a market for better beds. The new generation of backpackers, substantially more addicted to comfort than its parents, would dearly love softer, warmer, cheaper, lighter, more comfortable, and less bulky beds. Sleeping bag manufacturers respond with a swing away from increasingly expensive down to gradually improving synthetic fills.

The bed is the backpacker's last line of defense. It's his protection during the most vulnerable third of his trip—while he sleeps. Probably nothing is more essential to the success of a trip than a good night's sleep at the end of a day of strenuous (and probably

this snug sleeper is shaded from the early morning sun and sheltered from the chilly night sky.

unaccustomed) activity. Sleeping on the ground outdoors in the wild (or in a confining tent alongside a companion) is startlingly different from the familiar bed at home. Even if there's no altitude, wind, or cold to contend with, it takes some getting used to—every trip for most people. As the old prospector I used to travel with liked to say, "A man's no good for anything if he can't get his rest."

SLEEPING COMFORT VARIES

But getting a good night's sleep means something different to everyone. Down Home proprietor Chuck Kennedy has spent 20 years cataloging the sleeping habits of backpackers. His custom-made bags are tailored to individual sleeping patterns. Whether you "sleep warm" or "sleep cold" can make a 60-degree difference in the bag rating that's right for you. Almost as critical is whether you toss or turn, and how you do it.

If you move very little or move within the bag, so that the bag doesn't roll, then it's safe to buy a bag with less fill on the bottom, because the bottom stays on the bottom. Such a bag can conveniently be turned upside down for warm weather use. But if, like the majority of sleepers, you move enough in the night to make your bag roll with you, it needs to have uniform thickness. Otherwise, you'll get cold in the middle of the night with only a thin bottom layer covering you.

Sleeping bags reflect the beliefs and habits of their makers. Chuck gives top priority to the toss-and-turners—because he feels they constitute the vast majority—and feels a bag must nestle cozily around you for true comfort. He says, "The perception of comfort by the customer is even more important than comfort itself." His highly advanced bags nestle around you. When you curl up, so does the bag.

Jack Stephenson builds beds (not just bags) with a stiff foam or Down-filled Air Mattress (DAM) built into the bottom. His

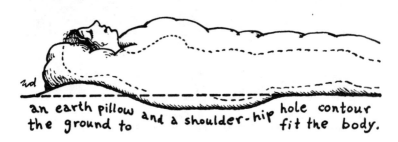

an earth pillow the ground to and a shoulder-hip hole contour fit the body.

bags stay flat, so they have to be roomier to give you space to curl up inside them. He also feels strongly about weight, so his fabrics and zippers are ultra light, and his down tubes are not over-filled.

CHOOSING THE RIGHT BAG

Picking the best bag for your purposes means giving a good deal of thought to your intended use, the way you sleep and your priorities regarding weight, price, warmth, and so forth. It's a highly subjective process and psychologically individual. We all have strong feelings about the way we want to sleep, and most of us have definite peculiarities to be addressed. We have favored positions and strict views on covering up. We're sensitive to light, wind, cold, and ventilation—as well as warmth.

Identifying "intended use" immediately presents problems. Ninety percent of backpacking is done in warm summer temperatures, but buyers dependably buy more bag than they need, looking for a margin of safety to combat ignorance and anxiety. What if it turns cold? What if I want to use it in the winter? they ask. Too often they end up buying too warm a bag—and baking their brains out. A better solution is to buy what you really need and obtain your margin from long johns, a vapor barrier liner, tent, or a bag cover.

Assessing needed warmth is just as tough. Bag makers all issue low temperature ratings, but they tend to be optimistic for competitive reasons. Ratings are only useful as a rough guide to differentiate between bags of an individual maker. There are just too many variables. And how are you supposed to know what the temperature is going to be on your trip anyway? Chuck Kennedy says men tend to sleep warmer than 90% of women and children.

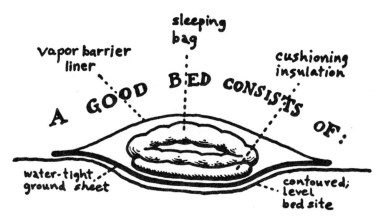

Addressing temperature ratings, Chuck has three categories: warm, average, and cold sleepers. The spread between warm and cold may be as great as 60°F (+10° for the chilly and −50° for the hot blooded). He also offers an upper temperature range, so you can rate the likelihood of sweltering. But the environment, your condition, and other circumstances can easily make all these numbers meaningless.

Consider this comparison. A well-upholstered, slightly weary, well-fed and watered, acclimated backpacker on a quiet evening in a good tent with a well-insulated mattress under him won't need a heavy-duty bag on a 20°F night. But a skinny, hungry, dehydrated, exhausted, unacclimated woman sleeping outdoors on poor insulation in the wind—at the same temperature—may easily freeze in the same bag.

Price considerations may reflect how much time you'll spend in the bag. If you're just starting out and uncertain about future use, it's probably hard to justify buying the best bag available. (You might be better off renting a bag for several trips.) If you're gearing up for the Pacific Crest or Appalachian Trail, on the other hand, you won't want to skimp. You're probably better off with down—if only for its durability.

Intended use may also determine the type of fill you choose. First-timers and casual backpackers would probably be wise to choose comparatively inexpensive synthetic bags, because they won't wear them out. Down bags may easily cost 50% more, but down bags maintain their loft a lot longer. A climbing guide who spends 200 nights a year in a sleeping bag said, "I can't afford to buy synthetics." He found the cost per night was lower in a durable down bag because synthetic fills go flat so much sooner.

Roominess is another subjective consideration. One man feels claustrophobic in a bag that seems roomy to another man his same size. Sleep patterns and likely activity will also help you decide. Body-hugging mummy bags are warmest because they minimize the volume of air to be heated. But many people find them too confining. Rectangular bags are more like your bed at home, but there's a lot of waste space to heat and no protection for the head. Semi-rectangular or modified mummies (also called "barrels") offer a decent compromise for most people.

To some people, light weight comes first. Others feel strongly about bulk (compressibility). Ventilation is vital if the weather turns warm or you've bought too much bag. A full-length zipper is essential on a sweltering night. Field-drying speed is all important where rainfall is high and sunshine is scarce, making frequent airing difficult. Many bag makers are turning to darker colored shells because the morning sun dries them so much quicker.

Other use considerations include type and length of intended trips, whether the bag's zipper should mate with that of your boyfriend, whether the bag will be used in a tent, whether the shell needs to be waterproof. Do you want the capability to snap or tie in a VB or breathable liner? What's the likelihood of winter use? What do you wear in the wilds when you sleep? And what kind of protection do you need or want for your head?

Taking care of the sleeper's head is the bagmaker's biggest headache. A bag is only as good as its protection of the head. The head causes designers problems because it's the most vulnerable part of the body to heat loss. That's because the capillaries in the head and neck don't constrict when it gets dangerously cold. The head's swiveling action drives bag makers crazy, figuring out how to protect the head but keep the face free to breathe—at various angles.

Finally, there's the problem of the constant supply of moisture in the water vapor being spouted during breathing—at the rate of 2.7 quarts per night. In deep cold a mask may be needed to preheat incoming air to cut down inescapable respiratory heat loss. Cold sleepers are often unable to keep warm while inhaling a steady supply of frigid air. They get chilled just from breathing.

Bag makers have come up with various strategies for protecting the head, most common of which is an integral hood. But there are helmets, cowls, detached hoods, collars, and shoulder baffles of many kinds—all designed to protect the head while promoting comfort in any sleeping position. It's a tall order, and there's no single best solution.

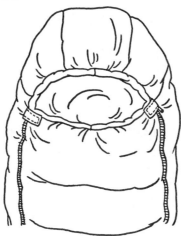

Before looking at the bags themselves, it's important to consider the suitability of the prime insulators for sleeping bag construction.

DOWN VERSUS SYNTHETICS

Down is still the best filling on balance, but it's no longer the most popular with bag makers. Down has become so expensive that it's forced up the price of bags to more than the mass of casual backpackers care to pay. As an insulator, however, down reigns supreme for substantial reasons, chiefly because of its unexcelled lightness, bulk, long life, compressability, and resiliency. Down pods compress to one seventh their expanded size with virtually no loss in resiliency. And even after a long period of compression, an ounce of good down will expand (if unrestricted) to stop convective air flow in a volume of more than five hundred square inches.

down pod:

Unfortunately, down's attributes have decided drawbacks. Its compressibility, a virtue when cramming a sleeping bag in its stuff bag or your pack, causes the down beneath your body to be squashed so flat that its insulating value is virtually nonexistent.

Because down is made up of individual, unconnected pods, it is the least uniform of insulators. Since it is capable of enormous expansion and compression, it tends to migrate if not carefully contained, producing unsuspected thin or empty places in the insulating layer. The small (4–8 inch) pockets required to keep its insulating layer even half way uniform, involve complex construction, which increases weight and cost.

Because of down's sensitivity to weight and tendency to migrate, bag design and construction are often as important to sleeping comfort as the quantity of fill or total bag weight. Infrared cameras measuring heat escape have shown a shocking volume of loss in impressively thick bags because of poor design, down shift, inexpert filling, etc.

EXPLODING SOME MYTHS

The big rap on down has always been its alleged vulnerability to wetting. I've reinforced the myth myself many times—unfortunately. The complementary myth is that synthetics are "warm when wet." Not surprisingly, there's a connection. We learned about the dangers of wet down from the hucksters pushing synthetics 15 years ago. Their fibers, they explained in full-page ads, don't accept water. And that's true. But that doesn't mean that they're warm when wet, or that they dry in a flash. Those claims are both false and dangerous—dangerous if you make the mistake of counting on them!

In 30 years experience, Jack Stephenson has never known of a down bag that lost warmth from exterior wetting. Neither have I. Rain, frost, snow, dew, or fog, Jack says, wouldn't be enough, because the down pods themselves don't absorb water. You'd have to hold the bag underwater to wet it enough to destroy down's insulating ability. So don't be afraid to take a down bag snow camping, or even river running, as long as you can keep it from being soaked. Down doesn't mean automatic hypothermia, despite the marketing hype of the synthetic bag merchants.

Now let's look at synthetics' resistance to wetting. Polar traveler Will Steger a few years back took a 13-pound Hollofil bag to the Arctic. After three weeks it weighed 52 pounds! Condensed body moisture had added 39 pounds of ice! Steger almost froze because his bag absorbed moisture and didn't give it up! So don't rely on synthetics to keep you warm when wet or filled with ice. They aren't foolproof. And remember that down's vulnerability to wetting has been greatly exaggerated.

That points up the real problem. All bags, down and synthetics, are vulnerable to moisture given off by the sleeper's body and condensed from his breath. So it's important to air your bag as often as you can. Fortunately, it takes 3–5 nights without any drying before a down bag begins to lose loft. It isn't well understood that in a single night the moisture from body and breath will weigh more than $3\frac{1}{2}$ pounds, and $2 - 2\frac{1}{4}$ pounds of it regularly condenses invisibly in any bag! If you don't or can't dry your bag you'll not only carry that moisture, your bag will lose a significant portion of its loft (warmth capability) as a result.

Down is difficult to clean, capriciously migratory, and highly variable in quality, but it's still the best insulator currently being used for sleeping bags. Unfortunately, it's becoming prohibitively expensive.

Polyester, on balance, is substantially worse—when looked at objectively. It's much cheaper, more uniform, and less absorbent than down. It's claimed to be more cushioning, but beneath the body's weight it has no real advantage. We have already seen that while it's water resistant, it *isn't* warm when wet, and while it dries faster than soaked down, it still holds substantial amounts of moisture. It *is* easily cleaned, non-allergic, and is far less sensitive to weight loading.

Unfortunately, it takes 2–4 times the weight of fiberfill to match down in loft and fiberfill has only three quarters of down's compressibility, making bags bulkier. It could be forgiven these defects if only it had a reasonable life. But it doesn't. The terrible truth is that fiberfill often "dies" before a buyer can get his money's worth, even at comparatively low prices, unless he babies his bag.

FIBERFILLS YOU'LL ENCOUNTER

A few synthetic bag makers have their own private fills, but the vast majority of them rely on the Big Three: Hollofil and Quallofil from DuPont and Polarguard from Hoechst-Celanese. Hollofil is the budget Dacron polyester chopped fiber. It has four microscopic hollows in each fiber to trap insulating air. Hollofil 88 is a still-cheaper version with only one hollow.

Quallofil, DuPont's premium polyester, boasts seven hollows, making it somewhat more compressible and downlike. Polarguard, the oldest of the three synthetic fills, is a continuous filament polyester that's spun into batting instead of being chopped. Polarguard bag and garment construction is very different from that of chopped fiber.

HOW SYNTHETICS DIE

By their very nature, fibers pressed together and allowed to move and work will gradually align and interlock. The process is aggravated by compression and heat. Neither silicone nor a heat crimp can prevent inevitable matting. And when matting occurs resilience (the ability to spring back) disappears and the loft that yielded insulative value is permanently lost. After 6–8 years experience, bagmakers, to their sorrow, have confirmed the fact that polyester batting dies in a comparatively short time. I have participated in the autopsies of a number of bags that have been returned because they "went flat."

When cut open the bags reveal locked, knotted batting that looks more like compressed cotton, wool, or Thinsulate than it does the original light, fluffy fiberfill. A continuously used or abused bag probably won't last one summer. A bag infrequently slept in and kept cool and uncompressed may last for years and give the illusion of long life. But it is generally (though not publicly) acknowledged by people who know that, on the basis of actual use, fiberfill bags won't last long enough to pay for themselves.

VAPOR BARRIER LINERS—THEY WORK!

Even the die-hards who won't try vapor barrier clothing because they're sure they'll get wet, reluctantly admit that it's valuable in a sleeping bag, especially one of down, to protect the insulation from picking up 2–4 pounds of body moisture in the night. But that's just half the problem. The heat lost along with that water, it has been calculated, would be sufficient to melt 27 pounds of ice! That's a tremendous amount of wasted warmth.

Since it's being generated in an effort to maintain body warmth and skin humidity, why not give the body some help by retaining heat and moisture and at the same time preventing dampness from penetrating your insulation? Much of that wasted energy can be saved by using a vapor barrier, because heat and moisture generation will drop sharply when proper humidity and warmth level at the skin are maintained. But the biggest payoff for many people is that a vapor barrier liner can increase the warmth of any bag by an impressive 20°F.

The application of vapor barrier to sleeping bags is much simpler than it is in clothing because there's no change in the body's activity level and temperatures remain constant or change very slowly. Offsetting this somewhat is reduced human awareness. When you're asleep you're unaware of overheating, chilling, or dampness until discomfort is sufficient to wake you.

There are four different ways to apply vapor barriers to sleeping: (1) You can use a sleeping bag with coated fabric on all interior surface, (2) You can snap or tie in a detachable coated-fabric liner (VBL) in a conventional bag, (3) You can wear a vapor barrier shirt and a free-floating half sack VB liner, or (4) You can wear a VB shirt and pants, not to mention gloves and socks, in any bag.

The first and most comprehensive sleeping system to utilize vapor barriers, not surprisingly, was Jack Stephenson's Warmlite

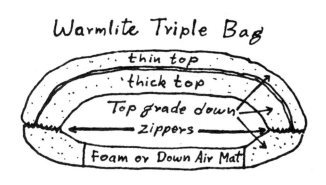

Warmlite Triple Bag

thin top
thick top
Top grade down
Zippers
Foam or Down Air Mat

foam offers a new alternative:

↑
flattened-down down provides no insulation.

↑
foam bags insulate under the body.

Triple Bag, available since 1968. The refined version is still revolutionary in the nineties. Unique features include an integral foam pad or down air mattress (DAM) instead of down on the bottom, reflective fabrics to reduce radiant heat loss, a vapor barrier interior fabric for warmth, down protection and sweat reduction, a removable multi-layer top, a down-filled collar to stop neck drafts, and double zippers at the openings to prevent heat loss.

Made from 1.2-ounce ripstop nylon, the outer fabric is windtight, water repellant (to dew, not rain) and aluminized on the inside. The interior fabric is coated on the inside, where you can't feel it. If you get wet from sweat it feels slippery instead of sticky. And when it quickly dries (once you ventilate) there is no lingering clammy dampness emanating from damp down.

THREE BAGS IN ONE

This bag has two separate down tops, one twice as thick as the other. Small nylon coil zippers make them entirely removable. In the warmest summer weather you use only the thin top; in colder spring and fall you use only the thick top; in the coldest winter weather you stay warm beneath both. Thus you have three bags in one, with a comfort range unknown in down beds, and four-season capability, yet you carry only what you expect to need on any given trip. In the coldest weather a down-filled collar snugs closely around the top of the neck and the hood is formed with zippers and the face opening closed with a drawstring.

The 3-inch DAM (or optional 2-inch foam pad) replaces a down bottom that was uselessly crushed beneath the sleeper. It also simplifies packing, makes it easy to turn over, reduces rolling, and eliminates the need for a separate mattress. Warmlite uses the finest available goose down, no matter what the price, because it provides maximum loft/weight and the best possible resiliency and durability. Loft varies with the supply from 700 to 850 cu. in./oz., loaded. Because the inside fabric is coated, the down never gets damp or heavy, the bag never needs washing, and the interior can be safely and effectively cleaned with a damp soapy cloth. The Warmlite Triple bag, with both tops and foam pad costs about $400–650, depending on size, and weighs $5\frac{1}{2}$ pounds.

Equipped with the Down Air Mattress instead, the cost range is $480–900. The DAM, which is custom made to fit your bag (or your specifications) is $95 separately. When I first heard of this intricate, cunning creation, put together with sewing, heat sealing and glued foam, I thought Jack had gone too far. I should have known better. The DAM is now the preferred mattress because of its reduced weight and bulk and its easy, dependable operation. It must not be inflated by mouth, to keep moisture from the down, but an ingenious adaptation permits easy inflation by using the sleeping bag carry sack as a pump. The purpose of the down inside the mattress is to prevent the convective air movement that has always made air mattresses cold.

THE VBL EXPERIENCE

A couple of my experiences with my Warmlite Bag will give some idea of how it functions. On the very first night that I slept in it there was still some snow on the ground at the High Sierra campsite and I was using the heavy top to be sure I was warm enough. After an hour or two I awakened, sweating, and groaned at the thought of spending the rest of the night wet and clammy. Then my head cleared and I remembered the vapor barrier lining. I jumped out of bed (naked), zipped the bag clear open (down one side and across the bottom) and waved it in the cool dry air. In no more than two minutes both myself and the bag were thoroughly dry, whereupon I climbed back inside, set the zippers for greatly increased ventilation, and slept comfortably dry for the rest of the night.

On a steaming August night in the Pennsylvania woods it was impossible to get cool and I was sweating heavily, even with both sides and the foot of the thin top unzipped. But while my companions' bags were soaking up sweat, mine was damp only on the surface. And sometime after midnight when a tiny night wind slipped into camp, I was the beneficiary of evaporative cooling that also dried both me and my bag. These examples are meant to reassure people who imagine that vapor barriers will get them wet and keep them that way. Just the opposite is true. The nylon interior feels just like the inside of any other bag, but it doesn't pass water into the down, keeps you warmer, and reduces your sweat output and dehydration on chilly nights.

A VB liner or system can add warmth capability as well as protection to any bag you own. Shortly before I was to leave for a month in the Bolivian Andes all of my bags but one were stolen. What remained was a light polypropylene summer down bag that North Face had given me to test years before. As a further experiment, I took it back to North Face to be fitted with a light custom-made VBL held in place by a half dozen velcro tabs. The liner boosted the bag's warmth about 20°F, so that, dressed night and day in a VB shirt, I was always warm in a bag with much less loft than those used by any of my companions. And when we left the peaks and descended into the Amazon jungle, I stored the bag and slept comfortably in the liner, well protected from the insect population.

THE DEWOLF SLEEPING SYSTEM

My friend Bob DeWolf employs application number four on protracted ski touring trips. Dressed from head to toe in VB clothing, he enjoys substantial advantages over any VBL system. He can easily roll over without moving his bag, he saves the weight and cost of the liner, his VB suit is usable during the day, and he can control his comfort over a wider temperature range by the selection of clothing he wears over his VB suit. But best of all he's fully dressed, which means he avoids the chilling agony of getting dressed on a frigid morning. He doesn't have to wait for the morning sun to warm his bed to avoid the shock of cold air, and, even better, he can get up in the night when nature calls without traumatizing his body.

Bob regulates his insulation levels to suit conditions and the bag he's using. Next to the skin he wears Patagonia Capilene long underwear. Over that goes a VB shirt tucked into side-zip coated (VB) rain pants. On his feet are plastic bags and his hands are protected by poly gloves. If he's winter camping he might wear zipper-ventilated pile pants, pile sweater, mittens, down booties, and two balaclavas (heavy wool outer over a light silk inner).

With this outfit to prevent heat and moisture loss, he can save several pounds by carrying a summer bag instead of one rated for winter—and he still has no clothing that he doesn't need anyway during the day. In fact he recently returned from a 20-day high Sierra ski tour on which he carried only one pair of socks! Protected at all times by VB (Baggie) liners, they never got dirty or damp.

In the summer Bob might add a pile vest to his wardrobe and leave his sleeping bag at home, relying on his tent for shelter and sleeping inside a one pound bivy sack, which he carries anyway for climbing. "It's a little mind-blowing," he reports, "just to lie down and go to sleep without anything around you—no covers to pull up, nothing to crawl into—that's where the bivy sack helps." I agree. The bivy sack adds significant (10−20°) warmth by holding heat and keeps off the inevitable chilling drafts. Bob finds traveling without a sleeping bag marvelously carefree, in the spirit of the happy hobo or John Muir going into the wilds with nothing more than a greatcoat.

Many people will find his system too extreme, but it makes perfect sense. Why should a weight-conscious backpacker carry two complete sets of insulation systems, one for day, the other for night? Why not avoid the duplication and save pounds? Even the most conservative outdoor traveler can probably trim his load by rethinking his needs along these lines.

At the most fundamental level, that means carrying a lighter bag and relying on the clothing you have to take anyway to provide some of your nighttime warmth. By using a VB suit you can then reduce the clothing you need, as well as protect it and your sleeping bag from loading up with condensed perspiration. For instance, you shouldn't wear a down parka to bed unless you wear some sort of VB shirt to protect it from sweat—and even then it may get damp from the moisture you exhale during the night. Pile, foam, or polyester clothing would escape the wetting problem.

THE "DOWN HOME" APPROACH

Down Home is a tiny mom-and-pop maker of sophisticated sleeping bags in backwoods Deadwood, Oregon. Chuck and Denise Kennedy only make 20–30 bags a year, but Chuck is respected throughout the industry as an innovator who's been talking to people, studying sleeping habits, and experimenting for more than 20 years in hopes of learning how to build a better bag. The experts say he's succeeded. Chuck builds individual custom bags, tailoring each to fit the customer's needs, planned use, priorities, and idiosyncrasies. He spends an average of four hours on the phone with the client before deciding exactly what's required.

"I ask a lot of questions and put the answers in my computer. When you add up all the choices, I have more than a thousand different combinations of components," he says. "I believe the best bag is the simplest one that satisfies all of the customer's needs, but I've got a lot of bells and whistles at my disposal to make a bag work. I have to find out what customers mean by 'warm' and 'comfortable.' I have to discover their entirely subjective attitudes and expectations. I've spent a lot of time finding out how people sleep."

Chuck believes that the vast majority of people want a bag that nestles around them snugly, that moves with them when they curl and stretch and roll. So most of his bags have uniform fill, top and bottom, but he will use a two-thirds fill bottom in bags for people who don't roll their bags. He doesn't like stiff bags with rigid foam or air-filled bottoms because you can't curl up in them.

Most buyers, out of vague anxiety, try to buy more bag than they need. Chuck does his best to talk them out of it. If their brains bake from too much bag, he feels he's failed them.

While he personally believes in VBLs, he finds he talks most of his customers out of buying them, because they aren't really needed. His VBLs tie into the bag and can be detached when it's too warm for them. "VBLs seriously cut a bag's comfort range," he explains. "They're only justified when it's really cold. I make mine with a full-length zipper for increased temperature management. VBLs are also useful in high rainfall areas to keep bags dry inside that can't easily be aired out."

After years of serious experimentation, Chuck invented the trapezoidal baffle to prevent down from clumping or shifting to leave cold spots. He and Jack Stephenson are good friends, though they disagree on many aspects of bag design. But they share a painstaking, scientific, thoughtful approach—which may explain why their bags are among the best ever made. Chuck's labor-intensive, made-to-order bags cost $300–600.

Down Home, like Warmlite, provides double zippers to protect against heat loss and a unique form-fitting design that assures full insulation thickness over the shoulders. But its most revolutionary feature is a "Floating Hood" that you wear like a gigantic helmet. Being entirely detached, it permits you to sleep on your stomach or side with full protection without twisting hood or bag. Almost as unusual is the optional boxed hood, an integral version of the helmet that provides far more warmth than do the hoods on conventional bags which are formed by cinching down on a drawstring.

Acquaintances of mine who used to rave about Goretex and sneer at vapor barrier bag liners recently came back from a high Sierra ski tour on which the weather was so foul that they made only 18 miles in 7 days. In that time a fine 5-pound. Goretex down bag, used in a tent and aired whenever possible, more than doubled in weight (and lost half its loft) due to condensed body moisture. After barely escaping frostbite, its owner will never be without vapor barrier protection on that sort of trip again.

WHAT TO LOOK FOR IN A BAG

Needless to say, you don't have to spend $600 to buy a good down bag, but the above described bags provide a standard against which other bags can profitably be compared. The buyer is in no position to judge down quality but he can easily see whether a bag is minimally filled (and highly vulnerable to down shift that creates cold spots) or plump and firm. Dependable down bags are decidedly billowy, but light. And billowy but heavier is far better in terms of warmth than flat and flabby but light. Other keys to bag quality are small stitches (at least ten to the inch), true differential cut, full-length nylon zippers backed by plump (or double) draft tubes, a foot section that toes won't penetrate, draft protection at the shoulders, and a hood that maintains loft when closed up tight.

Sleeping in a mummy bag on the ground in the wilderness is not much like sleeping in a heated home, but too many people, it seems to me, blame the resultant strangeness and likely wakefulness on the shape or confining nature of the bag. The mummy bag is so much more satisfactory in the long run than its larger relatives that an effort should be made to accept its confines. People shopping for a bag who are skeptical of their ability to adjust to its dimensions would be well advised to rent or borrow one for several trips to give themselves a chance to discover its virtues.

Before selecting a bag, the buyer needs to ascertain whether he sleeps warm, cold, or just about average. This determination, along with intended use, will largely determine the minimum temperature rating required for comfort. A bag to be used in wind and rain at high altitude by an exhausted, hungry climber will need to be warmer than one used by the same person at the same temperature under milder conditions. It is always a good idea to question backpacking friends about their bags.

When buying a bag it is worthwhile getting inside to check length, foot room, snugness, and the ease with which the hood can be closed from the inside to a face hole the size of a baseball. Drawstrings should be supplied with some sort of spring loaded clamp that can be operated with one hand.

Although design and down quality vary, Sierra Designs, North Face, Marmot, Kelty, and Feathered Friends all make dependably good down bags. Moonstone, Caribou, North Face, and Kelty make good fiberfill bags, but remember that the lower price of synthetic fills is reflected in their shorter life and greater weight.

THE NEW INFLATABLE "COCOON"

Back in the eighties, I sat on the board of directors of a small company developing, among other things, an inflatable sleeping bag. Because of my background, the scientist in charge invited me to participate in the bag's design. I did so with enthusiasm. I even invested in it.

When the first prototype was shown, I was shocked to discover that a $2 army surplus helmet had been stuck on a bag designed for −70°F! My input had been ignored. As earlier explained, because the capillaries in the head don't contract in the cold, heat loss from the head and neck is enormous. That's why a sleeping bag is only as good as its hood. But the designer scientist couldn't handle criticism. Since I protested, I was fired.

That prototype evolved into the Cocoon 4, an all-inflatable down-filled bag whose makers (Envirogear) make extravagant claims for it, like a comfort range of –45 to 70°F and infinite adjustability. The down prevents convective heat loss. Just inflate or deflate the top to dial the thickness of the insulation blanket desired. It fits "all shapes and sizes" and eliminates the need for a mattress because the bag's bottom holds the sleeper 3–4 inches above the ground.

Individual inflator sacks pump air into the top and bottom compartments. There is a canopy and fly that can be folded back when not needed. Being airtight, the structure is completely waterproof. The Cocoon 4 weighs more than 8 pounds and sells for nearly $800. Not surprisingly, I haven't seen or tested it. Jack Stephenson asked to examine it but received no response. He was curious because he had experimented with an all-inflatable down bag 20 years earlier. He junked it because of its heaviness.

But a friend of his, Larry Amkrant, tested the Cocoon on a hike to the Bering Sea a few years ago, and pronounced it very uncomfortable, especially around the head. The bag didn't come close to living up to its claims. Larry found it heavy, awkward, and stiff, with a very poor hood and collar. He felt is wasn't suitable for temperatures below zero, despite all the advertising and media hype. It was okay in the heat, but who needs a heavy expensive bag for warm weather? You can buy a light one for $50 in a department store.

Time will tell whether this 8-pound, $800 bed that floats is anything more than a curiosity. In the meantime, I wish I'd put my money into a foam bag. I *know* they work.

POLYESTER VERSUS FOAM

In the early seventies down's drawbacks and sharply rising price caused bag makers to seriously investigate two synthetic alternatives: polyester fiberfill and polyurethane foam. When it came time to tool up they put their money on fiberfill. I said at the time they were making a mistake, and that was before it was known that polyester dies young. I am still convinced that foam has the potential to be the premier insulator, bar none. Consider its impressive credentials. Foam's resiliency is marvelous: It springs back to 100% of its loft almost instantaneously and is essentially unaffected by fabric loading. Its weight is lighter than polyester, even though existing foams are primitive compared to the material's potential. Foam is comparatively cheap, non–allergic, wind resistant, ridiculously easy to fabricate into bags, surprisingly durable, and its insulative value is unaffected by wetting because it doesn't hold water.

When soaked it wrings out easily and evaporation by body heat quickly completes the drying process. But foam's greatest virtue is its perfect uniformity. By comparison both down and polyester are pathetic. Combined with its stubborn springiness, sheet foam's uniformity of thickness provides dependable insulation without thin or cold spots.

It's hard to convey what insulation uniformity means because few people have experienced it. Uniformity is what permits me to sleep in the snow without a tent in the wind and stay toasty warm in a foam bag with a total loft of 2 inches: an inch on the top and one on the bottom! It's what permits me to state that, as veteran winter travelers know, a better snow bag can be made at home out of one-inch foam, plastic sheeting, and rubber cement than the most expensive down bag on the market!

Testing Foam Bags

When I ski into my snowbound cabin at 7400 feet in the winter I sleep in a bag of one inch foam because of its 70°F comfort range. At bedtime, thanks to a roaring fire, the cabin may be 70°, but when I climb into the bag I am perfectly comfortable. The superb ventilation keeps my feet from sweating, a problem for me in down bags on much colder nights. The slight bellows effect produced by my breathing drives out excess warmth. I can feel it pumping out past my shoulders and neck.

Sleeping in a foam bag is a little like sleeping in a coffin because the tunnel of foam doesn't drape against the body. It takes a little getting used to, but I find the sensation extremely pleasant and free, now that I know I don't have to bundle up to sleep comfortably and warm. As you can see, I'm not a toss-and-turner who needs his bag to nestle around him and curl up with him. Predictably, Chuck Kennedy doesn't like foam, but Jack Stephenson does.

One night while testing the bag outdoors I awoke with a cold damp foot and discovered the foot of the bag had slipped off the pad and was in direct contact with the snow. When I swung the bag back onto the bed, my foot dried and warmed up with amazing quickness. Thus, this somewhat primitive old bag made of one-inch foam kept me comfortable over a range of 70 degrees, a feat inconceivable in any other kind of bag.

As the exposure of the foot of my bag to the snow illustrates, foam is breathable to a degree never approached by other insulation, including pile, thought it comes closest. And foam doesn't store the moisture that passes through it. You can hold a foam garment underwater until it's saturated, squeeze it 96% dry by hand, put it on comfortably, and let body heat complete the drying in a matter of minutes.

Zippers Aren't Needed

Believe it or not, zippers really aren't needed, except for convenience when getting in. And because the bags are so firm and smooth, one slides easily into foam when it would be a struggle in a conventional bag. The absence of a zipper keeps down cost and weight and enormously boosts warmth because there's no seam to lose heat. The continuous, uniform layer of foam around you is uninterrupted.

In down or polyester bags a double-slider, full length zipper is essential for ventilation (as well as entry) to combat sweaty feet with hoped for air circulation. Because of foam's unexcelled breathability and ventilation, zippers simply aren't needed to keep your feet dry and comfortable, even on the warmest nights! And because you're lying on cushiony, resilient foam instead of crushed flat down or fiber, you have insulation and mattress comfort beneath you. Nothing else is really needed, saving you the weight, bulk, and cost of a separate mattress, unless you (like me) want the luxury of additional cushioning. Ensolite-type closed cell foam is more than adequate on snow or any terrain. Anything more is delightfully decadent.

It has accurately been determined that there is no adverse air circulation (convective heat flow) in insulation as long as pockets of air have no dimension larger than $\frac{1}{4}$ inch. If a foam could be blown or baked to a sponge-like consistency with quarter-inch bubbles, it would be far lighter, much less bulky, and considerably softer. Such a foam in the top of a bag should improve drape and cut bulk and weight—without losing any insulative value. It would probably make my dream bag.

For years Dave Curtis and friends have tested foam bags and clothing in the snow at 14,600-foot Wolf Creek Pass, Colorado, where winter temperatures are commonly −25° to −50°F. Since Dave and Gil Phillips are both scout commissioners, it's not surprising that they often take scout troops to Wolf Creek Pass to teach them winter travel skills. Total reliance on these trips is on foam. Participants usually make their own gear under the supervision of Dave and Gil. They wear foam hats with face tunnels (which inspired the "Wood Hood"), foam mittens and foam mukluks over bare feet, and the arms, legs, and torso are wrapped with sheet foam which is held against the body by loose clothing.

How to Build a Foam Bag

Using Dave's foam and patterns the scouts make highly professional bags with only scissors and rubber bonding cement, substituting 4 mil plastic for nylon covers. If time is short, they simply take along sheet foam and sheet plastic and make safe, cozy burrows in the snow.

Here's Gil's design for a better snow bed than the finest down bag made. On one half of a 12-foot square of 4 mil polyethelene,

A snow bed good to −50°F!

4 mil plastic →

1" foam bag →

1" foam mattress →

uncoated
  nylon sheet →

foam body | foam-lined pants

... and you can make-it-yourself

spread on the snow, position a 4 × 8-foot sheet of uncoated nylon. On top of that goes your mattress, a simple sheet of one-inch foam, without cover. Next comes either a homemade foam bag, or simply two sheets of 1-1½-inch urethane foam about 3 feet wide. Now fold the free side of the plastic over the bed and tuck it securely underneath on the far side.

Fold the plastic under at the foot of your bed and you're ready to crawl into the open end and go to sleep in your foam clothes, controlling ventilation and carefully maintaining a supply of air to breathe through the open plastic tunnel above your head. Dave has slept comfortably wrapped in sheet foam and plastic at 50 below!

You can snuggle deep into your bag and fold the foam over your head securely because foam is so porous you can easily breathe through it. Moisture given off from your body (and breath) during the night passes out through the foam to condense to frost when it hits the plastic and collect as ice in the nylon sheet beneath your mattress, which is there to act as a blotter-collector. In the morning you "snap" the ice from your sheet and shake the ice dust from your plastic before packing up. The rest of your bed is bone dry.

A number of people have been privately experimenting with foam for some time. Jerry Pournelle, a California novelist with aerospace industry experience, for instance, told me he had built several bags out of one-inch upholsterer's foam rubber stitched together with nylon fishing line, sealed with rubber cement, and lined inside and out with uncoated nylon. "After several nights at about zero," he reported, "I concluded that it was the best bag I'd ever had. Materials cost me about $20, with an investment of about five hours work."

And Anthony E. Sowers, a New Mexico engineer, built four different foam bags, each in a different design, but all utilizing vapor barrier linings. For extreme conditions he constructed an 8-pound bag with $3\frac{3}{4}$ inches of soft foam on the bottom and 4-inch loft down on the top, with a VB liner of coated nylon. It was warm and comfortable at $-10°$F, and he felt confident it could handle much colder temperatures.

CLEANING AND STORING BAGS

Many a good sleeping bag has been ruined by overly enthusiastic cleaning. Prevention of soiling is the first step. You'll postpone the need to clean for years if you'll use a liner (especially a VBL) or wear long underwear to bed and use soap and water after every trip on the grime around the opening and hood. When cleaning is indicated, don't go to the dry cleaner or stick your bag in a home washer. The cleaner's chemicals can destroy both down and synthetics, and agitator washers can turn insulation to clumps and break fragile baffles.

Instead, take your dirty bag to your local laundromat and tuck it in a drum-type front-loading washer. Use mild detergent and cold or lukewarm water. Then put the sodden bag in a big dryer at low heat (or no heat) and run several cycles before taking it out to give it a gentle shaking to break up the clumps of down or fiberfill. Repeat until the bag seems dry, then take it home and hang it in the sun, kneading any remaining lumps.

When the bag is bone dry, don't roll or cram it back in the stuffsack. Stuffsacks are *only* meant for use on the trail. The rest of the time, to make your bag last, hang it in a dry closet or fold it loosely into a large breathable sack and hang it someplace dry until your next trip.

PROTECT YOUR BED

Bivouac sacks and sleeping bag covers are an important part of the beds that some of us carry, but they are discussed, along with tents in Chapter 8, Shelter. Because of the success of Goretex bivy sacks and the new lightweight tents, fewer people now entrust their beds to a mere ground cloth, even though it's by far the lightest, cheapest, simplest protection that can be provided—and often all that's needed. Where once we "rolled up" in heavy canvas tarps or army surplus ponchos that weighed more than today's bivy sacks, it's now possible to cut bed protection weight to a few ounces. The choice is between plastic of varying thicknesses, which is cheap but punctures easily, and coated nylon tailored tarps, which may cost four times as much but last four times as long.

What you choose will also be determined by the type of terrain, weather expected, your inclination to baby your gear, and the extent to which you prepare your bedsite. Four mil plastic can be made to last if you groom the ground first. Since the job of a ground cloth is to protect the top of the bag from dew and showers, as well as ground moisture, it needs to be big enough (at least 5' × 8' and better 7' × 9') to generously fold over and tuck well under on the open side and ends—ideally with all your gear underneath. To save on the cost of a tailored nylon tarp, you can buy 6 yards of 45-inch coated nylon off the roll at your local mountain shop (or from a catalog), cut it in half and sew the two strips together with a lap-felled double-stitched seam down the middle.

PILLOWS

Pillows used to be only for women and wimps. Real men were supposed to prop their heads on their boots—or rolled-up clothing in their sleeping bag stuffsack. Now you can get special pillow-sized stuffsacks with a flannel or fleece facing—or even an inch of Polarguard lining a pouch designed to hold your parka. And there are lots of inflatable pillows in different sizes and shapes, all weighing about half a pound.

They're fine—if you sleep on your back. But those of us who insist on sleeping on our sides find they aren't high enough or are smothering or too hard. By 2 a.m. my ear is so sore it wakes me up. I have to have a plump pillow of resilient foam. For decades I carried a luxuriously decadent 12-ounce Abercrombie & Fitch foam pillow, but I recently replaced it with a 4-ounce, 4-inch thick Pak N Travel foam pillow that's deep egg crate on the bottom and smooth soft EVA on top. It cost $6.50 with case and I love it.

Anyone used to a pillow—and that's most of us—must find some way to elevate and cushion his head if he wishes to sleep in any kind of comfort. Half the problem is solved during site preparation by making an earth pillow. Cushioning is generally supplied by a down parka stuffed into one of its own sleeves or the sleeping bag stuff bag filled with spare clothing.

MATTRESSES

Mattresses, too, were once scorned by real men. For years we had relied on ensolite (heavy and short-lived) to provide primitive, minimal cushioning but excellent insulation and protection from dampness. Egg crate urethane foam pads, often with nylon covers were excellent, if bulky and short-lived for drier conditions. Plastic air mattresses, though cheap and light, were certain to leak.

Ensolite has now been replaced by a generation of tougher, lighter, more durable closed-cell foams like Evasote (EVA). Egg crate urethanes are still with us, somewhat improved, but the big breakthrough is in air mattresses. The Air Lift combines 10 individual 3 mil plastic tubes, each filled with a single breath, in a light nylon zipper-closed cover. A puncture in the night affects only 10% of your bed and a spare tube can be substituted in the morning if patching isn't convenient. There's also a foam-filled model contoured to fit your body called the Equalizer.

A more sophisticated entry in the new wave of air mattresses is Stephenson's DAM, mentioned earlier, in which down effectively prevents ground cold from reaching the sleeper.

The best known, best liked mattress remains the Therm-a-Rest, although many people complain that they're too heavy and not thick enough. It's simply a nylon air mattress built around open-celled foam. The foam makes it self-inflating, prevents convection currents and increases cushioning. The foam squashes flat when you open the valve and roll it tightly into a 4-inch diameter cylinder (the $\frac{3}{4}$ length Backpacker). To inflate, simply open the valve and toss it where it can expand. By the time the tent is up it's fully inflated.

The Therm-a-Rest rarely leaks, doesn't leave you flat (thanks to the foam) if it does, and is easily patched. Like any air mattress, it requires a bedsite free of sharp objects and protection from a ground cloth or tent floor—or an EVA pad in winter. The mattress is so tough, effective, and foolproof that it survives rental well—the ultimate test of gear durability. As with bags, foam and foam/air mattresses should be stored unrolled and with the valve open.

Keeping pace with demand, Therm-a-Rests are gradually getting thicker. Originally a skimpy inch, there are now several models that claim two full inches, but they weight 3 pounds and no longer are cheap. We use our Camprests on river trips and when four-footed mules are carrying the loads. But on desert trips, for the same 7 pounds, we can take a 9-inch double air mattress for "like-home" cushioning—proving that sleeping comfort is where you find it. Don't leave all the innovation to manufacturers!

Food and Drink

I used to eat the All-American diet, both at home and on the trail. I was addicted to sugar, ate fat without restraint, and was always ready for hamburger or steak. Not any more. I haven't turned vegetarian, but I've learned a thing or two about food over the years and, like millions of others, I've modified my menu accordingly.

But problems arise when I try to take my new eating habits to the wilds on my back. The foods I prefer aren't the kinds one takes backpacking. They're too heavy, bulky, and juicy. I've resolved the conflict by making a sacrifice on short trips to eat what I want, and I dine more conventionally on longer trips. To give you the same opportunity/flexibility, I'm presenting both menus. You can take your pick—or combine.

John Muir, we are told, regularly set forth into the high Sierra provisioned solely with bread stuffed in the pockets of his greatcoat. Tibetan monks sustain themselves with little more than nettle soup. An Indian cowboy with whom I traveled in the Mexican desert subsisted on tea made from herbs he picked along the way and a scrap of meat slapped on the coals of our evening campfire.

These gentlemen's somewhat extreme approaches to eating have one thing in common: simplicity. And it's a measure worth heeding. Most of us would benefit by simplifying our grub lists. The efforts I've made in that direction in recent years have substantially reduced my cooking chores and made my trips more carefree. Life in the wilds should be simpler, not more complex. After all, it's supposed to be a vacation!

That doesn't mean I skimp on planning. Just the opposite. I'm willing to put a little more effort into planning and preparing at home in order to be more carefree in camp. I've learned the hard way that food can make or break a trip. Backpackers, like armies, travel on their stomachs. The scenery will pale if the food doesn't satisfy. And the pitfalls of poor planning are many. You can carry far too much, bringing half of it home. Or you can run out and go hungry. Excess weight becomes a burden, and so does excessive preparation. Balance may be bad, power insufficient, or the taste so dreary that eating becomes a chore. I therefore urge you to take food planning seriously, even if it bores you, and to put your emphasis on simple as well as succulent meals. The rewards can be great—and the alternatives grim.

PLAN AHEAD

My chief strategy for reducing the burden of meal planning is taking notes. By writing down briefly what I'm taking before I leave (items, quantities), then making notes as soon as I return on how things turned out (surpluses, insufficiencies, failures, unfulfilled cravings, ideas), I produce a record that makes planning food for the next trip twice as easy. Why start from scratch every time? By making notes—and keeping them—food lists are continually refined, the planning ordeal is greatly reduced, and you eat better each trip.

A principal pitfall in food planning is the instinctive urge to produce city-type meals in the wilds. One must set aside the rigid and ritualized habits of urban eating. Forget the three square meal structure of city life, which frowns on between-meal snacks. One eats in the wilds to keep the body continuously fueled, happy, and capable of sustained effort. The easiest way to stay continuously fueled is to eat small quantities continuously. Small meals and frequent snacks provide easier digestion during activity and better energy production. The food planner should concern himself with weight, ease of preparation, calorie production, balance between fat, protein and carbohydrates, bulk, resistance to spoilage, palatability, and cost—not necessarily in that order.

There is no such thing as the perfect menu. On an easy summer overnight or weekend trip with my wife and daughter I use one criterion. If I am planning a long and strenuous cross-country trip my priorities are much different and so is my food list. Weather and climate have strong effects on food selection. Snow, jungle, and desert require different menus. I know backpackers who happily go heavily laden to the wilderness to sit around camp and practice their gourmet cooking. I know others who think nothing of eating the same thing every day for a week to cut weight and preparation to the bone. I put myself somewhere in between. What I carry depends on trip length, terrain, weather, and whim.

I'm not fanatic about lightness—providing my pack isn't heavy—but when it comes to preparation in camp I'm very finicky. I've spent too many hungry, miserable hours struggling to put meals together under adverse conditions. In my view the importance of easy preparation can scarcely be overemphasized. After a long hard day on the trail in bad weather, the weary, starving backpacker, crouched in the dirt over an open fire in the cold, wind, and dark needs all the help he can get. At such times boiling a pot of water and dumping in the food can be heavy, demanding, exasperating work.

Ease of Preparation

Preparation that would be trivial in the city becomes somewhere between difficult and impossible. In the wind, cooked food may be five times as hard to prepare as cold food. A recipe that calls for milk may be twice the work of one that merely requires water. At high altitude, raw dry food may take ten times as long to cook as a precooked freeze-dried dish. And there's nothing more frustrating after an exhausting day than trying to read complicated recipes by flashlight while nursing a smoky fire. Even walking gourmets will therefore be well advised to include a supply of zero-preparation meals.

Foods designed specifically for backpacking are improving every year in terms of both appeal and simplified preparation. The same is true of lightweight dishes packaged for the housewife in supermarkets, health food stores, and delis. But there are still a great many foods that will make the backpacker salivate that are

simple directions on the package mean easy preparation in camp.

basically city meals and require a real kitchen for "easy" preparation. If the directions run more than a sentence, or if more than one pot is required, I quickly lose interest.

Two dishes designed to be eaten at the same time I pass over quickly. Dinners with low caloric yield are swiftly rejected. Packages containing three or four separate packets make me suspicious. Freeze-dried foods form the nucleus of my menu, but I manage to buy the majority of my provisions from sources other than mountain shops. I'm always on the lookout for suitable backpacking foods when cruising places that sell food. And I do my experimenting at home. The trail is not the place to gamble. It's also not the time to diet.

Tastes Change Outdoors

A backpacker's tastes usually change in the wilds. The body's needs are altered by heavy outdoor exertion, and these needs frequently are reflected in cravings for carbohydrates, (liquids, salty foods, and sweets) and a corresponding disinterest in other foods (like fats, meat, and vegetables). Individual meals lose much of their significance. To keep the body continuously fueled, the backpacker should eat or nibble almost constantly. Many snacks and small meals provide better food digestion, which means better energy production.

As *Freedom of the Hills* puts it, "As soon as breakfast is completed the climber commences lunch, which he continues to eat as long as he is awake, stopping briefly for supper." I generally start

nibbling an hour or two after breakfast if I am hiking, and I eat two lunches instead of one, the first in late morning and another in mid-afternoon. I know hikers who go a step further to escape food preparation altogether: they abolish distinct meals, eating every hour and fixing a larger or hot snack when they feel the need.

A hiker living outdoors should drink at least as often as he eats. If he is shirtless or the weather is warm his body may easily lose a gallon of water in a day! Since dehydrated food absorbs water from the body after it is eaten, still more water is needed. A backpacker can scarcely drink too much—provided he takes only a little at a time. Severe dehydration results if most of the fluids lost during the day are not replaced before bedtime.

Since water loss means salt loss, salty foods are unusually welcome. Although the body replaces salt lost normally, continuous, excessive sweating may justify taking salt tablets. A salt deficiency (from extreme water loss) can result in nausea, aches, or cramps. But overdosing on salt is dangerous too. To protect yourself, take no more than two salt tablets with every quart of water you drink.

TREATING SUSPECT WATER

Only a decade ago, we cheerfully drank any running water that looked clean, and never gave it a second thought. If it came from a murky pond or looked a little suspicious, we tossed in a few Halazone tablets. And nobody got sick—at least nobody I knew. Then came the discovery of Giardia, followed by The Great Giardia Scare.

People were told by the "authorities" that the water wasn't safe to drink anymore. It had to be boiled, treated chemically, or pumped through a filter. Many serious backpackers have dutifully, unquestioningly obeyed. But I believe the threat has been greatly magnified.

Giardia is a nasty but nonfatal protozoan infection that—so we're told—might be lurking almost anywhere. It has proved to be extremely hardy. Almost as mysterious as AIDS, Giardia has scared a majority of the people who've heard about it into taking elaborate steps to purify their drinking water. Giardia is no myth. A hiking partner of mine contracted it in Central America—and suffered for a year. But I think there's been an overreaction. Fear of the violent symptoms—diarrhea, vomiting, abdominal cramps, fatigue, weight loss—has caused rational people to treat it like the plague. I regularly meet people in the wilderness who go to great lengths to purify their water—even after they learn that there's never been a documented case of Giardia in that region.

Let me therefore try to ease this blind fear by pointing out that Giardia has been around almost forever. It's only in recent years that the connection has been made between its symptoms and drinking unpurified water. In other words, if you've been drinking water in the wilds for 40 years like I have, you've very likely been exposed to Giardia. If you haven't gotten it, it's probably because—like the vast majority of people—you're not susceptible to the little protozoa.

James A. Wilkerson in *Medicine for Mountaineering* says that less than half of those who drink water heavily contaminated with Giardia become infected; of these, only about a fourth actually develop symptoms; and these symptoms, even if untreated, usually go away of their own accord in 7–10 days. So Giardia is hardly the scourge that's been depicted.

The U.S. Health Department estimates that somewhere between 1.5 and 20 percent of the U.S. population are carriers of Giardia, but are asymptomatic—because they apparently aren't susceptible. In that respect, it's a lot like the dreaded polio (infantile paralysis). More than 90% of the population has been exposed to polio and is immune. Only 1 to 2% of those who contract it suffer any degree of paralysis. So I have to question the need for treating *all* running water—just because it may contain Giardia protozoa. So does many a municipal reservoir!

The U.S. Forest Service says, "Even clear running water should be purified before drinking. Boil it vigorously for at least three minutes before drinking. Chemical treatment or filtration may purify water, but is not considered as effective as boiling." Experts agree with Smokey. The Halazone tablets of yesteryear are no match for the bugs found in today's suspect water.

Today's hiker must take responsibility for judging the safeness of the drinking water supply along the way. I can't give you a rule of thumb, except to use common sense. Some people are so scared of Giardia and other pollutants that they won't drink anything that doesn't come out of a tap, carrying the considerable quantities they mean to drink. Others drink anything that halfway looks like water and rarely get sick. I regularly drink vigorously flowing water in the high Sierra as long as there aren't livestock or campgrounds upstream, but I realize I'm taking a chance.

Any authority you talk to will naturally take the most conservative position, to be on the safe side: "If in doubt," they'll say, "treat the water." Your family doctor, the Park Service, the Sierra Club, and the Forest Service all have to worry about being sued if they tell you it's safe to drink the water...and then you get Giardia. So do I.

But I continue to drink water I judge safe...without treatment, even when everyone else is treating it or lugging their own supply. I don't own or carry a water filter because I don't like the weight and bulk and the fiddling around. Filtering water is slow work and, some say, of questionable effectiveness. It's far from foolproof and may even be undependable. If I'm afraid to drink the water available along the trail, I much prefer to render it bacteriologically safe by adding a tasteless, iodine-based tablet to my quart (or liter) water bottle. Potable Aqua is the brand sold at REI. Just wait three minutes, shake, and serve.

The Sierra Club advocates adding 2 drops of fresh 7% iodine solution (a poison) to every quart or liter of suspect water. Shake well and let stand twenty minutes before drinking. But don't use it if you're pregnant or have thyroid problems. Iodine dosing is easy enough, but the water smells and tastes like iodine—sort of rusty. The easiest way to use it is to carry two canteens, so one is always ready to drink.

I'll reluctantly use iodine on the trail (or river) if I have to—adding Tang or lemonade crystals to mask the taste—but I've found something far better for treating a quantity of water in camp. It's the Sierra Water Purifier Kit, consisting of two little bottles and costing about $15.

A New Alternative—Chlorination

The Water Purifier Kit employs the system used worldwide to disinfect municipal water systems. Concentrated chlorine crystals disinfect the water and kill all living organisms known to cause illness in humans. Then an oxidizing agent (hydrogen peroxide) is added to neutralize any remaining chlorine, leaving clean pure water. The tiny 5-ounce kit will treat 160 gallons of water, about enough for two people for a month and a half. That's the good news. The bad news is that you have to be careful.

The concentrated chemicals are extremely potent and toxic. The makers asked me to emphasize that. They say their kit is "only for expert wilderness trekkers and world travelers. It takes a drug-free, alcohol-free, and emotionally competent, intelligent person with a steady hand." Maybe so, but if I can handle it, so (probably) can you. I first tested the kit at my High Sierra Echo Lake cabin, where we think we have the world's best spring water. We call it Echo Champagne.

Following directions, I scooped about 17 tiny chlorine crystals into a single glass of water, then stirred until they (quickly) dissolved. Then I smelled and tasted the water to make sure it was heavily chlorinated. Ten minutes later, I added a single drop of hydrogen peroxide to neutralize the chlorine. The treated water tasted sweet and good. For a comparison I tasted a glass of our spring water (the control). No difference. The second stage of the treatment had restored the full flavor of our Echo Champagne.

My second test was on a 3-day late summer backpack to tiny shallow Hidden Lake, a pond with no flow in or out. Trout lived in it, but the water was murky and there were signs of heavy use. It easily qualified as "suspect." Campers at nearby lakes were all filtering their water, though rangers later confirmed that there were no confirmed cases of Giardia in the region.

With a gallon plastic bottle, using the kit in camp was much easier. My wife filled the jug with water, used the kit's scoop to dump in about 100 crystals, screwed on the lid and gave the contents a good shaking. Then she took a whiff and sip, and nodded. Unmistakably chlorine. Ten minutes later she dropped in 6 drops of oxidizer, shook again and poured herself a cup. "Tastes like Echo Champagne," she reported. I tried it and agreed. More to the point, we felt confident that, having been chlorinated, the water was now quite safe to drink.

The flyer that comes with the kit gives detailed tips and instructions, like: settle the sediment out of very muddy water for some hours before treatment. Don't chlorinate until visibility is four inches . . . too much oxidizer can't hurt you . . . the longer the chlorinated water sits, the more bugs it kills . . . the process can be repeated to supertreat especially suspicious water that must be drunk. And so forth.

We're convinced. We're going to take the kit with us this winter on a 5-week hiking and river running trip to Costa Rica—to be prepared.

If You'd Rather Filter

If you're afraid to drink the water and you don't want to chlorinate, iodize, or boil it, you're a candidate for a filter. I dislike them because they're heavy, clumsy, slow, and expensive, but lots of people like them—after they get used to them. I tried the popular First Need and found it hard to use. Even with refinements it takes 3–4 hands to hold it, pump, hold the pre-filter in the water source, and keep the filter in your water bottle. The new bracket and a water bottle lid with attachable tube help some, but even pumping clean water wasn't easy.

The First Need is rated at a pint of water a minute, but that's just the first minute with a brand new filter and clean water. With dirty water, five minutes per quart is more like it. And when your filter gets clogged—it doesn't take long in really dirty water—you need a new one for $25. The apparatus screens down to .4 microns but tests show it doesn't always screen out all the Giardia. The rig costs $50 and with attachments weighs a pound.

The Cadillac of filters is the Katadyn, which filters down to .2 microns. It only costs $225 and weighs a pound and a half, but you better carry a spare filter (at another $90) in case you want to turn the Ganges into rainwater. PUR's two models both draw the line at one micron, good enough theoretically to catch Giardia bugs, perhaps because it has iodine matrix in the filter. At least the large pump is inside the filter and works twice as easily as First Need.

A big feature of filters is the alleged "no waiting time," but what about all the time you spend balancing your bottle and pumping? If all you care about is screening out Giardia, the comparatively cheap 2 micron Timberline is good enough—for a little while. But as the Sierra Water Purifier Kit people point out, filters don't screen out all disease. And if you don't clean them after every use, you risk contamination from bugs growing in the collected dirt.

You have to make two decisions before you leave home: Do you drink the water or treat it? If you treat it, what method will

you go prepared to use? The first is a mental/emotional decision, because it's based largely on fear. Wouldn't it be worthwhile to call the rangers beforehand to ask if there's ever been a confirmed case of Giardia where you're going? Give yourself some basis for that first decision. If you've made the decision to treat, you have four options. Let's summarize them.

COMPARING THE FOUR MEANS OF TREATMENT

1. BOILING   Everybody agrees it's the safest method, but it's tedious, inconvenient, and eats up fuel. It's often impossible, especially in the winter. And the experts disagree on how much heat is needed. Guesses range from 1–20 minutes boiling at sea level and five times that long at 10,000 feet.
2. IODIZING   It's the easiest, simplest, lightest approach, but the water smells and tastes like medicine if you drink it straight. Tang or lemonade powder helps some.
3. CHLORINATION   Dependably produces safe, sweet water, but requires twice measuring out potent chemicals.
4. FILTERING   Messy, heavy, expensive, vulnerable to contamination, and undependable, but slightly quicker than the other methods.

Treating water, by whatever method, is a chore—and far from foolproof. It takes some of the fun and spontaneity out of adventuring in the wilds. That's one reason I resist it. I also believe I've been repeatedly exposed to Giardia—and found immune. But once you've made the decision to treat water and chosen the approach that fits your personality, you'll soon develop the habit and a proficiency with your system that will make it a comfortable part of your routine.

TIPS ON WATER USE IN THE WILDS

DRINKING: A good rule of thumb is to drink every time you eat. To avoid dehydration, drink 3–4 quarts a day. Drink every time you can. Ice water is a shock to the system, so drink it cool if you can. If you're coming to a waterless stretch of trail, drink a little extra before starting out. If your urine is darker than usual, it means you're not drinking enough. Air is drier in the cold so you need to drink more in winter, even if you're not thirsty.

WINTER WATER: When melting snow on a camp stove, start with at least an inch of water in your covered pot, adding snow as it melts. If water is short, top off your water bottle with clean snow after each drink. Beware pink or yellow snow, which is contaminated by microorganisms that can make you sick. If you'll have to melt snow for water on your snow camping trip, bring plenty of extra stove fuel—or water. They weigh the same 2 pounds per quart.

PHYSIOLOGY: Dehydration not only jumps your blood pressure, it drops your overall energy. Just to maintain yourself you must replace the 3 quarts of water you lose breathing, sweating, and eliminating. Cold and altitude increase the loss. At high altitude you breath faster and deeper, losing water vapor faster, so you need to drink more. At 12,000 feet you may lose 5–7 quarts daily. Dry cold windy conditions can steal another two quarts.

The food you eat will replace about a quart of water daily—unless it's dehydrated, in which case you have to drink an extra quart. Avoid caffeine and alcohol, which flush water from your system. It's a good idea to drink at least a pint before you hit the trail so you start out well watered. Don't rely on feeling thirsty to tell you when to drink. By then you may already be dehydrated! If you're not producing clear urine five times a day, you're not drinking enough. Most backpackers would feel better if they'd make themselves drink more water.

WATER BOTTLES: Use wide-mouth bottles so you can get in to clean the bottoms where bacteria grows. And don't forget to clean the threads regularly. If you have to drink muddy water and have no way to treat it, pour it through a funnel made from your bandana in the wide mouth of your water bottle. Then let time and gravity filter your water through sedimentation. The longer you can wait, the better it is. Overnight is ideal. That's our main treatment in the Grand Canyon.

At first glance, a $2\frac{1}{2}$-gallon (Sunshower) shower bag seems like a luxury, but it's also great for lugging water from a distant creek. You can chemically treat the water in it for drinking. And when you hang your bag from a high tree limb you've got running water in camp for cooking as well as washing and showering. Finally, the bag makes a decent water pillow.

CUT DOWN ON COOKING

Since heating food greatly increases preparation, requires weighty equipment (pots, stove) and provides only psychological benefit—cooking only reduces nutritive value—more than a few backpackers avoid cooking in the wilds altogether. They find the saving in time, labor, and weight more than offsets the lack of comforting warmth. Denton W. Crocker (*Wilderness Camping*, Vol. 6, No. 2) after careful experimentation devised a menu of precooked meatless foods that kept him looking forward to mealtime even after eating the same thing every day for nearly two weeks on the trail. Cost and bulk of his provisions are low, food weight is less than 2 pounds daily, and leaving home pots and stove reduced pack weight by another 2 pounds. The menu produces a balanced 3000 plus calories/day, and meal preparation is almost zero.

For breakfast Crocker eats a prepackaged $\frac{2}{3}$ cup of home roasted potent granola that contains oats, wheat germ, brown sugar, salt, oil, corn syrup, vanilla, sunflower seeds, and raisins. He also drinks a cup of Tang. For lunch there's a mix of equal portions of peanut butter, honey, and milk powder, plus chocolate, crackers, dried fruit, and a quart of Kool-Aid. Dinner consists of a home-baked trail bar composed of whole wheat and soy flour, wheat germ, skim milk powder, salt, currants, raisins, chopped dates, eggs, oil, molasses, and vanilla. In addition there is a drink made of skim milk and malted milk powder. Needing only a spoon and a one-pint plastic bottle, Crocker found "there is something remarkably peaceful about an evening meal where I can just reach into the pack, pull out two small packages, and, with a cup of water, have my supper ready."

SPICE IT UP

Another approach to simplicity in the outdoor kitchen relies on the creative addition of spices and condiments to simple dishes to produce variety without complicating food preparation. For instance, on a relatively short easy trip, I might increase both the power and the flavor of a packaged stew by adding several of the following: freeze-dried sliced mushrooms, a pinch of Fines Herbs (spice mix), a gob of butter or margarine, parsley flakes, onion or garlic powder, a lump of cheese, crumpled bacon bar or vegetable bacon bits, tabasco sauce, and so forth. I could eat the same basic stew for a week but enjoy a different flavor every night by the restrained use of these and other seasonings. Or take another of my staple foods, applesauce. I keep it exciting day after day by the judicious use of cinnamon, raisins, lemon powder, vanilla, chopped dates, nutmeg, ginger, nuts, honey, and coconut in varying combinations.

On a long hard trip, seasonings and spices become even more vital in the battle against boring, bland meals. A dash or two of chili powder and a shake of onion flakes will turn a dreary pot of beans into spicy chili. A little curry powder will liven up the rice. Jazz up a dreary casserole with dry mustard and Worcestershire sauce. If trout are on the menu, I briefly shake the dampened fish in a plastic bag containing a few ounces of my cornstarch, cornmeal, salt, pepper, onion and garlic powder mix before frying. Trout are also good baked in a butter sauce with sage and basil.

Other versatile ingredients include sunflower and sesame seeds, slivered almonds, fruit crystals, wheat germ, coriander, bouillon cubes, tomato, beef and chicken base, peanuts, banana flakes, various freeze-dried fruits and vegetables, bay leaves, and oregano. For packaging seasonings for the trail, waterproof plastic medicine and cosmetic bottles and vials are best for the vanilla, Worcestershire and tabasco sauces.

Film cans and snap lid plastic containers are far better than plastic bags for dry spices. If you're going to be out for more than a weekend you'll find your condiments will be easier to find and use when kept together as a spice kit in their own drawstring bag. Don't turn your back on seasonings because you're not a cook. Neither am I, but I've learned that, with a little practice, anyone can turn dreary food into exciting fare with a little magic from a spice kit.

Sometimes flavor isn't the only reason for embellishment. If a stew or casserole is suspect in the realm of caloric punch, the deficiency can be corrected by fortifying it with TVP, freeze-dried meat, margarine, bacon bar, instant potato, wheat germ, cooking oil, or other items of known caloric clout. In this manner a mere soup can be transformed into a high potency stew.

In case you noticed that I didn't list sugar as a sweetener, it's because I'm convinced that it's a poisonous drug. Sure, it's the quickest source of energy—but at a price. It's a chemical that gives you a rush of energy by whipping the body's adrenal system. This unnatural stimulation doesn't last very long (an hour or two at the most), and when it's gone you droop lower than before.

I still carry a little sugar to flavor my applesauce, and I'm well aware that I eat foods that contain it, but I don't depend on it in the form of candy, jello, and chocolate. Having mercifully lost my sugar addiction, I can't tolerate very much of it anymore. So I substitute honey and molasses which are far less refined than white sugar. I like their distinctive favors, and molasses keeps me regular in the wilds.

A BETTER WAY TO EAT

Would you change your morning menu if you could double your energy on the trail and lose unneeded weight—without feeling hungry or deprived? That's what my wife and I did. It began with my discovery, in a wrecked car on a Hawaiian lava field, of a diet book called *Fit for Life* by Harvey and Marilyn Diamond (Warner Books). I've never been on a diet in my life, having always been slim, but my wife Deanne tried their scheme and loved it. The diet in a nutshell: eat only fresh fruit in the morning, instead of the obligatory pigout.

That had some appeal for me. I've always rebelled against the All-American big breakfast on the grounds that it's dumb to eat if you're not hungry. Besides, whatever I ate gave me mid-morning heartburn, so I rarely ate any breakfast at all. I was cautiously willing to consider something better.

The authors claim that fresh fruit on an empty stomach will zip through the stomach and into the intestines in 20–40 minutes where it immediately begins generating energy. By comparison, any other food (or combination of foods) sits in the stomach for at least two hours (and probably twice that long) before it's digested, consuming vast amounts of energy in the process. In fact, digesting most meals takes more energy than running or sex, say the Diamonds!

The fruit diet sounded like the perfect prescription for a day-hiker's breakfast—quick energy for a running start. Since I was writing a book called *Dayhiker* (also from Ten Speed Press) at the time, I decided to experiment. I tried playing tennis or taking identical hikes on fresh fruit, other foods, and nothing at all. With nothing at all I ran out of gas by mid-morning. After a mixed-food breakfast I felt lead-footed and heavy on the tennis court—even two hours after eating.

I Lost 5 Pounds

But after a bowl of fresh fruit—not frozen, canned, or dried—I was brimming with energy and a feeling of lightness in less than an hour—ready for swimming, tennis, or strenuous hiking. Without anything "solid," I expected to be hungry in an hour, but I wasn't. And I've never had a moment of heartburn—because I don't combine anything with my fruit, not even a cup of tea. And in less than a month my wife and I had lost 5 pounds apiece.

That was nearly two years ago, and we're still happily eating nothing but fresh fruit in the morning. It turned out to be the perfect breakfast for dayhiking. In a group, we always lightly prance past our panting fellows who are vainly trying to digest the sausage and eggs lying leaden in their stomachs. Around the middle of the morning, if we get hungry or our energy begins to fade, we stop for a second breakfast of peeled oranges in ziplock bags, bananas, dates, and grapes, maybe an apple.

Sure, fruit is heavy because it's full of water. But they supply all our water needs, so we don't need to drink or carry extra water. Fruit is liquid high-energy fuel.

Within minutes the fuel is transformed into energy, and we're back at our accustomed pace, propelled upward by fruit power. We try to do all our heavy dayhiking and climbing on fruit, so sometimes we eat two or three fruit snacks to get us to the top of the mountain, before we have lunch. Often the last several feedings are on dehydrated fruit, which works less well but keeps us going.

We carry dried—not bone-dry dehydrated—bananas, papaya, pineapple, raisins, and dates. We avoid sulphur-dried fruit—like most apricots and peaches—because they cost your body valuable energy to rid itself of toxic sulphur. Once the switch is made to dried fruits, of course, it becomes necessary to drink lots of liquids. If you don't rehydrate them, they'll dehydrate you!

At lunchtime while dayhiking, we switch to what the Diamonds call the four "fruit vegetables": avocado, tomato, cucumber, and bell pepper. They are compatible with fruit and can thus be eaten with it. We either split one of each, or we make them into buttered sandwiches with whole grain wheat or rye bread. We find them delicious and they maintain our energy and feeling of lightness.

We also eat other veggies (onion and lettuce in our sandwiches), carrots, crackers, and Nu-Tofu Jalepeno cheese (free of dairy, cholesterol, and lactose), as well as nuts (ideally raw). And Deanne makes a delicious egg-free mayonnaise out of raw almonds, lemon, and safflower oil, to keep our sandwiches tasty and moist.

The Diamonds scrupulously avoid meat, eggs, and all dairy products except butter, because (1) they're non-essential, (2) they steal energy during digestion, and (3) they fail to fuel the body. Since there's no nutritional reason to eat them, we stopped carrying meat, gorp, cheese, chocolate, tuna fish, candy, etc. At first I was anxious about running out of energy, but the Diamonds were right. We hike far better all afternoon without them. Our wimpy low-octane-sounding vegetarian diet gives us power and lightness that doesn't quit.

After switching to other foods, we don't go back to fruit. In combination with *any* other food, say the Diamonds, fruit merely rots in your stomach. It only does its magic on an empty stomach.

After lunch the Diamonds' diet starts to get complicated because combining starch and protein is a no-no, which rules out good old meat and potatoes. That's tough enough to manage at home. While backpacking in the wilds it would be impossible. So it's reassuring to hear that two-thirds of the diet's benefits come from merely eating fresh fruit in the morning.

Mixing Fresh Fruit and Backpacking

The *Fit for Life* scheme of eating, while ideal for dayhikers, who eat breakfast and dinner at home, poses certain problems for backpackers. We don't want to sacrifice the benefits of our diet, but we can't carry an unlimited supply of heavy, bulky, juicy, fast-spoiling, ripe fresh fruit, either. What to do? We solved the dilemma with a compromise. On short 2–4 day trips in easy country or on trails, we sacrifice weight and carry fruit and avocados, with dried fruit as backup.

On difficult or longer trips—which we seldom take—we'll take enough fruit for 2–3 mornings, then sadly fall back on a more traditional menu. Our love affair with morning fruit has us doing more dayhiking—and making shorter carries on backpacking trips. We now rely more on dayhiking from a backpacked basecamp for soul-satisfying exploring, solitude, and peak climbing. See *Dayhiker* for strategies for having your cake and eating it too.

Of course, you don't have to stop eating fruit at noon. The Diamonds recommend "all-fruit" days for maximum energy (like climbing a peak) and maximum weight loss. But try it first at home or on a dayhike before you rely on nothing but fruit while backpacking. I don't do all-fruit days, but I rely on morning fruit, because my aim nowadays is to make it up the mountain *because* of what I eat, not in *spite* of it!

The choice is yours. You can trudge up the trail with a miscombined breakfast rotting in your stomach, expending vast amounts of energy to digest food that will never produce energy—essentially hiking with the brake on. Or you can charge yourself with fruit, doubling energy, freeing your muscles to propel you lightly up the trail in high gear, happily walking off excess weight as you go.

If you think this eating strategy is radical—as I would have five years ago—face the possibility that you're behind the times, out of step with modern research.

There is ample evidence that the traditional All-American diet is a disaster. Nearly two thirds of the nation is at least twenty pounds overweight. Some 200,000 bypass operations are performed each year because our arteries are clogged. The best-selling prescription drug in America today is anti-acid. Heart disease kills four thousand Americans every day. "A vegetarian diet," says the conservative AMA, "could prevent 90 to 97 percent of heart disease deaths."

Clearly, meat is the culprit. Maybe it's time to consider the alternative, since meat isn't essential to nutrition and doesn't provide any great benefits. If, like me, you aren't quite ready to go vegetarian, the *Fit for Life* diet is a good place to start—especially if you'd like to gain energy and lose weight.

COUNT CALORIES PER MILE

Since backpacking is decidedly strenuous, it is hardly surprising that the body's fuel intake must increase significantly in order to keep up with demand. The body's energy requirements and the energy production of food are both measured in calories. It takes twice as many calories to walk at 3 mph as it does to walk at 2 mph. Walking at 4 mph doubles the calorie requirements again, and it take $2\frac{1}{2}$ times as many calories to gain a 1000 feet of elevation as it does to walk at 2 mph.

EATING HABITS CHANGE

A variety of studies have shown that—depending on innumerable factors (like body and pack weight, distance covered, terrain, etc.)—it takes 3000–4500 calories a day to keep a backpacker fueled. Easy family trips might require 2000–2500 while climbers may need 5000.

Backpackers who take in fewer calories than their systems need will find the body compensates by burning fat to produce energy. Stored fat is efficiently converted to fuel at the rate of 4100 calories per pound. The backpacker who burns 4000 calories, but takes in only 3590 (410 fewer), will theoretically make up the difference by burning a tenth of a pound of body fat, although individuals vary widely where fat conversion is concerned.

Backpackers unused to strenuous exercise will usually lose weight, but probably not from lack of caloric energy. Exposure to the elements results in water loss, and the change from the high-bulk diet of civilization to low-bulk dehydrated foods tends to shrink the stomach. For most people, a little hunger and a loss of weight is beneficial to health and need not be construed as the first signs of malnutrition—as long as energy levels remain ample.

The wanderer who carries concentrated, low-bulk dehydrated food on his back needs to know something about the calorie power it will deliver—if only to prevent overeating. If the food is well chosen, about 2 pounds of it (before rehydration) will provide the approximately four thousand calories necessary to keep the body well stoked under load at high altitude.

In the city we customarily eat till we are full. In the wilds, where energy expenditure is far greater, we tend to be anxious about keeping the body fueled; consequently there is a powerful instinct to stuff ourselves with food until we feel comfortably full. In the process it is easy to eat two days' ration at one sitting and get up feeling slightly sick and bloated. The extra power is wasted since the body will not accept any more than it can use. It requires some knowledge of the caloric output of foods and the body's likely needs, but if the traveler can muster the necessary self-discipline and restraint, he will discover he can eat less with no loss of energy.

This tendency to overeat, in my experience, is as little recognized as it is fundamentally important. Think back to those trips on which you ran out of food. Instead of trusting the menu you originally devised, you probably decided—on the basis of bulk alone—that you weren't getting enough to eat, so you increased the rations. You damned the company that labeled your dinner "serves four," because it barely filled up two of you. It probably didn't occur to you that there might have been enough calories for four and that you didn't have to eat till you were stuffed. With a little knowledge of caloric production, the veteran traveler realizes that the slightly empty feeling in his stomach—and even loss of weight—reflects a healthy lack of bulk, not a dangerous shortage of nourishment.

Because freeze-dried foods cost 2–3 times as much as comparable dehydrated dishes, many hikers (and writers) dismiss them as too expensive. But cost per ounce can be a poor measure of value. A menu liberally supplied with freeze-dried foods will still cost less than $10 per day per person. Where can you vacation and eat in modest restaurants that cheaply? Considering the shortness (four days) of most backpacking vacations and the necessity of carrying everything on one's back, skimping on prime quality seems foolish. After a hard day in the wilds the best is sometimes barely good enough!

Freeze-dried food is often best for wilderness travel because of its ease of preparation, low bulk, rapid rehydration, nutritional values, superior taste, texture, form, color, and long shelf life. Air or vacuum dehydrating loses some proteins and vitamins. Weight is usually about the same for both dehydrated and freeze-dried foods, since both processes leave about 5% water and 25% of original weight, but dehydrated foods take 2–3 times as long to rehydrate (soak), a severe drawback when you're ravenous even before you stop to camp for the night. Air-dried food contains as much as 25% water. I'm willing to simmer my precooked, fresh-tasting freeze-dried stew for 20 minutes at high altitude, but an hour (and sometimes two!) is too long to wait for a less-appetizing air-dried dinner to cook. At such a time, cost is meaningless. The weight of cooking gear can often be shaved because precooked freeze-dried foods need only the addition of hot water to the package. I'm not a spendthrift, but when it comes to food I'm going to carry on my back, I want the best I can buy.

When it comes to shelf life, it's the packaging that counts. Food in polyethelene bags is always good for a year, but the safe maximum is two years. Vacuum packed foods in foil are good indefinitely—as long as the seal isn't broken. When the vacuum goes (easily determined visually) shelf life drops to the polyethelene level. Food vacuum packed in nitrogen in cans has no known shelf life limit, except for high-fat foods (butter, buttermilk, peanut butter powders) which have a five-year life expectancy.

CLASSIFYING FOOD

Food is divided into three major components: fats, proteins, and carbohydrates, all of which are essential to the backpacker's diet. The ideal proportions are essentially unknown and vary according to the temperature, individual, environment, and type of activity. A decade ago it was believed that we needed only about 50% carbohydrates, but a generous 25–30% protein and 20–25% fats.

The proportions were based on the myth that the more strenuous the activity, the more protein was needed. And fat was believed essential to provide power. Now we know that fresh unrefined

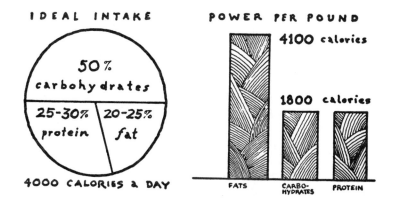

IDEAL INTAKE

50% carbohydrates

25-30% protein

20-25% fat

4000 CALORIES a DAY

POWER PER POUND

4100 calories

1800 calories

FATS   CARBO-HYDRATES   PROTEIN

carbohydrates are what generate most of the body's energy, with minimal need of protein and fat. But many Americans—and therefore many backpackers—persist in believing that meat makes them strong and fat keeps them energized. So they load their menus with meat, cheese, milk, eggs—and sugar.

Actually, protein requirements are unaffected by activity. Excess protein can be a liability in that it is comparatively difficult and slow to digest. Large intakes are poorly assimilated and provide no immediate energy. Furthermore, protein at 1800 calories per pound provides less than half the energy per pound of fat (4100). Most protein-happy hikers would do better to switch their enthusiasm to fat, in which they probably are deficient.

The National Academy of Sciences says we eat 50% more protein than we can utilize. Protein serves only to maintain existing muscle. On a rigorous trip, all that's needed is .015 ounces per pound of body weight per day. That means a 100-pound woman needs only an ounce and a half, while her 200-pound boyfriend needs a mere 3 ounces. More than that is wasted!

Fats are no easier to digest than proteins, but they supply more than twice the energy and release it gradually over a long period of time. The principal fat sources for backpackers are oil, butter, margarine, nuts, meat fat, and cheese. The digestion of protein and fat demands the full attention of the body's resources for a considerable period of time. Consumption should be spread through breakfast, lunch, and snacks rather than being concentrated in a heavy dinner. Even relatively small amounts should not be eaten before or during strenuous exercise. The blood cannot be expected to circulate rapidly through exercising muscles and digest complex food in the stomach at the same time without failing at one function or the other—usually both.

When heavy demands are made on both the digestion system and the muscles, the body is likely to rebel with shortness of breath, cramps, nausea, and dizziness. The first signs are low energy and fatigue. Carbohydrates may conveniently be thought of as pure energy. Digestion is rapid, undemanding, and efficient and the energy is released within minutes of consumption.

But fast energy release means that carbohydrates are completely exhausted of their power in as little as an hour, and more must be ingested if the energy level is to be maintained. The backpacker who lives on carbohydrates must eat almost continuously to avoid running out of fuel. The common sources of carbohydrates are fruits, cereals, vegetables, starches, honey, and sugars.

EAT SELECTIVELY

Back before I switched to fruit exclusively in the morning, I still was careful to climb on carbohydrates, not fat or protein. For example, one January day in the high Sierra I set out on snowshoes to climb the steep mountain that rises behind my cabin. In my daypack I carried a banana, chicken leg, cookies, a chunk of cheese, and raisins. The going was strenuous and hot and despite a good breakfast I began to grow faint and tired around ten, well below the summit. I found a shady flat rock thrusting up through the snow, and I sat down to eat the carbohydrate portion of my larder: the banana, raisins, and cookies. After resting for fifteen minutes flat on my back, I started off again feeling noticeably stronger and without any discomfort.

An hour and a half later when I reached the top I polished off the fat-rich chicken leg, the cheese, and the last of the cookies. After a nap and a relatively easy hour exploring the summit ridge I made the quick trip down feeling comfortable and strong.

If I had eaten the fat and protein components of my lunch instead of the carbohydrates before reaching the top, I know from experience that I would have been very uncomfortable when I resumed the climb. I would also have been further slowed by the lack of quick energy which the carbohydrate provided me.

Since fat digestion yields the most heat, it makes sense in cold country to partake just before retiring on a cold night for leisurely digestion while you sleep. There is no more potent source of fat calories than cooking oil, so I take a pull on the bottle or pour a dash in the stew when calories are needed and there's time for digestion.

With the exception of vitamin C (which is a natural antibiotic and prevents infection and is best taken in pill form), vitamins and minerals can usually be forgotten since they are provided in adequate quantity by any reasonably balanced diet. Even though storage is comparatively small, there is virtually no effect on the body for at least a month if vitamins and minerals are absent under normal conditions.

Severe conditions are different. For instance, on a month-long mountaineering trip above 14,000 feet in the Bolivian Andes I daily took Stress Potency Vitamin C and B Complex for better body performance. A climber friend takes along Vitamin E because it aids oxygenating his blood at high altitude. And people who are going to feel weak or uneasy without their vitamin pills should certainly take them along.

GLYCOGEN LOADING

In recent years, there has been considerable study and experimentation in an effort to produce maximum work capacity in climbers, runners, backpackers, and cross-country skiers. It's now well known that work capacity can be increased as much as 300% by careful dietary preparation. Studies show that a carbohydrate-rich diet several days in advance of heavy prolonged exercise greatly improves the body's respiratory quotient (oxygen supply) and thereby improves capacity for prolonged hard work. (Utilization of carbohydrate depends on the rate at which oxygen is supplied to working muscles.)

The most startling increase in work capacity comes from emptying the body's store of glycogen about a week in advance, then building up a fresh store just a few days before the trip. Glycogen is a starch normally stored in the body in small quantities. It can be quickly converted into glucose to answer sudden energy demands upon the body. The higher the body's glycogen content, the greater its work capacity.

For instance, a man who can do one hour of heavy work on a fat-protein diet could do two and a half hours of the same work after that diet had been heavily supplemented with carbohydrates for three days. When the man flushed the glycogen from his system a week in advance and followed the same diet, he was able to produce up to four hours of work.

So the backpacker who wishes to start a trip on Sunday with the greatest possible capacity for prolonged exertion should, the Sunday before, load up a pack and take a practice hike that thoroughly tires him out. Then on Sunday, Monday, and Tuesday he should eat fat and protein exclusively to keep his glycogen down—avoiding carbohydrates—get plenty of sleep, and limit his exercise to a walk around the block. On Wednesday, Thursday, Friday, and Saturday he should gorge on carbohydrates while continuing to consume ample protein and fat. On Sunday he should be admirably prepared for the most strenuous hike.

To prepare balanced, potent menus the backpacker obviously needs to be able to evaluate any given food. The best source of information I know is Agriculture Handbook No. 8, entitled *Composition of Foods* (available from the U.S. Government Printing Office, Washington, D.C. 20402).

For each of the thousands of foods listed the number of calories per pound or per 100 grams (equal to $3\frac{1}{2}$ ounces) is given, as well as a percentage breakdown into water, protein, fat, carbohydrates, vitamins, and minerals. Food combinations like granola are not listed and cannot be computed accurately, and brand names have been excluded, but it is possible to estimate the quantity and types of fuel contained in most backpacking foods with reasonable accuracy.

A SAMPLE MENU

Before considering individual foods, it might be worthwhile to take a look at what I eat on a typical summer day at, say, 8000 feet in the California Sierra.

making dinner — the hard way

DINNER : Invariably I begin with a Maggi, Knorr, or Lipton Soup Mix that yields $1\frac{1}{2} - 2$ cups of thick, hot soup per person, the first step in replacing liquid lost during the day. For maximum potency I fortify the soup with a gob of butter or a slosh of cooking oil and perhaps some TVP. Any leftover jerky or milk powder may also get dumped in the soup. We cook it in our one big pot and drink it out of our oversized plastic cups, accompanied with a few crackers from the lunch supply.

When there is still half an inch of soup in the pot (for flavor) I empty in the contents of one of my favorite AlpineAire dinners and stir in the required amount of cold water. This may be contrary to the directions on the package, which call for adding boiling water, but by mixing ingredients before heating I maximize valuable soaking time.

At 8000 feet the time needed to rehydrate the casserole may be twice the five minutes advertised, and twenty minutes is better than ten if you don't like your meat hard and rubbery. When the meal is half-cooked (i.e., the meat portion is no longer rock hard) I add my salt and pepper mix (to taste), mushroom slices, fine herbs mix (with restraint), and whatever other flavors or fortifications that seem appropriate on that particular evening.

With the aid of big spoons we eat the resulting stew in our unwashed soup cups. The moment the pot is empty and scraped, I fill it with water to simplify future cleaning because experience has taught me that stew allowed to dry will set up like concrete! Once the stew is off the stove a small pot or teakettle containing about three cups of water goes on—saving stove fuel. When the water is half heated we use a little in our empty cups to clean out the grease, polishing with a piece of paper towel. Into the hot water goes applesauce, probably pre-mixed with cinnamon and nutmeg. By the time a few raisins and a dash of honey have been stirred in, this precooked dish is ready for consumption in the cleaned soup-stew cups. The final course is hot tea, along with snack foods, and it continues until bedtime.

BREAKFAST: As already explained, I rely on fresh fruit exclusively all morning—if I can get it—for quick and bountiful energy that sends me bounding up the trail. If I can't carry enough heavy, juicy fruit to keep me stoked every morning, all morning, my first choice is dried fruit. If that won't do it, I go to an all-carbohydrate breakfast of sugar-free (and fruit-free) cold cereal or hot cereal with a touch of honey or molasses.

I hate to cook in the morning and I wouldn't dream of fixing hotcakes or sausage and eggs. I don't drink coffee and I have no appetite in the morning for sugar-rich Tang. But I know others do. Jack Stephenson likes to cook in the morning just to wake himself up and plan his day. He tells me he met a foreign backpacker on the Appalachian Trail who was so in love with his new discovery, American hotcakes, that he'd brought along nothing else to eat. When Jack met him he'd been living on hotcakes for three weeks and hadn't gotten tired of them yet! So tastes differ.

LUNCH: It begins for me when I'm through eating fruit and starting to get hungry for solid fool. I usually don't stop eating fruit until I've done my morning's hiking/climbing. If the trip is short, my preference is to dine on avocado, tomato, bell peppers, and crackers or sandwiches made from the four vegetable-fruits and onion. I often add Nu Tofu cheese and finish up with nuts, preferably raw. And I drink water.

I don't eat meat, eggs, or dairy when I'm hiking—if I can help it. But if the trip is long or somebody else planned it, I eat what I'm offered and enjoy it. Only a few years ago I ate the standard American backpacker's lunch. I quote from the 1980 edition of this book.

> At lunch we customarily break out the thin-sliced, compressed Pumpernickle and make sandwiches with butter, cheese, salami, peanut butter and jam and make up a quart of lemonade. If the morning has been strenuous we may substitute Gookinaid ERG, a sugarless electrolyte that's less tasty but more thirst-quenching.
>
> We may also dip into the dates or banana flakes to satisfy a sweet tooth, or break open the bag of gorp. Traditional

lunch time..

gorp is equal parts raisins, peanuts, and M&M chocolate drops. I substitute carob drops for difficult-to-digest chocolate and salted almonds or cashews for peanuts, and I use honey-dipped raisins. My gorp may also include banana flakes, sunflower seeds, date nuggets, and so forth. I like my gorp salty and will shake in salt if needed. Gorp is concentrated and potent and should be eaten in small quantities, along with plenty of liquid to avoid a stomach ache. Together with dried fruit it keeps me going until dinner is ready. I try to remind myself that what I'm eating is low on bulk but dehydrated and concentrated: so I must drink lots of liquids and restrain myself from the urge to eat until full.

There are too many potentially good backpacking foods for anyone to list, much less try, them all. Over the years I've developed a list of foodstuffs that meet my criteria and continue to satisfy. Listings are alphabetical.

APPLESAUCE, apple slices, etc.: The apple is the most widely available, generally most pleasing of dehydrated or dried fruits, and it has the highest calorie count (353 per $3\frac{1}{2}$ ounce) of the common fruits. As indicated earlier, applesauce lends itself to a variety of spices and additives. There are myriad brands to choose from, some raw, some instant, some with sugar, some without. I buy mine freeze-dried in bulk and prepackage it by the meal with cinnamon, etc.

BACON, RAW: While delicious and a great source of fat calories, bacon is heavy, prone to spoil, messy, difficult to prepare, and 80% of its calories end up in the grease which is difficult to handle and generally thrown away. Furthermore it requires carrying a skillet. I love crisp bacon but I wouldn't think of taking the raw stuff backpacking.

BAKING: A great many people enjoy baking biscuits, cornbread, gingerbread, bannock, coffee cake and the like, and fresh baked breads are extremely welcome, even craved, after a number of days on the trail. Bakery products can provide considerable power, especially the sweet ones that are cooked with (or eaten with) butter or margarine. However, pre-baked products (bread, cake, doughnuts) are seldom practical for backpacking trips, usually being mangled and squashed into an unrecognizable paste.

BEANS: A staple for travelers since the beginning of time, beans provide a fair source of carbohydrate and bulk and a popular starch base for many one-pot dinners. The raw bean is virtually uncookable at high altitude. Only precooked, dehydrated, or freeze-dried beans should be carried.

BREAD: The problem with breads is bulk, spoilage, ease of crushing, and drying out. Generally speaking, the harder and darker the better. Pumpernickle, rye, oatmeal and German black are all good, yielding about 250 calories per $3\frac{1}{2}$ ounces. A variety of small unsliced exotic loaves are now available at organic and health stores, but one must beware of labels that brag of absence of preservatives, for mold will quickly grow.

My favorite bread in recent years has been either of two brands by Orowheat: Westphalian Pumpernickle squares and Oro d'Oeuvre. A one pound "loaf" of either contains two packets, each with a dozen compressed, cracker-thin slices of strong delicious dark rye. Amazingly enough it keeps for more than a year, spreads easily and resists mangling and crumbling.

BOUILLON: Virtually weightless, ageless, foil-wrapped cubes are ideal for flavoring soups and casseroles and for impromptu broth when the body is too tired for food or a sudden storm makes a hot drink at lunchtime desirable.

BUTTER (MARGARINE): Only oils and animal fats surpass butter and margarine (about 720 calories per $3\frac{1}{2}$ ounces) as a source of fat. Served in Sherpa tea at breakfast, on bread or crackers at lunch, and in soup or stew at dinner, butter palatably provides an ideal source of high-yield, long-lasting energy. Parkay offers margarine in a lock-top plastic squeeze bottle designed for camping.

CANDY: Because candy is mostly sugar, which I believe harms the body, I no longer carry it, substituting honey and such sweet fruits as dates, raisins, pineapple, and bananas. But candy provides quick carbohydrate energy and is often craved in the wilds. Favorites are lemon drops, toffee, caramels, hard candies, sour balls, butterscotch, and bitter orange.

CANNED GOODS: Many a backpacker still carries canned tuna, corned beef, Spam, sardines, Vienna sausage, etc. for lunch or to bulwark a starchy dinner. Not only is such food unjustifiably heavy, the cans, when empty, are often left in the wilds. With all the good inexpensive dehydrated food available in the markets nowadays, there's no excuse for carrying canned foods into the wilderness. And in some areas glass and cans are now banned.

CASSEROLES: Made from scratch they allow experienced trail cooks to concoct their favorite one-pot dinners for any number of people with some cost savings over prepackaged freeze-dried dinners. See the end of the chapter for recipe sources.

CEREALS, COLD: Birchermuesli, with an energy yield of about 350 calories per $3\frac{1}{2}$ ounce serving, is a longtime favorite backpacking dry cereal, but the profusion of packaged and home-made granolas are just as powerful, especially when fortified with wheat germ, nuts, fruit, milk powder, etc. A pre-mixed sackful that allows close to a cup per person per morning conveniently solves the breakfast problem for many, especially those who don't care much for breakfast.

CEREAL, HOT: Cold cereal, of course, can provide additional comfort if made with boiling water, but in heavy weather with a strenuous morning ahead nothing provides long-lasting power better than fresh-cooked oatmeal or other high-potency hot cereal, especially if fortified with butter, milk, honey, raisins, etc. Single serving packets of precooked instant oatmeal with fruit or spice and sugar are wonderfully convenient—but too sweet for some of us.

CHEESE: Deservedly a mountaineering staple because of its high energy output (almost 400 calories per $3\frac{1}{2}$ ounces for Cheddar—divided about equally between protein and fat), cheese, nevertheless, produces little more than half the energy per ounce of margarine. And even relatively dry Cheddar and Swiss have a very considerable (34–40%) water content. Soft cheese like Jack, Edam, and Blue are often more than 50% water. The driest cheeses are Italian Romano, Parmesan, Provoloni, Kasseri, etc.

CHOCOLATE: This is one of the most difficult-to-digest foods known to man, partly because it's more than half fat and protein. It's a grave mistake to think of it as candy. Eaten during strenuous exercise it's more likely to provide a queasy stomach than a burst of energy. In addition it contains more caffeine than coffee, and eaten before bed it may easily inhibit sleep. I mention it only because its sweetness has made it popular with trail travelers, not because I ever carry it. Be warned! Cocoa mix is likewise popular because of its sweetness, but I avoid it because of its chocolate content. Carob (bars, drink, chips, etc.) is a delicious high-potency carbohydrate substitute for chocolate. It is available wherever natural or health foods are sold.

COOKIES AND BARS: These are always popular in the wilds because sweets and bakery goods enjoy enhanced appeal. The fig newton is the classic backpacking cookie but oatmeal cookies have always been my favorites. An increasing number of fruit and granola bars on the market are augmented by numerous recipes for homemade creations. Basically these are compounded of the ingredients of granolas, gorps, and fruits mixed together with eggs, water, shortening, and salt and baked in the oven. At some point cookies merge with...

CRACKERS: Hard biscuits and crackers, hard-pan, pilot biscuit, Triscuit and the like, though subject to breakage, are preferred by many to bread, because of the reduced bulk and water content and freedom from slicing and spoilage. Wheat thins, rye saltines, Rye-crisp, Melba toast, and Zweibach all have their fans. The chief drawback to crackers is their tendency to shatter and crumble, but I like them well enough to carry a lightweight plastic box that keeps them intact for lunch, soup-dipping, and snacks.

DRINKS, FRUIT: Lemonade mixes, Kool Aid, and Tang are most popular, but fruit juices made from citric powders, orange and grapefruit crystals aren't far behind. Artificially sweetened drinks are lighter and less bulky. Tea and coffee, though easy to make with bags and freeze-dried powders, offer zero food value unless fortified with butter (Sherpa Tea), milk powder, honey, or sugar. The stimulation they provide comes from caffeine. Herb teas won't keep you awake.

making lemonade

EGGS, OMELETTES: Powdered eggs have come a long way since they gagged the foot soldier in World War II; they now are available from every food manufacturer in a variety of highly edible forms. Omelet fanciers and those for whom breakfast is not breakfast without eggs can easily find a different featherweight dish for every morning of the week packed in foil or plastic, usually with ham or bacon bits. Calorie content is very substantial (usually upwards of 600 calories per $3\frac{1}{2}$ ounces). I don't carry eggs because I'm not fond of them, dislike the preparation and cleanup entailed, and rarely carry the necessary frying pan or skillet.

FREEZE-DRIED FOODS: Proof that backpackers care about what they put in their stomachs is the emergence of firms offering natural, vegetarian, unadulterated food. AlpineAire's fare is sugar, MSG, and preservative free, with no artificial flavor or color. All Harvest Foodworks dinners are meatless. Even old-timer Richmoor leaves out MSG in its Natural High Foods. Backpackers Pantry (Dri Lite) and Mountain House continue to offer good freeze-dried meals.

FRUIT, DRIED: Sun-dried apricots, peaches, dates, figs, prunes, bananas, etc. contain 25% water and are consequently heavy, but their chewiness makes them delightful as snacks on trips where weight is not critical. Whereas sun-dried apricots yield

260 calories per $3\frac{1}{2}$-ounce serving, the dehydrated version, with only 3.5% water, provides 332 calories.

Fruit is excellent stewed, with cereal, and baked in breads or cake. When I go dayhiking I nearly always carry sweet, dried bananas from Hawaii, honey-dipped pineapple from Taiwan, or Greek figs. On longer trips I lean toward lighter banana chips, date nuggets, and freeze-dried peaches and strawberries.

GORP: Recipes are legion. While the traditional mix is salted peanuts, M&M chocolates, and raisins, gorp can be broadly defined as a sack full of mixed dry high-potency savory snack foods. Extremists live on it or dislike it. It will flavor and fortify breakfast hot oatmeal and serves as dessert for lunch or dinner. I no longer carry it because it combines fruit, nuts, grains, seeds, and often chocolate—more than the stomach can handle at one time. That's why it never gave me the energy boost I expected. Now I take Sesame Sticks or Corn Nuts instead.

HONEY: Indispensable for those of use who don't carry sugar. Although sticky, heavy, and liquid, honey behaves well enough in a sturdy screw-capped squeeze bottle. There is no quicker source of potent carbohydrate energy (300 calories per $3\frac{1}{2}$-ounce), and honey is only 17.2% water. Its sweet delicate flavor makes it valuable as a spread, dessert, syrup, frosting, and sweetener for drinks.

INSTANT BREAKFAST: On the face of it, Instant breakfast and its relatives like Tiger's Milk should be ideal for backpacking, but my friends and I have reluctantly abandoned them because they dependably produce diarrhea within an hour if we are hiking. I have not tried them on inactive layover days, but I suffer no ill effects in the city where fresh, rather than powdered milk is used.

JAM: Like honey, jam and jelly tend to be messy and should be packed in reusable tubes. They offer slightly fewer calories and nearly 30% water, but are extremely welcome in the wilds.

JELLO: Has its fans as a drink, hot or cold, and as a chilled and set dessert, often with fruits or vegetables mixed in. I no longer carry it because it's mostly sugar and because preparation and cleanup efforts do not seem justified.

MEAT, FRESH: For years I carried a fresh, juicy steak to broil the first night out. Gradually I discovered that it was my city-oriented association with steak, not the steak itself, that seemed appetizing. On that first night in the wilds, steak usually has less appeal for the weary hiker than soup, starchy stew, and cold lemonade.

MEAT, DRIED: Freeze-dried chicken, beef, and meatballs are invaluable when making stews from scratch, but ham and corned beef offer more flavor. Allow maximum time for rehydration, preferably in hot bouillon, if you don't want it rubbery because water penetrates meat cells slowly. Beef jerky is a tasty trail food, but cannot be reconstituted and is therefore unavailable for cooking (it will flavor soup, but bouillon is better and cheaper). Dry salami, though 30% water, yields 450 calories of fat and protein per $3\frac{1}{2}$ ounces and keeps very well unsliced inside its skin.

MILK, etc.: Like dried eggs, dehydrated milk has gradually come to taste almost like the real thing—especially when allowed to stand fifteen minutes, and served cold. Most convenient are 4-ounce foil packages of Milkman instant low-fat dry milk product, which make a quart with a few shakes of the poly bottle.

The flavor is better than that of whole, skim, or non-fat milk products. A few drops of vanilla or a little coffee or cocoa mix help mask the slightly artificial flavor. Malted milk powder and milkshake mixes are favored by some, but the latter, including sugar, seems excessively heavy. Milkman probably yields over 400 calories per $3\frac{1}{2}$ ounces.

MOLASSES: This raw, crude liquid cane sugar, though nearly 25% water, quickly converts to energy and is used like honey or jam by those who like the strong sweet flavor. And a teaspoon or two works beautifully as a gentle natural food laxative—often necessary after a change from city fare to a steady diet of low bulk, dehydrated food.

molasses—a natural laxative

NUTS: Dried, roasted, salted nuts (almonds, walnuts, pecans, peanuts, etc.) contain very little water and yield 525–700 calories per $3\frac{1}{2}$ ounces, divided roughly into two parts fat and one part each of protein and carbohydrate. Nuts are an ideal snack and a perfect complement to high-carbohydrate candy, fruit, and bread. Peanut butter, though sticky, is a fine source of protein and fat when carried in a squeeze tube or a can. Sunflower, sesame, and other seeds are equally potent and popular as snack food and in gorp or granola.

OIL: Carried mainly for frying pancakes or fish, oil is the unexcelled source of pure fat calories, producing 884 per $3\frac{1}{2}$ ounces. Ultra weight-conscious extremists have tried to subsist on periodically ingested oil capsules, severely taxing their digestive systems and inviting difficulty during strenuous activity. Vegaline is easier to use than butter or margarine for greasing the skillet. I generally carry a small plastic bottle of cooking oil, even though I am not equipped to fry, and use it to fortify stews and other dishes when there is leisure for fat digestion. And I sometimes take a pull on the bottle before retiring on especially cold nights.

PANCAKES: I shudder when I think how many hours I have spent cooking pancakes in the hot morning sun and then cleaning out the gluey batter pot. Pancakes, in my view, belong to the dark ages of backpacking on the basis of preparation alone.

PEMMICAN: The legendary wonder food on which the mountain men of the early west lived almost exclusively, takes some getting used to and is therefore not ideal as a steady diet for recreational backpackers on comparatively short trips. A balanced diet, strong on carbohydrates, will produce more energy and contentment. True pemmican is half lean dried meat, half cooked animal fat, with the two mashed together into a paste. Recipes for pemmican and jerky are widely available.

POTATOES: Like beans, potatoes are a favorite base and source of bulk in one-pot dinners. Instant potato powders easily produce genuine-tasting mashed potatoes, and the leftovers can be fried for breakfast. Potato cubes are great in stews, hash, and french-fried.

PUDDINGS: Satisfying desserts that contrast well with sweet trail snacks can be a problem in the wilds where sweets are craved. Puddings (like Jello Instant) can be bought cheaply in the markets and shaken with milk powder in a plastic bag; since they set promptly without regard to temperature, they are a boon to backpackers. Mountaineering shops offer a number of excellent puddings, as well as strudels, cobblers, pies and cheesecakes, many of which (ideally) require neither cooking nor containers.

SALTS: Individual shakers for various salts and peppers are a nuisance to open and close in the dark. After struggling with various clever designs, I have returned to a single shaker loaded with two parts salt to one each of pepper and onion, garlic and celery salt. This all-purpose seasoning is just as good on eggs or

Coating the catch with "Trout Mix"

SPICE KIT

stew as on trout; my companions have yet to complain. With my salt mix in one shaker and Spice Islands Fines Herbs in another, I am well equipped with flavor for short trips.

SPICES: As earlier detailed, spices are the essential ingredients I rely on to transform comparatively simple fare into exciting eating. A word of warning: use restraint. Too much of the wrong spice can impair edibility. On overnight or weekend trips I rely solely on my salt mixture and Spice Islands' "Fines Herbes," a mixture of thyme, oregano, sage, rosemary, marjoram, and basil. A half teaspoon of this safe, all-purpose seasoning will perk up any one-pot dinner.

SPIRITS: Except for beer in warm weather I'm not a drinking man, but I've learned that a small belt of something potent can be marvelously beneficial under certain circumstances. Spirits are low at the end of a hard day when you ease the pack off weary shoulders and grimly contemplate setting up camp and cooking dinner in the wind and dark.

At such a time, nothing restores cheer by blotting out discomfort like a shot of painkiller, even if you don't drink. Some like the shot of 151 proof rum in a cup of snow; others prefer a tall one to help relieve thirst. I nearly always carry a few ounces of something potent in a sturdy plastic bottle for those tired times at the end of some days. My surprised companions, even the non-drinkers, are delighted to share it.

STARCHES, OTHER: Like beans, potatoes and pancakes, spaghetti, noodles, rice, and macaroni form the heart (and provide the bulk) of a backpacker's casserole. Kraft Dinner, which served me in Boy Scout days, is still a good bet, especially when cooked with a packet of freeze-dried chicken, slivered almonds, sliced mushrooms, and the above mentioned herb mix.

Precooked Minute Rice is the quickest of starches to prepare, but pasta has more protein and a shade more calories. The most convenient starch I know is Top Ramen, now widely available in markets. Three ounce packets of precooked, dry Chinese noodles are packaged with pork, chicken, beef, oriental, or onion bouillon mix. With three cups of boiling water, Top Ramen is noodle soup for two in three minutes. With only one cup, you have the starchy base on which to build a satisfying noodle dinner.

TVP stands for "textured vegetable protein." Made from de-fatted soybean flour, this widely available product contains more than 50% protein and 10% fat. Far superior to "hamburger helpers," it comes flavored to taste like ham, beef, chicken, bacon, hamburger—especially if simmered in the appropriate bouillon

base. Although soy protein lacks some of the amino acids found in meat, milk, cheese, or eggs, it has been a boon to the backpacker as a potent, fast-cooking meat substitute additive, economically stretching expensive freeze-dried meat. In fact, TVP has revolutionized backpack cooking.

VEGETABLES: Despised by many (at home as well as on the trail), they are indispensable as components of balanced, interesting one-pot dinners. For short trips I carry fresh mushrooms, onions, garlic, and whatever is in season. We either lightly steam them or eat them raw. On longer trips I depend on dried or dehydrated mushrooms, onions, peas, carrots, celery and tomato flakes to add bulk, flavor, and calories to an over-concentrated low-bulk diet. The longer I am out, the better they taste—especially if some of them are fresh.

FRESH SPROUTS: The best source of fresh vegetables in the wilds is—sprouts. You can grow them on the trail in as little as two days. All you need are seeds sold expressly for sprouting, a wide-mouthed quart plastic bottle, a piece of cheesecloth, and a few rubberbands. The best candidates are mustard seeds, wheat, sunflower seeds, peas, and sesame seeds.

You soak the seeds of your choice in clean sun-warmed water, wait for them to sprout, give the sprouts a few rinses—and they're ready to be eaten raw, made into salads, mixed in scrambled eggs or what have you. Sprouts are easy to prepare, lightweight, nutritious, compact, and delicious. For more information on growing your own sprouts, get *Rodale's Basic Natural Foods Cookbook* by Charles Gerras from Rodale Press Books.

If you'd like to start the day with more energy than you've ever known and a feeling of lightness, I urge you to try the power of fresh fruit for breakfast. To test it, give it a whirl before your favorite dayhike, and if it works take it overnight in the wilds.

Another source of delicious, spicy, satisfying gourmet meals you can easily prepare in the wilds is the 112-page *Wilderness Ranger Cookbook*, put together by people who live and work outdoors for weeks at a time. The recipes contained have stood the test of time. See Sources.

SE

PLEASURE PACKING

142 •

pour gas in the wilds
of its butane fuel
propane/butane mi
gral tank liquid
it's heavy and
Wilder
heavily t
of area
grow
m

Stoves and Cooking

*Picking Your Stove ... Rating Stove Power ...
Wind Protection is Vital ... White Gas and Kerosene ...
Butane and Propane ... Stoves are Dangerous! ... The Most
Popular Stoves ... Liquid Fuel Stoves ... Stove Accessories ... Wind
Protection ... Fireplace Design ... To Build a Fire ... Cook
Kits ... Choosing Utensils ... Handy Containers*

For most backpackers, unfortunately, cooking in the wilds is a necessary evil. So anything that promotes greater comfort in the kitchen will surely enhance the pleasure of a trip. As with most aspects of backpacking, the simpler and easier the arrangements, the smoother things go. Unless you're a gourmet, cooking will be easier if you carry a stove.

The trend is inexorably toward greater dependence on stoves. And stoves are getting both easier to use and safer. The field of stove makers has narrowed in recent years—and polarized. Nowadays, the basic choice is between stoves that burn liquid fuel fiercely in any weather and those that use cartridges of gas for a more controllable flame in warmer weather.

Two companies dominate: MSR builds compact blow torches operated from a separate gasoline tank, eliminating the need to

. Bleuet has improved the cold tolerance
̷ith the development of isobutane (IB) and
x (PB). Peak 1 offers a compromise in an inte-
uel stove that can be turned down to simmer. But
may have to be refueled in the field.

ess managers increasingly urge the use of the stoves in
aveled country or where fire danger is high. The number
where wood fires have been banned altogether is steadily
ing. In the California Sierra, for instance, burning wood is
ostly prohibited above 9600 feet. The improvement and refinement of stove offerings has led to their increased popularity. Then
there is the growing disinclination to deal with sooty pots and
smoky fires, and the trend toward simple one-pot dinners—aided
considerably by the proliferation of good freeze-dried and dehydrated meals in local markets.

In summary, people nowadays want cooking to be as easy as
possible. They carry a stove to avoid mess, uncertainty, and extra
hours in the kitchen—as well as to conserve firewood. They have
learned that a stove means even, dependable, controllable heat,
without the need to build a rock fireplace, hunt for wood, nurse
a fire, fight smoke and falling ashes, and deal with wildly varying
heat output that often means scorched or uncooked food. Backpacking stoves have not only gained acceptance, they have become
a badge of outdoor knowhow and ecological awareness—heavily
used areas are beginning to benefit.

Stoves, of course, have drawbacks, too. The small single
burner means only one dish at a time can be cooked, and the first
course will not stay warm while the next is cooking. The small
concentrated circle of heat makes cooking on large surfaces (frying
pancakes or trout) difficult. No stove works well, if at all, if not
well sheltered from wind. A shelter must be built if none can be
found. Then there is the fiddling with fuel, the assembling, priming, and preheating, and, of course, the weight of the stove and
fuel. But I view the lack of a second burner as a blessing rather
than a limitation; it forces me to employ one-dish dinners or eat in
courses, which enormously simplifies meal planning and automatically rules out fussy, difficult-to-prepare city-type meals. It also
means each course is served hot.

Many backpackers have never purchased a stove because they
look so intricate, because they are rumored to explode, or simply
because the catalogs and shops offer such a bewildering assortment.
With as many as three dozen models to choose from, how does
one know which is best? The guidelines that follow should reassure

the buyer as to intricacy and safety and help him narrow the field to not more than two to three models.

PICKING YOUR STOVE

The majority of stoves can be eliminated, for instance, if your stove must work in the snow. Conversely, if temperatures will always be above freezing, you can afford to carry lighter, cheaper stoves. But even if you're a summer camper, high-altitude use means your stove must have cold weather capability. Will your stove have to cook for only one or two, or will you require a stove able to handle big pots? If your family or group usually numbers four, will you prefer two small ones or a big one? Do you need a torch for melting snow, or a stove that will simmer a delicate dish?

Stove weight isn't critical any more. Weight comparisons become difficult because the fuel supplies in a growing number of stoves are detachable—and the majority of the weight is in the fuel. A detachable fuel source means the stove (essentially a burner with legs) can be folded and packed more easily. Where stoves used to be one piece, now they're often three to four: fuel bottle, burner, and 1–2 windscreens—which makes for less bulk and easier packing.

Stoves tend to bring forth strong emotions. People often discover they have strong—and sometimes contradictory—feelings about one or more aspects of stove ownership and operation, and these feelings usually have a strong influence on choice.

Stove weight cannot be considered arbitrarily. Heavy stoves offer more power and sometimes other advantages, such as simmering ability, stability, durability, etc. And stove weight cannot be considered without regard to the fuel weight needed to do the necessary cooking.

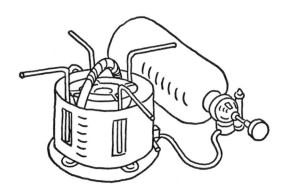

Light stoves tend to cook more slowly and use more fuel to accomplish their work. Over a period of a week, a light but inefficient stove might use so much more fuel that its weight advantage completely disappears when compared to a heavier but more efficient stove. So the lightest stove is not always best, or even the lightest source of the needed heat. Don't choose your stove on weight alone.

Ease of operation can also be a snare. While operating instructions are often mind boggling the first time your read them, be assured that they become routine and automatic once learned—and the learning can and should be done at home. Don't reject a stove on the basis of what look like complicated instructions. After fiddling at home for an hour or two you'll be able to forget the directions and set forth confidently, knowing you'll be able to run the stove without inordinate thought—except for safety procedures. Nevertheless, some stoves are far easier to operate than others, and since simplicity is the watchword I would urge you to pick the simplest stove that meets all other criteria.

The MSR stoves are virtually impossible to adjust. They're either on or they're off. They're indispensable for melting great quantities of snow efficiently for essential water, but they're hopeless for simmering. If you hope to turn down your stove to a low flame, don't buy an MSR liquid fuel. But since most packaged freeze-dried dinners merely require the addition of boiling water, it's possible to cook them without simmering, especially if you're cooking your food in its pouch. If you build your stew from scratch or enjoy gourmet cooking in the wilds, choose your stove accordingly.

RATING STOVE POWER

Heat output or stove power is usually measured (for purposes of comparison only) in the time required to boil a quart of water. It is vital to evaluate stove performance under the worst conditions you expect to face. Remember that heat output can be sharply reduced by cold and virtually destroyed if the stove is not protected from wind. Kept above freezing and sheltered from the breeze, most stoves will perform adequately, and boiling time will not be an important factor—unless conditions are always cold, the cook is impatient, or the trip is unusually long. As with other criteria, you'll be happier in the kitchen if you do not skimp on stove capability.

People can get quite emotional about refueling and carrying extra fuel, with all the risks of spilling, puncture, explosion, etc. Some travelers carry butane stoves solely to avoid the necessity of ever having to worry about a bottle of gasoline or kerosene in their pack. Be sure to carefully consider burning time before you purchase a stove. With any stove you're going to have to compute before each trip just how much fuel you'll have to take along. You'll feel sorry for yourself if you bring home too much—worse if you run out ahead of time.

While a good many of the best backpacking meals only require adding the contents of the package to boiling water (turn off stove, stir, wait five minutes, then eat) I insist on good flame adjustability, and the best new stoves provide it. It's exasperating to try to cook on a stove that burns whatever is on the bottom of the pot and goes out when you try to turn it down. To me, simmering (low flame) ability is important for even primitive cooking. Gourmets feel even more strongly on this point.

Easy starting is another endearing attribute in a stove. The procedure, as it will be seen, is quite different for each class of stove and type of fuel. A great many people will choose a butane stove solely because it starts just like the gas stove at home, whereas liquid fuel stoves require a more involved and often alarming procedure. Lighting a pool of gasoline and watching the stove enveloped in a flaring flame can produce great anxiety, especially inside a tent. Still, the anxiety disappears in most people once proficiency is attained and the process becomes automatic.

Stove stability may not seem important until you've had a stove fall over and the dinner you've been hungrily awaiting ends up in the dirt. Stove makers have put insufficient thought into stability design and a good many of their creations are still dangerously wobbly. Beware a stove that has skimpy pot supports, tips easily, has a small base, or stands inordinately tall. Poor stability in the kitchen will produce anxiety in the cook.

WIND PROTECTION IS VITAL

Wind resistance is of prime importance. It is placed near the end of the list because comparatively few stoves offer adequate wind protection. It isn't so much a matter of choice as it is of placing the stove thoughtfully out of the wind. Wind protection is something you arrange or construct in the field out of what you've brought and what you find in camp. Veteran backpackers have spent a lot of time and thought on creatively, cunningly building their own windscreens and positioning their stoves.

Because the lightest zephyr strongly affects stove performance—especially on simmer—wind protection remains the largest unsolved problem in the operation of the most backpacking stoves.

Safety is the other great concern. The subject is complex because it's part psychological. All stoves, by their very nature, are potential bombs. Caution is always required. There are no foolproof stoves, but the dangers differ greatly in different kinds of stoves. Fuel connections, starting procedures, fuel volatility, and the refueling process produce the greatest potential dangers. Experience, patience, common sense, and caution, however, reduce the hazards for most people to acceptable levels. Specific danger areas will be discussed for each fuel and stove type.

The final considerations are durability, dependability, and cleaning. Stoves that have been on the market for many years have proved durable and dependable. The bugs have been worked out, design has been refined, and safety levels are usually good. Beware a brand new stove. Very few come to the marketplace without some flaw—and in some cases the flaws have been extremely dangerous. It's better to stick to the tried and true stoves described below rather than hope for miracles in an untried offering.

All liquid fuel stoves need to be cleaned, some more than others. Cleaning is either manual (with a fine wire that you run through the burner orifice) or built-in (the cleaning needle is integral, operated by a lever or valve). When impurities in liquid fuel cause inevitable clogging, the stove stops or runs poorly until the orifice is reamed out.

WHITE GAS AND KEROSENE

White gasoline (or the cleaner commercial versions: Coleman Fuel and Chevron Blazo) is highly potent, extremely volatile, and quite capable of exploding. Unlike kerosene, spilled gasoline lights readily on clothes, hands, or tent. Its cost is reasonable, it is generally available in this country, and it tends to be clean smelling, oil-free, and produces less soot than kerosene. There are two classes of white gas stoves: those that require priming to heat the generator, and those that do not.

On the one hand the volatility of white gas permits it to be used as its own priming fuel, so no separate priming fuel is needed. On the other hand this is a distinctly hazardous procedure—probably the greatest source of gas stove accidents—and ought to be avoided at all costs in tents. A variety of safe and convenient priming fuels (solid or paste) are available as an alternative, and I strongly urge readers to use them. Kerosene, once the favored small stove fuel, is making a comeback—despite the fact that very few stoves are made for it.

Kerosene is slightly heavier than white gas but it is also somewhat hotter. It produces more odor and soot, and since it does not light readily a separate priming fuel (again solid or paste primers are far safer than gasoline) is generally prescribed.

Kerosene is far more likely to be available in the distant corners of the world favored by expeditions and trekkers than is white gas, but the biggest reason for its recent gain in popularity is its safety. It will not explode under ordinary circumstances and spilled fuel will not turn into an instant fireball if accidentally ignited. If the winter camping trend continues (often requiring cooking in tents) more kerosene stoves will probably become available.

BUTANE AND PROPANE

Butane and propane are compressed gases sold in pressurized metal cartridges. The liability of explosion is low, providing used cartridges are not thrown in the fire. Both fuels are considerably less potent than kerosene or gasoline, comparatively expensive, and the least readily available. But both are clean and soot free. Since butane and propane stoves require no filling, priming or pre-heating, they are unquestionably the easiest and most convenient of backpacking stoves.

Bleuet has upgraded its fuels with the development of Isobutane (IB) and propane butane (PB) to replace butane, in order to gain greater cold weather tolerance for its stoves. Butane was notorious for its refusal to flow in cold climates because pressure in butane containers is comparatively low. And toward the end of a cartridge, as pressure decreased, heat production slipped, increasing boiling time. But fuel cartridge pressure is increased at high altitude where air pressure is lower. It takes experience to estimate the amount of fuel remaining by hefting and shaking the canister.

Isobutane is marginally better than butane in cold tolerance, but it's still a summer fuel. Propane/butane mix (20% propane) is significantly better, dependable in the chill to be encountered in spring and fall. But don't dream of taking either IB or PB where it's cold enough to snow. For winter camping, liquid fuel is essential. There are also stoves that run on alcohol, even some that burn twigs.

Propane is stored under great pressure, which means that flow is excellent in cold weather or when the canister is nearly empty, but canisters must be thick walled to withstand the pressure. Although burning time is an impressive 6 hours, they are too heavy (2 pounds, full) to be carried by most recreational backpackers. Propane stoves are used chiefly by large groups that have porters (or boy scouts) to carry the fuel. The greatest advantage of butane and propane is that lighting the stove is no more difficult than lighting a kitchen stove that has no pilot. Simply hold a lighted match to the burner an instant *before* turning on the gas.

Since all stoves are designed for maximum heat output, there are a number of operating hazards that the user should be aware of. In gas stoves the principal dangers occur during refueling. Funnels overflow, fuel bottles get knocked over, gas gets spilled on a hot stove, fuel tanks get too hot, campfires ignite nearby gasoline supplies, the cook panics during a flareup and knocks over the stove, burning himself and catching the tent on fire, a fuel check while cooking causes burnt fingers, a spill or a flare-up.

Never forget that gas stoves can explode and spilled fuel can ignite in a flash. Because kerosene is far less volatile, all or most of these hazards are much reduced or nonexistent in kerosene stoves. But since the stove is red hot you can still get burned if you are less than cautious, and spilled kerosene can still burn up your tent.

STOVES ARE DANGEROUS!

Butane and propane stoves, because they're simple are considered safe by many campers—and this is a dangerous assumption. Cartridge-type stoves are just as dangerous as gas stoves, but the dangers are different, often unpredictable and less dramatically evident. Punctured canisters can turn into torches if ignited or foul your pack if undetected on the trail. And removing a canister that's defective or not yet empty, I can say from personal experience, can freeze your skin painfully. On rare occasions defective or poorly connected canisters spout fire like a torch without warming. Empty canisters thrown in the fire can explode, and butane stoves can erupt in tent-burning flareups when the canisters have been shaken vigorously or the temperature is too low.

Any kind of stove will produce dangerous levels of carbon monoxide if run in an enclosed space (tent). Carbon monoxide is sneaky stuff, invisible, almost odorless. The product of inevitable incomplete fuel combustion, it reduces the blood's ability to transport oxygen. Since high altitude has the same effect, it can be seen that the two are additive: the higher you are the more lethal carbon monoxide poisoning will be.

If tent ventilation isn't vigorous—as when buttoned up tightly against wind or storm—a burning stove consumes all the oxygen, causing the occupants of the tent to sweat, gasp, and complain of headache and nausea. The danger is greatest in tube, Goretex, or sealed fabric tents without vents. It is likewise greatest with the larger stoves, owing to their greater energy output and greater oxygen consumption. Pans so close to the burner that they deform the flame also contribute to incomplete combustion and therefore carbon monoxide production. If you cook in the tent, what you imagine to be high-altitude sickness may, at least in part, be carbon monoxide poisoning. Beware!

an eye-dropper fills the spirit cup.

Kerosene stoves can be lighted without a priming fuel by creating a wick. A twisted square of toilet paper tucked into a circle in the kerosene-filled spirit cup will light easily enough. But solid or paste primers are safer, cleaner, and much easier to use. And their value goes up if you must cook in a tent. But don't use lighter fluid, which is just as dangerous as white gas.

THE MOST POPULAR STOVES

With this background, you will hopefully be able to evaluate the stoves you are considering. Here are the most popular stoves of the nineties, starting with those fair-weather cookers that use gas cartridges.

BLEUET 206 uses a 190-gram cannister of PB that cannot be removed until empty. The stove weighs 10 ounces, will boil water in 4.5 minutes and runs for 2.5 hours, which is usually long enough for a long summer weekend for two people. The collapsible plastic base is distinctly unstable and the optional windscreen will only handle light zephyrs, but this is probably the most popular warm weather stove for weekend trips, especially for beginners. Just light a match and turn it on and you're ready to cook—and simmer. Bleuet cannisters are available everywhere.

BLEUET 106 is the baby brother of the 206. With its 90-gram cartridge, it packs in its own pair of cooking pots, so the kit weighs a pound. Burn time is a meager 1.3 hours. Since the cartridge is the base, stability is only fair. This small compact specialty stove

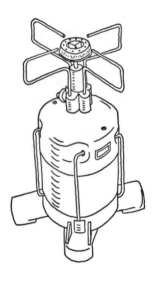

is strictly for solo hikers or bikers with severe space limitations, on a minimal cooking weekend.

BLEUET 470 is the newest entry in the stove derby. It offers a large burner sitting on a huge PB cannister with a burn time of 4.5 hours. With care it might last a week. Its greatest virtues are its generous size and the ability to detach the burner from the cannister, which after dinner can be plugged into the Lumogaz 470 lantern. Though made for car camping, this stove may well become popular with backpackers, now that Bleuet is putting PB in its cartridges instead of mere Butane. But it needs a real windscreen.

SCORPION II (from Olicamp) takes its own or the MSR IB cannister only, but instead of screwing directly onto the burner, it sits nearby, connected by a detachable flexible hose. This arrangement permits excellent burner stability and easier windscreening, due to its low center of gravity. The stove is compact, stable, quick to assemble, and simmers readily when protected by its windscreen. A safety device protects against explosion if the cartridge falls into your campfire. Inexpensive, it's a good starter stove.

MSR RAPIDFIRE, another IB stove with detachable cannister and excellent windscreen, is otherwise similar in most respects to the Scorpion. Both burn a maximum of 2.5 hours in warm weather.

PROPANE stoves (like the big three-burner Coleman) are excellent in the cold due to their high-pressure cannisters, but the latter are big and prohibitively heavy for backpacking unless the group is very large. Propane is excellent for horse packing, car camping, and river trips.

LIQUID FUEL STOVES

Veteran backpackers tend to favor liquid fuel stoves because they take longer trips, camp in the snow, appreciate efficiency, and aren't afraid of the dangers or the need to play mechanic if something goes wrong.

MSR WHISPERLITE is popular with long-distance trekkers, climbers, and serious backpackers, but some experience and mechanical ability are necessary before the stove becomes as "field maintainable" as represented. It's great for melting quantities of snow, but it's not for the casual weekend summer backpacker. As with the Scorpion and Rapidfire, the stable, ground-hugging burner is supplied by a flexible fuel line attached to various sized fuel bottles.

The Whisperlite folds compactly, runs quietly, weighs 12 ounces, and includes an excellent two-part windscreen system. But assembly is complex. You have to dress it first in its horizontal "heat reflector," open it up, connect it, pump up pressure, feed raw gas into the priming bowl, light it, wait until the flame goes out, then quickly light the burner before cooling can occur. Finally, you have to rig the vertical windscreen around the hot stove without singeing your fingers or eyebrows.

WHISPERLITE INTERNATIONALE can burn kerosene as well as white gas and comes equipped with a K jet and tool kit. Fuel bottles of 11-ounce, 22-ounce, and 33-ounce capacity are available.

MSR GK II is similar to the Whisperlites in that it's a burner attached to a fuel bottle. But the burner's round bottom isn't nearly as stable. The stove burns almost any fuel: white gas, leaded or unleaded auto gas, or kerosene. A heat reflector and windscreen are included. As with all the MSR liquid fuel stoves, simmering is nearly impossible, unless you start at low throttle. If you do achieve a low flame, the slightest breeze will blow it out. And don't over-tighten the gas line to the pump or you'll ruin the gasket and cause it to leak.

PEAK 1 FEATHER 400 is a redesigned traditional white gas stove with the burner mounted on an integral tank, which means it has to be refilled periodically by pouring, but fuel typically lasts through a weekend trip. Folding legs and low profile provide good stability. The burner is divided into four quadrants with an integrated windscreen. The stove requires no priming and the flame is moderately adjustable for simmering.

Filled with 11.8 ounces of gas, the stove weighs almost 2 pounds. The Peak 1 is rated as reliable and dependable by some

and subject to mechanical problems by others. But it offers an attractive alternative to the extremes of the warm weather BI and PB cartridge stoves and the finicky MSR blowtorches. As a compromise, it's valuable to many backpackers.

PEAK 1 FEATHER 442 burns unleaded gasoline at a fourth the cost of white gas and a fraction of the price of IB and PB canisters.

PEAK 1 MULTI FUEL stove is slightly lighter, has an improved windscreen, and burns kerosene as well as white gas.

OPTIMUS 8R and SVEA 123 are old-fashioned white gas stoves with integral tanks. Unlike the Peak 1s, they have no pump and therefore require priming. Performance drops in the cold and high altitude when tank pressure becomes hard to maintain. Once the premier stove maker, Optimus has failed to keep pace, and its few remaining models have become fearfully expensive.

STOVE ACCESSORIES

Though the number of stoves on the market has shrunk in recent years, there are doubtless other good ones. For better performance in the kitchen, one sometimes needs stove accessories. In the Campmor catalog we find the aluminum Sigg and MSR fuel bottles ranging from half a pint to a quart and a half, a 10 × 19-inch folding aluminum windscreen that won't blow over, tubes of Fire Ribbon for priming white gas or kerosene stoves, a circular windscreen for the Multi Fuel Peak 1, the expensive but effective wraparound MSR heat exchanger that clamps around your pot. PB gas cartridges for the Bleuet 106, 206, 470, and IB cannisters for the Scorpion and Rapidfire, plus stove bags, stove lighters, funnels, caps, and filters.

WIND PROTECTION

Wind is the number one nemesis of outdoor cooks, and veteran backpackers have learned that sheltering the stove from all but the faintest zephyr is an art that must be mastered if cooking is to be quick and efficient. Except for the MSR's effective circle of protection, windscreens that come with stoves are undependable at best. The burden is on the cook to build a wall or screen of rock or wood, get behind a downed tree, find a hollow, use a cooker or, as a last resort, retreat to the tent to find the still air essential to carefree cooking. If a part of the stove's burner will not stay lit or the flame blows out from under the pot, there is a serious loss of efficiency that should be corrected. Otherwise, fuel is wasted, cooking time is prolonged, or food may never completely cook.

The first step is to take pains to find a sheltered place to cook. Don't just set up the stove in the middle of camp. Number two, if shelter isn't sufficient, take the trouble to build an effective windbreak. Third (and easiest), don't set forth into the wilds without lids that fit snugly on every pot—and use them!

Fourth, for windy conditions, pick a stove with good protection, use the windscreens offered (even if you have to pay extra for them), and do everything you can to reduce the heat-stealing gap between pot and burner down to a quarter inch (if possible) by bending or modifying pot supports.

Don't settle for the wind protection—if any—that comes with your stove. I have seen clever homemade windscreens of cardboard, foil, and cloth that made a big difference. For instance, a friend of mine dislikes the MSR foil windscreens because they crumple, tear, pick up food and dirt, wear out, and blow over. So he augments his with that stand-up folding aluminum screen offered by Campmor. Sometimes in a windy camp, a windscreen makes the difference between a hot dinner and a cold one.

Sigg makes beautiful spun aluminum fuel bottles in pint, quart, and quart and a half sizes. MSR makes bottles that hold 11, 22, or 33 ounces. Backup fuel can also be carried safely in the leak proof plastic bottles in which you buy your motor oil. MSR also offers a Cooking System that includes its wrap-around-the pot heat exchanger and a cookset that includes 1.5 and 2 liter stainless steel pots, a frying pan that fits both pots as a lid and a pot lifter. The folded-up Whisperlite or Rapidfire stoves will pack inside the pot set.

The alternative to carrying a stove, of course, is to build one out of native materials and gather native fuel to fire it. Ease, efficiency, and effectiveness are generally doubled by carrying a small grill. The 4.5-ounce tubular, stainless steel Backpackers Adjustable Grill will do the job. It's 5.5 inches wide and extends from 13 to 22 inches long, and will accommodate 2 to 3 carefully placed pots. The cheapest grills are oven and refrigerator shelves and broiler racks, but they're heavy.

FIREPLACE DESIGN

My favorite cooking fireplace design is the half-dugout. There are two advantages: smaller, flatter rocks can be used to ensure a more stable structure, and the fire is easier to light and easier to protect from wind. If I were faced with rebuilding a heap of blackened rocks into an efficient cookstove—assuming the location is appropriate and safe—I would first clear a circle about four feet across and sort through the rocks in hopes of finding a matched pair about the size and shape of bricks. Such rocks are never to be found, of course, so I settle for the best I can find (concave upper surfaces are better than convex.)

Using the direction of the breeze, the lay of the land, and the pattern of branches on nearby trees to determine the path of the prevailing wind, I place my rocks parallel to that path and also to each other—about a foot apart. On the downwind end, I place a larger rock (or rocks) to form a chimney, so the resulting structure forms a squat "U." Then, using a sharp rock fragment as a trowel I excavate about four inches of earth and charcoal from inside the pit. Now I am ready to place my lightweight grill across the opening, supporting it on the two "bricks" as close as possible to the chimney. Care must be taken to see that it is solid and will not slide or wobble—or the dinner may end up in the fire!

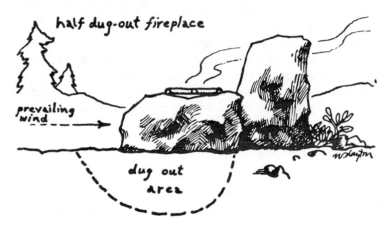

half dug-out fireplace

prevailing wind

dug out area

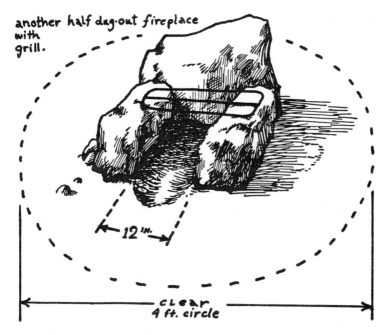

another half dug-out fireplace with grill.

12 IN.

CLEAR
4 ft. circle

I like to set my grill about 2 inches above ground level and 6 inches above the bottom of the firepit, but the proportions must sometimes be altered. On a windy day, I dig deeper and sometimes have to block the windward end with rocks to control the draft. Where there are no rocks at all and the grill sits directly on the ground, the firepit must be deeper still.

Inexperienced stove builders invariably build too large a firebox and set the grill much too high. Increasing grill height from 6 to 10 inches probably triples the volume of wood needed to cook dinner. Small fires are easier on the cook, easier on the wood supply, and heat is more easily regulated. Expert backpackers emulate the Indian and try to cook their food with the smallest fire possible.

TO BUILD A FIRE

The traditional structures for kindling a camp fire are the lean-to (match-sized twigs leaned against a larger piece) or the tepee (a cone of twigs). The most common mistake among fire builders is not having good quantities of dry twigs, tinder, toilet paper, and burnables of all sizes within easy reach before the first match is struck. I usually start with three squares of toilet paper loosely crumpled, cover that with a handful of dry pine needles, then build a tepee of the smallest, lightest twigs by tilting them against the paper from all sides.

After carefully leaning half a dozen finger-sized sticks against the pile. I crouch low to block the prevailing breeze (if it is strong, I block the entrance to the fire pit temporarily with rocks) and thrust a lighted kitchen match beneath the paper with one hand while I shelter the match from stray zephyrs with the other.

Once the paper is lighted, I add the match to the tepee and use both hands to shelter the embryo blaze until all the wood has caught. Care must be taken not to put the fire out by knocking down the tepee with fresh wood by skipping the intermediate-sized sticks and adding heavy branches or by letting the tepee burn up before adding fresh wood.

There are differences of opinion, not surprisingly, about matches and lighting fires. Some people carry only paper book matches, others (like myself) take only wooden kitchen matches: wooden safety matches that can only be lighted on the box are a bother in the summer but indispensable in the winter when snow covers the rocks. I have used commercially waterproofed and windproofed matches and found them excellent though expensive, for difficult conditions and emergency kits. Some people dip their matches in paraffin or candle wax.

Still others carry all their matches in waterproof matchboxes. My simpler, but probably less secure strategy is to stuff lots of matches in all the waterproof outside pockets of my pack. Another dozen are inside my watertight first aid kit. The climate of the California summer Sierra does not seem to me to demand a waterproof matchbox. A handful in a securely closed plastic bag makes a decent enough emergency supply. In wet country or for winter mountaineering, fire starters are valuable both for open fires and for stoves.

COOK KITS

Today there are a number of good cook kits on the market for small groups and a variety of good pots, pans, and kettles. But thoughtful backpackers will still be well advised to devise combinations suited to the particular requirements of their menus. And the Goodwill stores and supermarkets still offer bargains and a variety not to be found in mountaineering shops.

Since the evidence is strong that aluminum corrodes and poisons the body, pot makers have swung to stainless steel, which is no longer twice as heavy as aluminum. MSR has largely replaced

Sigg as the leader, but Open Country, with its wide variety of copper-bottomed pots is close behind. Coleman and Primus also offer attractive cook kits in light weight stainless steel. Or you can buy your pots and pans individually.

Ideal pot design depends somewhat on whether a stove or open fire is to be used. For stoves, pots need small, perfectly flat bottoms of small diameter for maximum stability. The thicker the bottom the less likely that the small concentration of heat will cause scorching or burning. Heat is not a problem at the handle, bail, or lid.

Pots for an open fire can be any shape and uneven on the bottom, but lids should be easily removed and handles or bails must be usable when flames envelop them. All pots should have rounded edges and no grooves or seams or cracks to trap food and dirt. Tin cans, or billycans, for this reason are poor except for making tea.

Frying pans or griddles are a nuisance for the backpacker because they require a wood fire, which blackens them, and thus require a heavy cloth or plastic case. Decent frying pans and griddles are not light because heavy gauge metal is needed to evenly spread the heat and prevent burning. The best compromise for the backpacker is a shallow 8- or 9-inch pan of thin steel or thicker aluminum, with either a ridged or waffled interior to spread heat, or a teflon coating to prevent sticking. Or cook your trout in the ashes—after first wrapping it in foil.

After making coffee or tea for many years in whatever pot was available, it dawned on me that I could do a far better job and leave one pot at home (not to mention avoiding a scum of grease from the soup) by carrying a real teapot.

People who are deeply attached to certain dishes, or who genuinely like to prepare fancy meals, are often obliged to carry additional equipment, like ovens, toasters, and pressure cookers. Fresh

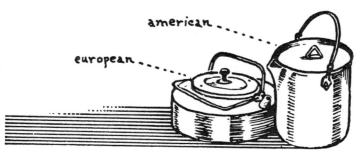

american

european

a tea or coffee pot is the ideal 'second pot'.

foil .... pie pan oven .... hot coals

office clamps ..... pie pans

bread, biscuits, gingerbread, and cake are extremely welcome in the wilds, more so after a week of dried foods.

The Bakepacker insert, which comes in two sizes, converts covered pots of 6 or 8 inches in diameter into an oven to bake food sealed in a plastic bag. You can bake a cake, biscuits, fish, rice, or an omelet. Dispense with the plastic bag and you've got a steamer for fresh vegetables or rice. Weight is 4 ounces.

Though it requires more fiddling—and a wood fire, not a stove—you can make a far lighter, cheaper "Mini Dutch Oven" from two pie pans fastened together with spring clamps. Just suspend the oven on a grill over a bed of coals and spread a layer of coals on top.

CHOOSING UTENSILS

Eating and cooking utensil requirements range all the way from the couple who carry a single large spoon and jackknife between them, to parties in which each person has his own knife, fork, and spoon wears a sheathknife, and carries additional utensils for the cook. Obviously, the larger the party, the more cooking gear required. Most experienced backpackers using easily prepared dishes forget about table knives and forks and carry only a soup spoon apiece and a good sized simple pocketknife. If you prefer full service "silverware" you can't go far wrong with Lexan's strong, unbreakable plastic knife, fork, and two spoons.

A steel knife is an absolute necessity in the wilds, so it's important to pick the one you need. Many people have strong and sometimes irrational feelings about what sort of knife expresses who they are. Most hikers carry more knife than they need to make a fashion statement or reach for status. The first decision in knife

my best knife

choice is to pick your steel. Carbon steel knives like the Boy Scout jackknife will rust and dull easily, but they're quick to sharpen, inexpensive, hard to break, and take a keen edge.

Stainless steel blades like the Swiss Army knife are hard to sharpen, don't get as sharp, but hold an edge longer. Because they're shiny they're easier to clean, but they tend to be brittle. Once the type of steel has been chosen, there are three basic knife styles to consider: the small folding pocketknife, which includes the Boy Scout workhorse and the Swiss Army toolbox, bigger folding lockbacks, and the heavy hunter's sheath knife. You'll probably choose the one that best expresses your personality, but don't completely lose sight of function and weight.

Only you can decide how many blades you need, what type they should be and how big. The best Swiss Army knives come from Victorinox and Wenger. Beware their many cheap copiers. The best lockbacks come from Buck, Gerber, Schrade, and Spyderco. Because of their greater weight they're too heavy for a pocket. For maximum utility and minimal chance of loss, you'll want to carry yours in a holster on your belt or pack strap. Nowadays the big heavy macho sheath knife is mostly carried by hunters who really need them.

The carbon steel knife I like best for backpacking has a big bread blade suitable for spreading crackers and cutting salami—and a shorter, slimmer sharply pointed blade for cleaning trout. Brightly colored handles help prevent loss. If I am traveling alone, I put a tiny single-bladed spare jackknife in the outside pack pocket containing the first aid or fishing kit.

Pot grippers or tongs or pliers may be needed to lift lids and serve as pot handles. Aluminum pot grippers weigh little more

sigg pot lids lift off easily when fitted with homemade knobs.

than an ounce and are fine for stoves, but the handle is too short for an open fire and the lack of a spring makes operation awkward. Longer, stronger spring-loaded steel grippers of similar design weigh a quarter of a pound. Neither fits all pots. I prefer a paicast aluminum hot pot tongs that, being a large pair of pliers, is a more versatile tool. Many of us find an old padded cloth pot holder indispensable.

Can openers will not be needed if canned food is left at home, but a good many of us, after many weight-saving economies, like to take along some canned luxury like sliced apricots in heavy syrup. Besides, copies of the army can opener weigh only an eighth of an ounce. Other sometimes useful kitchen tools are spatulas, forks, mixing and stirring spoons, and water dippers. Nylon spatulas though subject to fire damage are light, cheap, and needed for Teflon pans.

Every backpacker needs a cup, and the more experienced choose large ones and dispense with plates. In the west where the influence of the Sierra Club is strongest, the Sierra cup has become an object of worship to some, and consequently an object of scorn to others. This wide-mouthed, nesting, stainless steel cup holds 12 ounces and weighs 3 ounces. The wire handle which hooks to the belt, stays cool enough to hold when the cup is filled with boiling tea. But I much prefer a 12-ounce plastic cup that costs pennies, and weighs only $1\frac{1}{2}$ ounces, retains food heat better, cleans more easily and, when the bottom of the handle is cut, snaps more securely to a belt or nylon line.

HANDY CONTAINERS

For backpackers not yet ready to dine out of cups—or who cannot abide an oily film from the stew in their tea—a small, deep boilable polyethelene bowl is a greatly superior alternative to the sectioned plastic plate.

When it comes to food storage, plastic bottles, bags, Ziplocs, boxes, canisters and jars have—or should have—replaced aluminum containers. Many containers are so commonly available in markets that some mountaineering shops no longer bother to stock them. I make a habit of cruising the kitchenware section of supermarkets to hunt for merchandise adaptable to backpacking.

In choosing plastic containers, I shun all but screw-on caps likely to form a watertight seal and avoid corners and recessed seams that will trap food and be hard to clean. And I buy widemouthed containers whenever there is a choice. Some of my best

tube
&
clip
for
carrying
jam
or
honey

containers are recycled. When I spot an unusual bottle around the house, I wait until it is empty and then boil it out and add it to my collection.

Refillable squeeze tubes are invaluable for leakproof easy dispensing of jam, jell, catsup, butter, honey, peanut butter—anything of similar consistency. They boil out easily between trips and have yet to leak when properly assembled. Powdered milk presents a more difficult problem. When the wind is blowing the only way to avoid considerable spillage is to squirt the powder from a plastic catsup squirter bottle (available at large supermarkets) directly into the cup. Salt and pepper shakers come in a half dozen clever designs. Unfortunately, they hold enough for only 2–3 days per 2–3 persons. Salt companies now offer a variety of prefilled plastic and cardboard shakers which are handy and safe if carried in plastic bags. For many years, I carried an old tin spice can filled with a mixture of three parts salt and one each of pepper, onion, garlic and celery salts. It is still one of my favorite shakers.

For larger parties or where water is scarce, collapsible jugs and bags are extremely convenient. They range in capacity from 1–5 gallons and weigh as little as 7 ounces for $2\frac{1}{2}$-gallon bag. They roll up or press flat, and eventually they spring leaks, but if I am planning a dry camp on a ridge I carry a collapsible jug to fill at the highest water.

Though the quart poly bottle I carry for making lemonade doubles as a canteen in wet country, there are myriad plastic canteens and water bottles, some with drinking tubes or straws, designed for runners, that work perfectly on the trail.

To keep stoves and fire-blackened pots from spreading soot in one's pack means storing them in bags. Even heavy plastic does not do nearly as well as cloth. All kitchenware must be washed daily to prevent the formation of bacteria that can cause debilitating stomach illness. A few people scrupulously boil everything in soapy water after every meal; many only scrape out pots and pans and rinse in cold water—and cross their fingers.

My procedure lies somewhere in between. For a short 2–3 man trip, I carry a 4-inch square abrasive scouring cloth and a 3-inch square sponge backed with emery cloth. Both are soapless. For burned pot bottoms I take a "chore girl" and I always take a dish cloth. Completing my kit are a vial of liquid bio-degradable soap—which is very effective at cleaning skin as well as pots—and a clean diaper or small absorbent hand towel.

Old threadbare towels are inefficient. Fire-blackened pots are best wiped with wet paper towels, rinsed and allowed to dry before being packed away in plastic or cloth bags. And if you rub a pot with soap before putting it on the fire, the soot will come off with comparative ease.

Cooking, for most of us, will never rival good eating, but if you keep it simple—a good stove, simple menus, and ample advance planning—your time in the kitchen will be surprisingly pleasant and rewarding.

EIGHT

Shelter

*Domes... Advantages and Drawbacks... How
to Pick a Tent... Condensation Problems... Some
Mistaken Assumptions... How to Fight Condensation...
Tent Pole Considerations... Checking Out Tents... Doors and
Zippers... Vestibules Add Storage... The Prototypic Tunnel...
Individual Tent Makers... Other Forms of Shelter...
Bivys and Bag Covers... Features and Accessories*

There are various ways to classify the tents of the nineties. Let's start with shape. Nearly 90% of today's tents can be divided into (1) Domes, (2) Tunnels, or some combination of the two. (3) Frogs, the most popular new shape, are hybrid tunnel/domes. (4) A few modified traditional A-frames still linger. Of course, modifications and combinations of these four basic shapes abound. It's often hard to classify a given tent.

Tents have gradually improved as new technologies, designs, and configurations combine, but there have been no major advances. New tents are only marginally better than those of a decade ago. In fact, the shrinking number of major manufacturers turn out increasingly similar products. They haven't taken advantage of modern technology. They haven't discovered, for instance, the importance of built-in chimney venting to fight condensation.

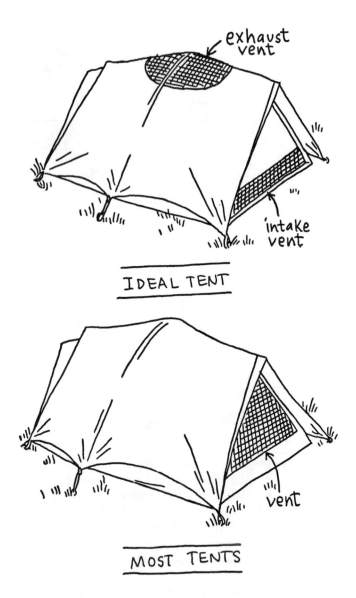

IDEAL TENT

MOST TENTS

They claim their tents are well vented, but they aren't. Vents are poorly located and netting panels often defeat vertical airflow. A chimney full of holes doesn't draw! To establish the needed vertical rise of air, intake vents must be at ground level, an exhaust vent must be located near the ceiling's highest point, and the area in between must be closed.

And most tent makers still think the chief benefit of double-wall construction is ventilation, i.e., maximizing the air flow between the walls, so they separate them to the max. Actually, the double wall's main benefit is to raise the inner wall temperature, thus reducing the potential for condensation by reducing the temperature differential. The inner wall stays warmer when air movement between the walls is reduced, not enlarged, so the walls should be closer together, not farther apart.

Maybe there's a connection between this tunnel vision and the fact that Sierra Designs, The North Face, Alpine Designs, Marmot, and others are all owned by the same multinational Hong Kong holding company. And the tents offered by North Face, Sierra Designs, Eureka, Walrus, and Quest are all made in the same Korean factory. Clearly, consolidation marks the backpacking industry of the nineties.

Shapes may differ, but the basic design of the vast majority of tents looks like this. An integral canopy of uncoated nylon and netting is protected from the weather by a coated, removable outer fly. The structure is hung from curved external poles of fiberglass or aluminum, above a waterproof floor.

The single-walled Goretex tent was such a dismal failure that Gore, to protect himself, now refuses to sell his over-hyped magic coating to tent makers. Goretex tents weren't waterproof and they didn't breathe. The demise of the Goretex tent also largely killed the booming Goretex bivy sack market. Maybe the public is beginning to figure out that Goretex doesn't work.

In response to public demand, more and more tents are designed to be "free standing." Comfort-loving Americans want their tents to self-erect if possible, and the makers are striving to give them their wish. Fewer people, say the retailers, are willing to study directions, practice setting up the tent on the front lawn, set guy lines, or drive tent stakes. So tents are either "free-standing" or they're not. That's another way of classifying tents.

Today's backpackers don't want to sweat or struggle. They'd like to shake the tent out of its bag, stand back and watch the heap of fabric and poles spring to life, producing a taut tent that can then be picked up and positioned on a suitable sleeping site. We're not lazy, we just want our tents foolproof. And ease of erection is definitely a blessing at the end of that first long day (or when it's blowing, dark, or raining—or some diabolical combination).

Tents can also be classified as (1) summer tents of netting for bug protection and shade, with a floor for cleanliness, sometimes with flies, (2) three-season tents with fabric walls, tub floors, netting skylights, doors, windows, and vents—all protected by a coated fly, and (3) winter tents of the same general design, but with less netting, sturdier poles, high-sided tub floors, and heavier all-around construction. There are also serious shelters (and emergency protection) built from (4) pitching tarps, (5) tube tents, (6) ground cloths and ponchos, and (7) bivy sacks.

DOMES

Domes vary so greatly that they're sometimes hard to recognize. They look vaguely like igloos and the tops are usually symmetrical. But vestibules, pole envelopes, and stretched flies tend to camouflage the basic shape. Rarely perfect hemispheres, some domes are flattened, others are elongated. Basically the tent is hung from 2 to 6 long curved fiberglass jointed poles that arc from the ground up over the roof and back to earth again. Since rectangular floors make more efficient use of both sleeping and storage space, domes increasingly are rectangular at ground level.

Tunnels grew out of A-frames, which in turn had their origins in the old army pup tent, with its vertical I-pole at either end that neatly blocked the entry. A-frames nowadays are hung from two A-shaped poles fore and aft. And they have floors and doors, netting and all the trimmings. By adding a pole down the ridgeline they can be made semi-free-standing.

Today's A-frames are both the cheapest tents and the most expensive. This paradox stems from the fact that the A-frame is easy to build so it's found in low-cost models at drugstores and dis-

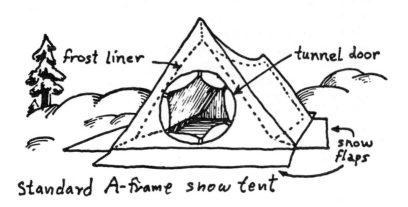

frost liner — tunnel door

snow flaps

Standard A-frame snow tent

count houses. Its shape is also well-suited to the most demanding mountaineering, hence the high-priced climbers' tents.

The tunnel begins with the rectangular pup tent configuration that neatly fits the shape of 1–2 sleepers, but the two straight poles that form the A-frame are replaced at each end by curved hoops, producing a stretched canopy like that on a covered wagon. Poles may be bent fiberglass or (better) curved aluminum.

The front (door) hoop is higher than the foot hoop. The catenary cut makes the hoops stick out like ribs and makes it impossible to connect the hoops with a ridgeline pole. So tunnels aren't freestanding even when the hoops are leaned away from each other. There are cone-shaped extensions for storage and entry both fore and aft from the hoops. Tunnels had their origins in the Warmlite tent.

The popular new Frogs are squat, tall stretched tunnels with a dash of dome. They are higher in the front, where a large dome-style door dominates, and lower in the back. The best-known examples of this small but growing fraternity of amphibians are the Sierra Designs Clip Flashlight and the North Face Tadpole.

ADVANTAGES AND DRAWBACKS

The greatest advantages of domes and tunnels over flat, slanting-walled A-frames are wind stability and usable space, specifically headroom. Because the walls rise more or less vertically on all sides, domes and tunnels have almost half again as much volume as an A-frame with the same floor area. You don't have to wriggle on your belly or sit in the middle to avoid rubbing against the wall. In stormy weather, when you must live in your tent around the clock, not just sleep in it, and when condensation and frost make touching the walls uncomfortable or worse, this extra living space is valuable—both physically and psychologically.

Domes are warmer when it's cold because the minimum possible fabric area is exposed to the weather for the cubic foot volume enclosed. And warmth is important because tent wall temperature is critical when there's a threat of condensation. The minimal surface is further reflected in lighter weight and lower cost. In theory, domes and tunnels are especially good in the wind because the smooth rounded surfaces offer nothing to grip on, but in fact domes are notorious for their "bowl of jelly" softness, because their poles are flexible instead of rigid.

Because most domes are self-supporting, they can be easily moved and positioned, and there are fewer stakes to set and no guylines to trip over. For many, the freedom from guylines is what sells the tent. As one tent maker puts it, "People will pay for something that's easier."

But domes, not surprisingly, have other drawbacks. Pitching can be complicated, at least at first, because they need up to four times as many feet of tent pole as tunnels require. If you've never pitched a dome you had better memorize or bring along the in-

struction sheet. All those miles of tent poles, however, cause other problems: they make a bundle in your pack that can be awkward and vulnerable. And because the poles are bent and under tension when the tent is pitched, they are considerably more vulnerable to stress and strain.

Just bending them into shape can use as much as 80% of their strength! Since each pole is made up of many short shockcorded sections, there are a great many joints under tension, and all are vulnerable to failure. Tunnels—and especially domes—are hard to ventilate because there are no vertical walls near the top. When flysheets are pitched the problem is compounded. Finally, these roomy new designs tend to be expensive.

HOW TO PICK A TENT

Back-
packing
tent

cav
camp
tent

The tent that will suit you, if you're shopping for shelter, depends less on shape than it does on the use to which you will put it, the emphasis you give weight and your willingness to spend money. There's no such thing as the ideal tent. If there was, it would have to weigh 17 pounds. Lightweight tents are designed for certain combinations of conditions. A snow tent would be useless in the jungle. A desert tent would leak in heavy rains. So the first thing to decide is the sort of conditions you'll generally encounter and the kind(s) of protection you'll most often need.

You can eliminate vast numbers of tents by setting priorities on sleeping capacity, weight, and price. Let's say you've decided on a tent for the summer high Sierra, which means you need protection against occasional wind, rain, cold, and bugs. You don't expect prolonged extreme conditions, so you don't need much extra storage space. The next decision is based on how many people the tent must sleep. The greatest choice will be found in two-man tents. Solo tents are rarest. Three- and four-man tents were scarce until domes became popular. Most tents for more than four are made either for expeditions of Boy Scouts and probably would be less satisfactory for most families than taking two tents.

Cost and weight limitations are largely arbitrary decisions. While some people are willing to pay more than they expected to get the tent that seems right for them, others will be unable to come up with extra money under any circumstances. If you can budget $300 you should be able to buy almost any two-man, three-season tent to meet almost any needs. If you're limited to $200 the selection will be much smaller.

Weight considerations are more personal. At one extreme is the often inexperienced buyer who falls in love with a piece of gear and doesn't stop to consider the weight. At the other extreme is the veteran who's allergic to an extra ounce. He cuts the handle from his toothbrush, tears the paper tabs from teabags, and he often goes tentless in the summer to save weight. He wants comfort on the trail, even at the expense of some comfort in camp. If he carries a tent it's got to be light enough to justify itself.

CONDENSATION PROBLEMS

Before looking at features to be assessed while shopping for tents, it is important to consider the problems presented by living in small portable spaces and the strategies tent makers have devised for solving them. The number one problem in tents—as in clothing—is condensation. Ironically, it's a problem that many have never encountered if their tenting experience is limited to dry, breezy conditions in moderate temperatures. But when condensation strikes, the experience is likely to be intensely unpleasant, even dangerous in extreme conditions.

When water vapor in the tent turns to water on the walls that wets everything it touches and runs down to form puddles on the floor and soaks your sleeping bag, that's extreme condensation. If the temperature is below freezing, the walls turn frosty instead of wet and the frost falls on your bed instead of making puddles under it. Since humans, as we have seen, are constantly producing moisture as they breathe and perspire, the concentration of water vapor in the small volume of a backpacking tent is unavoidably high. If the tent is closed tight against rain, cold, or wind, this concentration is likely to increase.

Condensation occurs when the tent wall is colder than the surrounding air—or the air on one side of it. There are three ways this can happen: (1) From cold radiation on still, clear cold nights (condensation is rare when the wind is blowing), (2) When cold rain falls on the tent, and (3) When there is excess heat and moisture within the tent so that the interior air is warmer than the tent wall. The last of these conditions almost always exists in occupied tents.

You typically lose about 8 cups of water during the night from perspiration and breathing. That vapor is confined in perhaps 70 cubic feet in the average two-man, A-frame. That much extra water (16 cups if there are two of you) is bound to overload the small volume of air unless it's somehow vented from the tent. If it isn't removed it is bound to condense on tent walls whenever they are substantially colder (highly likely) than the air inside.

There isn't much you can do about water loss from breathing—although one man rigged a breathing tube that ran outside the tent so he was breathing fresh air and not exhaling in the tent—except perhaps to acclimate yourself if the altitude is high, which will substantially decrease the volume of air you breathe and the water vapor you exhale.

Fortunately, air has a considerable capacity for holding moisture suspended as water vapor. The warmer the air, the more it can hold. It is only when the air reaches saturation ("dewpoint") that condensation must occur. So there is a combination of factors that lead to condensation and their interaction is subtle.

Knowledgeable designers of sophisticated tents know that small changes can make an enormous difference in the condensation level. Improve venting slightly or raise wall temperature a few degrees and you may manage to keep below the condensation level. Unfortunately, a good many tent makers either do not understand anti-condensation design, give it a low priority, or ignore it altogether. The subject is complex, beliefs have changed in recent years and there are several points of view.

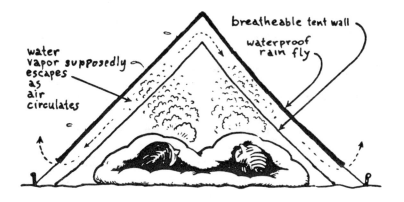

The first backpacking tents were made of heavy cotton. They leaked a little but condensation was no problem because the thick cotton fabric absorbed it and hid it. Of course, drying time was extremely long. When condensation was extreme inside the first coated nylon tents (coated because uncoated nylon passes water like a sieve) the coated nylon was blamed. It wasn't realized that the coated nylon did not cause, or even increase, the condensation level. It merely failed to conceal it because it was non-absorbent.

SOME MISTAKEN ASSUMPTIONS

The mistaken belief that coated nylon caused condensation gave rise to the double-walled tent with a space in-between. The inner wall was "breathable" uncoated nylon fabric. This was the tent itself. The outer wall was a separate rain fly or flysheet of coated (waterproof) nylon.

In theory the breathable tent wall would allow the warmth and water vapor generated by breathing, sweating occupants and their cookpots, to pass through into the space beneath the fly where air flow would dissipate it. Meanwhile the fly would protect the tent from wetting in case it rained. This arrangement worked moderately well: rain was kept out and condensation was distinctly less troublesome than it had been with a single wall of coated nylon. But at times condensation was still appallingly severe.

In the last 10 years it has been discovered that the major assumptions were false. Breathability, as was shown in Chapters 1 and 2, deserves little credit because the volume of vapor passed is so negligible. The apparent improvement in condensation levels was (again) partly illusion: the porous nylon inner wall sponged up a good deal of condensation, just as the old cotton tents had done. The actual reduction in condensation was due to the fact that two walls kept the inner wall warmer, thus raising its dewpoint.

Unfortunately, most tent makers have made no use of these discoveries. They still believe in breathability so they build their tents with porous walls and design their flies for maximum airflow underneath. And when conditions are bad enough their customers are still deluged with condensed water and ice.

Another group of tent makers, likewise ignoring the facts, has gone to single-wall tents of Goretex. Naively believing its unwarranted claims of breathability, they assert that double-walled tents are no longer needed to prevent condensation. Unfortunately, single-walled Goretex tents quickly proved themselves significantly more subject to condensation than old-style double-walled tents. Most of them are also heavier and prices are nearly double that of conventional tent fabrics.

But a few tent makers took advantage of what had been learned about fabrics and condensation, and they set out to make adjustments in design. The leader among these was Jack Stephenson, a former aerospace engineer. Because breathability had failed, he saw that some driving force would be needed to rid the tent of excess humid air. Wind could not be depended upon because it often was absent under conditions that caused condensation; besides, wind would chill the occupants and was difficult to control. Instead he took advantage of the fact that both warm air and water vapor are light and therefore rise.

Vents had been used before with only partial success, but Jack reasoned that, since venting had to work in still air, it could be greatly improved by imitating the chimney. Plugging holes in a chimney improves the draft. When he covered his tent with a plastic sheet to seal it, he found venting was improved and the tent stayed drier.

Finally, to maximize the draft he repositioned vents so that cool air could enter only at floor level and warm humid air could escape only at a vent in the tent's peak. Strong convection currents were generated that continually forced out warm humid air and replaced it with drier, cooler outside air. He also employed sealed double walls instead of a separate fly, and sought minimum air circulation between them to maximize insulation and therefore wall temperature.

HOW TO FIGHT CONDENSATION

There are a number of things you can do to keep down the moisture level, and they may easily determine whether or not you stay comfortable during conditions ripe for condensation.

1. Be careful not to spill drinking water.

2. If you must cook inside the tent, keep a tight lid on the cook pot and run the stove for a few minutes after dinner to warm up the tent interior so excessive moisture can easily escape from the vent you should have at the peak of the roof. A great many problems and dangers can be avoided by cooking outside. Do so if you possibly can.

3. Use a vapor barrier liner in your sleeping bag and wear vapor barrier clothing to keep you warmer, reduce sweating and dehydration, and avoid sweating up your clothes.

4. Don't dry those rain or sweat clothes in the tent. If you can't leave sweaty clothes outside, keep them in a closed plastic bag so they don't contribute dampness to the atmosphere.

5. If it's raining or snowing when you enter the tent, take the trouble to shake off excess moisture outside, remove wet outer clothing as you enter and fold it inward on itself to minimize exposure to the air inside. Best of all, use an umbrella!

6. If the tent leaks rain, try to find the trouble spot. Patch holes with tape and seal leaky seams with sealant right away if possible; otherwise mark leaks for between-trip repairs at home. Leaks generaly are small and water often flows unnoticed down walls or seams to form a puddle that may convince you it's the floor that's leaking. Don't be fooled.

7. Pitch your tent or trench around it so that water cannot run beneath it. The best tub floor should not be mistaken for a boat. Water under a tent is almost certain to enter.

8. Even in dry weather ground dampness has a tendency to rise through waterproof tent floors and condense inside. To protect against this phenomenon on damp ground or snow, place an unpunctured polyethelene sheet beneath the tent before you pitch it.

9. Nylon expands when wet, so rain or dew can make your tightly pitched tent sag and flap, which disturbs the insulating air gap between walls and thus cools the inner wall, inviting condensation.

If you do what you can to reduce moisture and pitch and vent your tent properly, you should rarely encounter significant condensation. But when you do, wipe it off with a small sponge periodically so it won't collect and drip or run down the wall to puddle beneath your bed.

In summary, tent design can minimize condensation partly by (1) providing effective vertical chimney venting and partly (2) by shielding the sealed inner wall from the cold outer wall. The object in both cases is to minimize contact of humid interior air with cold tent surfaces.

Don't be alarmed by this long dissertation on condensation and its control. Most of the time conditions are such that condensation is no threat, even without chimney venting and scrupulous attention to the water vapor level. Nevertheless, since heavy condensation can be brutally uncomfortable, it makes sense to understand its causes and cures and to buy a tent designed to resist it.

When Goretex appeared in the mid-seventies, ballyhooed by heavy advertising, it was hoped by many that a solution to the tent problem was at hand. Many tent makers jumped on the bandwagon, producing single-walled Goretex tents that were claimed to both shed rain and permit the water vapor generated inside to escape. They didn't do either, and tent buyers protested. Goretex tents were a flop and Gore withdrew his magic fabric coating, refusing to sell it to tent makers in order to escape the public outcry.

As reported earlier, the breathability of porous nylon really isn't great enough to pass much body-generated water vapor, and Goretex coating cuts that capacity in half. The notion that vapor pressure has sufficient driving force to help the process along just isn't accurate. And when it rains on a Goretex tent the wetness seals the pores and prevents the escape of water vapor from inside. The only time Goretex "breathes" is when conditions are good and "breathability" is of no help.

TENT POLE CONSIDERATIONS

Next in importance are the poles that must support your tent, holding it erect against the onslaught of the elements. Poles are either made of heavier stronger aluminum or weaker, lighter weight fiberglass. Pole sections of quality tents are shockcord loaded, which keeps them connected and takes the guesswork out of putting them together. Good poles are a large part of a tent's price, so assemble and bend the poles of bargain tents to try and figure out if they'll do what you require.

The development of domes and tunnels, with their curves and arcs, presented a need to produce poles that would curve. Most tent makers gave little thought to making curved poles. Instead they developed small diameter poles that would bend, first of aluminum, then of solid fiberglass and now of hollow fiberglass. Unfortunately, poles that bend when the tent is pitched, will bend further when the wind blows, distorting the tent, making it flap and function poorly.

Because all these poles are made up of short sections, enormous strain is placed on the many joints. Not surprisingly, joint failure is common in even moderate winds. The basic weakness is inherent in the fact that the poles are made to flex, and when flexed they are under tension and stress that weaken the entire system.

The problem is worst in domes because a considerable number of very long poles are required for pitching this shape, and there is no way to escape the need for all poles to bend. Domes are often soft and vulnerable and there is continuous strain on every single

Shock cord-loaded poles spring into shape.

pole and joint every minute the tent is pitched, even if there isn't a breath of wind. As a consequence, while the dome in theory is a good wind shape, in practice it is highly vulnerable to deformation and pole failure.

One possible solution (which as far as I know hasn't been tried) is detachable clamps. When domes are pitched there is considerable criss-crossing of poles. At present this provides little structural benefit. But if miniature clamps could be tightened to lock the joint at each intersection, the pole system would achieve enormously improved rigidity and double the strength. Inherent strain in the joints of bent poles would, of course, still be a problem, but the "bowl of jello" shakiness of domes might disappear.

Most tunnels use flexible aluminum or fiberglass poles, but in this design the vulnerability is sometimes slightly reduced because the configuration is different. Stephenson's tent escapes the strained pole problem by producing curved, rigid sections that form the necessary arcs without any more tension than is found in the equally troublefree A-frame. In flexing poles, generally speaking, solid fiberglass is heavy, vulnerable, cheap, and cannot be shockcorded.

Aluminum makes for a more rigid tent but is expensive, prone to "set" (stay bent), and split. Hollow fiberglass is lighter, also expensive, less rigid, and more breakable. Even more important than the material is the joint where sections meet, and there are many different kinds to ponder and test. Try the fit, bend it and take your pick. Shockcording is even more helpful on the maze of poles required to pitch domes than it is on A-frames. Good tent makers always provide it.

CHECKING OUT TENTS

The best tent makers take pains to build a floor that won't leak—until you puncture it. There are two styles of floors on quality tents: the traditional tub floor, which minimizes seams, and bias tape floors, which cost far less to replace. Quality tents have two or three coatings of urethane waterproofing on the floors, exposed sidewalls, and rainflies. All rain-vulnerable seams need to be sealed. If the factory didn't do it, the job is yours. Sealed seams are stronger than (and generally outlast) mere coated fabric.

hollows can turn into puddles.

To protect your tent floor, first clean the site of anything that might puncture it—twigs, sharp pebbles, dead roots, pine cones. Then put down a new 4-mil subfloor of polyethelene sheeting before you pitch the tent. It should be an inch or two smaller than your tent floor so it doesn't funnel rainwater runoff from the walls under the tent.

Once the tent is up and you're mostly moved in, dig a 3-inch deep ditch all the way around it so rainwater running off it flows away and downhill—not back under it. For mopping up rain leaks, mud tracked in and condensation, a small flat sponge is invaluable. One lives permanently in every tent I own.

Lap felled double-stitched seam

The once sophisticated catenary cut of a tent ridgeline that builds A-frame sag into the pattern to prevent flapping and insure taut pitch is now standard. Treatment of tent fabric with fire-retardant chemicals is now required by law in most states, but don't get careless. Treated tents will still burn. Good tents now offer one or more inside pickets per occupant, ideally made of netting with elasticized tops. And there are d-rings or loops in the roof for hanging clotheslines, lights, etc.

Check the stitching on any tent you're seriously considering. Seams should be secured with double rows of lockstitching, with 6–10 stitches per inch. Needle holes will leak so seams should be factory sealed—or the maker should supply you with a tube of seam sealant and instructions for using it. The protective reinforcement of seams, stake loops, pole tubes, corners, guy line tabs, and all other stress points still separates tents in terms of construction quality. Shoppers should look closely and critically at seams, loops, stitching, reinforcement, and finishing before buying any tent.

DOORS AND ZIPPERS

Tent doors and the zippers that operate them are critical to performance, comfort, and safety. A door that won't close is a nuisance

if there are bugs—and a menace if there's cold, wind, or snow. The best doors are large and zip up from the bottom with YKK zippers. Netting is increasingly used as a window in the door, but I like my netting independently zipped. Toothed zippers with brass sliders can be used on straight zippers, but continuous coil zippers with soft aluminum sliders are needed if they curve, as they often do on tunnels, frogs, and domes.

corner seams need sealing

Unfortunately, coil zippers under tension are vulnerable to spreading if fabric gets caught in them. If that happens, run them back to the beginning and squeeze the slider back together with pliers to effect a repair. This will work 4–5 times before the slider must be replaced. Toothed zippers are just as likely to fail but are more freeze resistant. The secret in avoiding zipper failure is gentle treatment. Don't rip them open or closed, and never force them if they're stuck. Best of all, hold the two edges together as you zip.

Tent makers rate their tents as to the number of occupants they will sleep. Like sleeping bag ratings, the numbers are suspect. Makers are inclined to be a little optimistic in order to be competitive. Beware! Many two-man tents will seem crowded even to honeymooners! If you'll need to bring your gear inside or—God forbid—cook inside, you may have to be a contortionist! Many two-man tents are barely big enough for one. And three-mans are ideal for two.

So when you're trying to decide between a big two-man and a skimpy three-man tent, ask yourself how much time you'll spend indoors. The longer the trip, the more unfriendly the environment, the more space you'll need. And ask yourself if bugs or weather or wildlife will require you to cook, eat, or store food inside? Pay more attention to the floor area than the maker's rating. If you can't possibly bring your pack inside, be sure you have a cover (a large garbage bag works well) to protect it from rain.

VESTIBULES ADD STORAGE

One way to gain needed space without gaining too much weight is to buy a tent that offers a vestibule—either as part of the design or as an add-on option. Vestibules—or sheltered entries—come in many cunning configurations, but the most common is merely an unfloored space immediately outside the door that's covered by the fly. In a pinch you can cook in it, employ it for storage out of the rain, wind, or snow, even use it in emergency for a bathroom. Bear in mind that when you take off the fly, the vestibule disappears.

Beware mosquito netting that doesn't zip completely shut on all sides. One mosquito is all it takes on a sultry night, and dozens will discover a dime-sized gap. Jammed zippers indoors are such a threat to safety in snow that some winter campers insist on a tunnel entrance in addition. Secured by ties, tunnel entrances are not only independent of zippers, they provide a convenient passageway for knocking off snow or joining two tents together. Vestibules do the same thing and sometimes provide cooking and storage space as well. Like tunnels they are chiefly found on A-frames.

When considering how much capacity will be needed in the tent you seek, don't limit yourself to sleeping area. Be sure you'll have the needed shelter for all the gear you must keep dry. A tent you have to live and maybe cook in should be substantially larger than one you only sleep in. Finally, give a thought to ease of pitching. It can be important if you move every day and may have to set up and take down the tent on the run or in the dark and rain.

THE PROTOTYPIC TUNNEL

Having looked at the major considerations in tent selection, let's look at individual tents. It will come as no surprise that the tent I

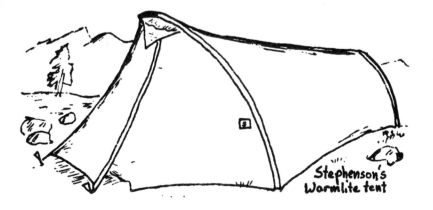

Stephenson's
Warmlite tent

know best and like most is made by Jack Stephenson. In the early 1960s Jack discovered that a half-cylinder with pointed ends had the best stability in wind from any direction and also provided minimum surface area.

Stephenson tents have a long-established reputation for peak performance in severe weather. But what lifts them above every other tent on the market is that in addition to their stormproofness and condensation resistance, they offer unexcelled lightness. For instance, the two-man model is 9 feet long, 5 feet wide at the front and weighs less than 3 pounds!

Though Stephenson's is a small company, with no retail stores and only mail-order sales from a rarely advertised catalog, its unique gear has long been the choice of experienced, veteran wilderness travelers. For instance, one night by a glacier in southern Patagonia a group of us were huddled over a windy fire when a young American couple (Greg and June Siple) pedaled up on battered, overloaded bikes and gratefully joined us for dinner.

They had been on the road for more than a year having started in Fairbanks, Alaska. They had ridden every foot of the Pan American highway and were now near its end at Tierra del Fuego. After sharing our dinner they unpacked the battered, faded, patched Stephenson tent they had carried all the way. Though it seemed to be in tatters it still pitched tight in the wind. The aluminized coating was gone and it was no longer waterproof (necessitating the use of a plastic sheet when it rained) but otherwise this lightest of tents was intact and fully functional. (It's now in the National Geographic museum.) More than half of us at the fire, we discovered, were Stephenson tent owners. It was like a reunion, and into the night we traded "There I was . . . " stories about the little tent's heroics.

Stephenson's makes just one tent shape, but it comes in different models with a wide variety of options so that it can be made to suit almost any use: from Arctic to Sahara. A number of its features are unique—or were until tent makers by the score began making copies.

The tent has a double roof (not a separate fly) and both are feather-weight coated nylon. The inner walls have an aluminized fabric. This makes tents warmer in the cold and cooler when it's hot. The double wall is constructed to provide an insulating layer of still air in between. By blocking the passage of water vapor, total condensation on both walls is reduced.

There are sheltered, zippered ground-level vents on both ends of the tent and a larger stormproof chimney vent in the roof peak. When the tent is inhabited (generating heat and humidity) and the doors are closed tight (essential for good draft), the sealed fabric enables the tent to draw strongly, like a good fireplace. Warm moist air rises directly to the chimney vent and the convection current produced provides suction to draw cool, dry outside air in to replace it.

A marvelous feature for mild evenings is the "drop front," which enables the wakeful occupant to reach out of his sleeping bag and unzip and drop the end of the tent for an unobstructed view of the stars. For people who find tents claustrophobic or confining, this option is a boon. When weather is foul and persistent wind has stretched the tent walls, internally adjustable guy lines make it possible to tighten the tent's pitch without leaving the warmth of your bed.

Most tent makers feel that durability and wind stability require comparatively heavy fabrics, then they try to save weight and space by using flexible poles. Jack achieves far lighter, more stable tents by using the lightest possible fabrics (1.6-ounce walls, 2-ounce nylon floors) in his aerodynamic-thermodynamic design, but controls tent shape by the use of rigid, thin-walled, large diameter, shockcorded, pre-curved pole sections.

Because the two poles form rigid unstressed arcs they are immensely stronger than tensioned flexible poles used by most other tent makers, and Jack's tents hold their shape and tautness in winds that deform or flatten tents equipped with flimsy, flexing fiberglass or small diameter aluminum poles. The curved pole sections easily plug into one another as you slide them into the pole sleeves—after you've done it once or twice. Other options include stake-out side windows, end liners, and middle poles on larger tents.

In fairness I must report that Stephenson tents are fragile. Some customers complain that floors lose waterproofing too quickly, pole sockets can rip out if the tent is allowed to flap, and the tent as a whole is distinctly delicate. The tent must be handled with consideration and respect. Jack doesn't pretend otherwise, in fact his instructions read, "the tent . . . is light enough to be rapidly destroyed by unnecessary rough abuse."

People who are hard on their equipment should not consider it. But a distinction must be made between fragile and flimsy. While the tent is fragile it will stand up far better than most to whatever abuse *nature* can muster—provided it is carefully pitched. And when it comes to saving weight here's a chance to save pounds, not ounces. It seems to me false economy to make sacrifices that shave an ounce or two, then choose a 7-pound tent instead of a 3-pound Warmlite!

INDIVIDUAL TENT MAKERS

Now let's look at some of the major production tent makers, especially those whose size and reputation provide widespread tent availability—as well as some smaller innovators and their intriguing products.

BIBLER tents are noteworthy in that they use an allegedly breathable/waterproof, single-wall/no fly design on their expensive domes—despite the failure of similar Goretex tents. Beware!

EUREKA!/JOHNSON tents, now made in Korea, offers a large selection (about half modified A-frames, half domes) of decent, inexpensive, mostly three-season shelters for 1–5 occupants.

GREGORY MOUNTAIN PRODUCTS, better known for its internal frame packs, offers a chimney-venting system in its handful of expensive domes.

KELTY provides a large selection of moderately priced domes and tunnels.

THE NORTH FACE offers several popular "frogs" in its Tadpole, Firefly, and Bullfrog. It's "No-Hitch-Pitch" system, in which rings (instead of sleeves) are permanently hung on the tent poles, and one end of each pole is already fastened to the floor, make for exceptionally easy tent erection of a few of its offerings.

SIERRA DESIGNS, long a leader in tent quality and innovation, provides the popular Clip Flashlight, an easily pitched two-man, 32 sq. ft. frog that weighs less than 4 pounds and costs less than $200, an unbeatable combination. The latest of my many Sierra Designs tents is the three-man Comet, 50 square feet of rectangular dome that weighs a hair under 7 pounds. Clips take the place of pole sleeves or rings for quick pitching.

QUEST tents, made by the owners of the same Korean factory that produces North Face and Sierra Designs tents, takes the best features of both and combines them in a line of serious, high-quality domes that are amazingly inexpensive. If a Quest tent fits your needs, it's easily the most tent for the money.

MOSS, who pioneered domes, makes beautiful, quality tents of unusual design.

WALRUS offers Korean lightweight tents for backpackers, and American-made, heavy-duty mountaineering tents.

OTHER FORMS OF SHELTER

For people who find tents claustrophobic, or are enterprising enough to improvise their own shelter, pitching tarps have some appeal, especially for group sleeping where bugs and wind are not a problem and the only need is to keep off the sun or dew. Tarps also appeal to those who are unwilling to pay for a lightweight tent or carry a heavy cheaper one. Mostly, however, they are for the rugged individualist who wants both minimal shelter and the feeling of being out in the open. Their numbers are dwindling in a day when convenience seems to hold top priority for most people.

For many years, shelter for the solitary camper was ignored. If you camped alone you had to carry a two-man tent or roll up in a tarp. But in recent years, tent makers have offered lightweight little tents for one, or bivy sacks, often with mini tents over the head and shoulders. Pound-and-a-half bivy sacks are made by Sierra Designs and Famous Trails, plus an all-Goretex model from Wild Things, and a Goretex-style bivy from Bibler.

Tiny tents just big enough for one often weigh 3–5 pounds, so before you buy one carefully consider whether it offers any advantage over the smaller two-man tents.

Tarp tents offer adaptability to the terrain. Tarps designed expressly for pitching can be difficult to find, and styles, prices, weights, and rigging points vary almost as widely as the ways in which they can be pitched. The best tarps have the fewest seams and the greatest number of fastening points. Black Diamond's 3.5 pound Megamid has a catenary cut and comes with a center collapsible pole.

Mountainsmith's tall "oval cone" tarps are the answer for people with claustrophobia. While avoiding "cabin fever," they are heavy and fearfully expensive, even if they do offer roll-down walls, optional floors, liners, and stainless steel stoves. But there are light, inexpensive pitching tarps for under $100, like the Campmor Parafly and the Eureka! Lean-to (with or without poles and netting).

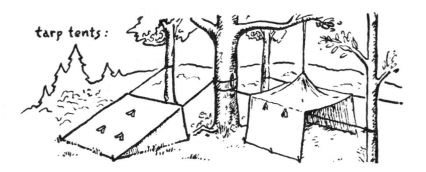

tarp tents:

Tube tents are not as popular as they were during the seventies because too many people have discovered that what sounds and looks like a good idea has definite limitations. Because a tube of plastic is completely sealed, it won't leak a drop as long as it's intact, but it may get you and your bed wetter from the oceans of condensation produced than the rain would.

Tube tents need both ends wide open to allow sufficient venting to hold down condensation. So for protracted rain they simply aren't practical. As lightweight emergency-backup protection against possible brief thundershowers (such as those that last only an hour or two on summer Sierra afternoons) or in dry climates when storms are not expected, however, they can be well worth carrying.

Ground sheet and poncho shelters are essentially emergency versions of the tarp tent. Though comparatively inflexible and inefficient, they yield short-notice shelter that often makes the difference between misery and comparative comfort. Sometimes their convertibility to shelter hinges on the presence of a few strategically located grommets or the possession of 50 feet of nylon line. More often it depends on the backpacker's foresight.

For several years I carried a 7 × 9-foot coated fabric poncho. When combined with the 6 × 8-foot plastic ground sheet carried by my partner, it provided us considerable shelter. After carefully preparing the bedsite to reduce the chance of puncture, I used it as a ground sheet, covering my bag on cold or dewy nights. Two corners on one side were fitted with permanent peg loops while the other two were fitted with 20-foot nylon cords.

When it threatened to rain, we tied off the hood, drove pegs to windward, tied the cords to trees to make a lean-to (or used pack frames for poles and pegged them down if it were treeless); we did what we could about controlling the drainage and wrapped our bags in the ground cloth. Many a short thunderstorm was weathered in this manner, and we once endured two days of solid rain on the shores of Lake Shasta without wetting our bags.

BIVYS AND BAG COVERS

The persuasive claims of Goretex were responsible for a revival of interest in bivy sacks in recent years. Although Goretex will not simultaneously breathe and shed water in bivy sacks any better than it will in clothes, tents, or sleeping bags, it is superior to coated fabrics in this application. For years when I carried no tent in

the benign summer Sierra (tents in those days were crude, heavy, confining, and beyond my means) I relied on a sleeping bag cover.

My cover had much more going for it than a mere ground cloth because it kept my bag and pad clean and provided a place to stuff clothes away from the dew. It was a dresser drawer during the day, and on cold nights it gave my bag extra warmth. On sweltering evenings I could lay beneath its cover on top of my bag without exposing myself to swarms of mosquitos. But most of all I like the snug, cozy feeling of security the cover provided—without the confinement of a tent. The sleeping bag cover functioned for me well as a one-man tent, largely, I'm sure, because I rarely got rained on.

Bivys, bag covers, ground cloths, and ponchos are generally light, but tarps and tube tents are as heavy as tents, sometimes heavier. As Jack Stephenson bluntly asks, "Why add the weight of a tent to avoid the tent, and how do you expect to get in and out of your bag in the rain?" Also remember that once your Goretex bivy sack gets wet, even from heavy dew, breathability is further reduced.

The problem with bivy sacks—in the rain, cold, and snow—is that you're drowned in condensation, since they're too small and snug to ventilate. The only way I know to stay dry is to use a vapor barrier liner inside your sleeping bag. That will take care of your sweat if not the condensate from your breath. Some people find bivy sacks more claustrophobic by far than tents, and they certainly are confining. But with me it's the other way around. If I can open my eyes and see the stars, I don't feel confined. But if the forecast is for other than clear weather, I'll take a tent.

FEATURES AND ACCESSORIES

Additional features to look for—and accessories to buy—can add valuable comfort and utility to your tent. Most good tents will provide at least one mesh-wall pocket per occupant (3–4 would be better). In our Sierra Designs Comet, the Attic, a handy net hammock with pockets, hangs suspended horizontally a few inches beneath the dome roof. It can also be hung vertically. It's wonderful as an organizer and a place to toss clothes.

Black floors dry faster in the sun.... No-seem netting (now virtually standard on good tents) should cover all openings: windows, vents, doors, and skylights.... Some windows have zip-down covers for greater nightime warmth.... Winter tents may offer zip-down storm flaps.... Back doors or entry tunnels can be valuable in winter tents, especially if you jam or break a zipper.... Repair kits (needles, thread, sealant, fabric, netting, etc.) are worth carrying under critical conditions, like hard or long trips.

The need for well-placed vents to assure chimney venting and the benefits of vestibules have already been discussed.... Some tents offer flies that can be pitched independently, so you can leave the tent home on a dependably bug-free summer weekend.... Many tents have sewn-in loops or rings in the eaves for hanging lanterns, clotheslines, stoves, organizers, etc.... Factory-sealed or taped seams, especially in the floor are essential. If they're not offered, you need to purchase (and use) seam sealant.

Campmor sells 6-mil polyethelene Floor Protectors in varying sizes. Position them under the floor to keep it clean and dry and protect it from puncture. It's a lot easier to wash a piece of plastic than the muddy underside of your tent floor, and it's cheaper to replace punctured plastic than rebuild a tent floor. Or you can use the Protector inside the tent to keep the floor clean. I like a plastic doormat in front of the door so I can stamp off dust and dirt before entering. And don't forget to equip your tent with an invaluable sponge.

Tent stakes are no longer included with many tents, so you may need to buy your own, even for free-standing tents. Free-standing doesn't mean stake-free, but many people don't learn that until they see their tent take off like a kite and cartwheel down hill in a sudden gust of wind.

tent pegs There are many different types of stakes, ranging from 10-inch nails for hard pan, deadmen for sand, forest stakes, wire pegs, and perforated stakes that fill with snow and freeze solidly in winter if you stamp them down and then pour a bucket of water over them, forming a cake of ice.

Sierra Designs offers a Shok Lok for repairing tent poles and a Grip Clip for fastening a guyline tiedown anywhere on the fabric to withstand a big blow. And there are doubtless other handy accessories to make your tent a home in the wilds.

So there you have it: a hundred different ways to find shelter in the wilds. Whether you choose a bivy sack, tube tent, flapping tarp, or sophisticated backpacking tent, you'll find the pleasure of any trip will be substantially increased by the security of having dependable shelter from the ravages of wilderness weather.

NINE

Getting Ready

*Trip Planning ... Altimeter/Barometers ... Route
Planning ... Figuring Trail Speed ... Preparation ...
Flashlights/Headlamps/Lanterns ... Cameras and Binoculars ...
Sunglasses ... Insect Protection ... Collect Your Gear ...·
Conditioning ... A Sample Program ... Hit the Trails ...
Check Your Toenails ... Setting Forth*

Nothing dooms a trip like slipshod preparation. It only takes one or two little mistakes. Many a veteran backpacker has seen a trip ruined for lack of a map, knife, salt, or match. Still more common is the beginner who, determined to camp in comfort, can barely stagger up the trail under a gargantuan load. The line between comfort and misery is far too thin for any backpacker to take getting ready lightly.

But preparing to go backpacking need not be drudgery. There is keen pleasure in working out a route for a fine summer trip on a dark and drizzly January night. And there is satisfaction in planning a trip into wild and distant country that delicately balances the weight of food and gear against the necessity of traveling light. The more that is accomplished beforehand at home—getting in shape, experimenting with foods, memorizing maps, breaking in boots—the smoother and more carefree the trip will be.

By systematizing the job to reduce the work, one can make getting ready a pleasant prologue to the trip. The subject divides itself conveniently into four distinct phases: (1) Trip Planning: where, when and how to go, (2) Preparation: deciding exactly what to take, then getting it together, (3) Physical Conditioning: getting in shape before the trip, and (4) Packing up: getting to the trailhead and making up packs.

TRIP PLANNING

As backpacking becomes more popular, it becomes easier and easier for the beginner to get started. Probably the best sources of help are the big organizations like the Sierra Club, Mazamas, and Mountaineers in the west, and the Adirondack, Appalachian, and Green Mountain Clubs in the east. Not only are they unexcelled sources of information about their respective territories, they offer organized outings of all types on which the beginner can safely become acquainted with the country and acquire experience with equipment and technique. You may also want to become part of the backpackers' lobby by joining The (nonprofit tax-deductible) American Hiking Society, 1015 31st St., Washington, D.C. 20007. And if you're wondering what's new in gear, where to go, what to take, and the latest news in hiking, I'd advise having a look at a pair of helpful magazines, *Walking* and *Backpacker*.

Trip planning, like wilderness travel, requires the ability to read and use maps. Probably no other skill is more important to all aspects of backpacking. No one should enter wild country unsupervised without appropriate maps and the ability to use them. Of course a map is useless if directions are unknown, so a compass becomes a necessity.

There is a tendency among amateurs and strangers to the outdoors to regard the compass as a toy for Boy Scouts. But in strange country where landmarks are unfamiliar, a compass is no less than indispensable. Many times I have worked out my true location or avoided a wrong turn by referring to a dollar-sized compass that weighs a fraction of an ounce and cost less than a dollar.

Navigation in the wilderness is a book-length subject in itself, and I urge all backpackers to become familiar with the rudiments. Proficiency could save your life, and it will certainly increase your confidence and security when entering new country. While a cheap floating-dial compass, used with understanding, will be adequate for trail travel in familiar country, an "orienteering" compass will be needed for genuine navigation. These instruments can be recognized by their movable dials and transparent bases.

Prime examples are the Suunto Leader and the Silva Ranger, weighing 2–3 ounces. The built-in protractor and locking device make it possible to quickly and easily determine bearings with a map. For greater precision and navigational capacity, consider the Brunton Elite. A large selection of Silva compasses is widely available.

With the aid of instructions, it is possible to teach yourself navigation in half an hour. Precision compasses rarely are needed in wild country simply because it's impossible for the hiker to measure distance accurately and maintain precise bearings. One degree of error in a mile amounts to only 92 feet, so compasses that can be read to the nearest 5 degrees will be accurate enough for most purposes. The sport of Orienteering, long popular in Europe and gaining ground in this country, provides valuable and stimulating practice for outdoor navigators.

ALTIMETER/BAROMETERS

Another useful (but rarely essential) aid to routefinding is the altimeter barometer. Besides measuring elevation gain, it can be used to compute progress, determine location, plan rest stops, and forecast the weather—especially in combination with a thermometer. Altimeters are also fun to play with if you like gadgets. To be useful they need to "compensate for temperature," and even then their readings will be far from precise.

Peet Bros. makes an inexpensive 2-ounce model whose watchlike dial reports 50-foot increments up to an elevation of 8000 feet. Or, for three times as much money, you can buy Peet's all electronic Ultimiter 8, which gives readouts in 10-foot increments up to 21,000 feet. Altimeters can be as valuable as your compass for finding your way in mist, cloud, and deep forest, or when triangulation points are non-existent, scarce, or unknown. They add a useful third dimension to navigation in new and difficult country.

Since there is no substitute for proficiency with map and compass, the inexperienced backpacker is well advised to invest his spare time in mastering both. The book *Be Expert with Map and Compass,* by Bjorn Kjellstrom, available from most mountaineering shops that handle books, covers the subject and offers instruction,

quizzes, drills, field problems, sample topographic maps, and related tools.

The single best map for the backpacker's purpose is the topographic (topo) map published by the U.S. Geological Survey in a variety of scales. Topo maps dependably offer more information per square mile than any other kind of map. It may be useful, however, to transfer to the topo map from more up-to-date local and Forest Service maps such useful data on "improvements" as trails, roads, campgrounds and the like. While the very large scale $7\frac{1}{2}$-minute topos provide marvelous detail, smaller scale maps that show distant landmarks will also be needed for orientation.

Though a first glance at a topo map is liable to be confusing, they are really not difficult to understand. Winter is an excellent time to study maps, plan trips, and become familiar with topography. USGS publishes free indexes and catalogs of topo maps for each state, plus a free brochure, "Topographic Map Symbols." See Sources for how to order.

ROUTE PLANNING

There are various ways to plan routes. Newcomers to the outdoors may want to car camp at the trailhead for a day or two and make exploratory day trips into the wilds until they become acclimated and find an appealing campsite that seems within their reach. Families and other groups with limited range often set up a base camp within an easy walk of the car and then make daily side trips into surrounding country.

Groups with greater mobility or the urge to move may decide to shift their base camp one or more times; others make a practice of packing up and moving every other day.

FIGURING TRAIL SPEED

How far one should attempt to go in a given day is equally hard to answer. The first day out is always the hardest, especially if the hiker has gained a mile or two of altitude between home and the trailhead, carries a healthy pack, and is in less than top physical condition. In these circumstances, 5 miles may be a full day's work. Well-conditioned backpackers who know their capabilities may cover 10 or more miles the first day and not suffer unduly, but most people will be happier if they schedule considerably less. On succeeding days it becomes possible to cover more ground with less discomfort. I have covered 15 or 20 miles on the third or fourth day with greater comfort than I felt after 8 miles the first day.

I customarily spend the summer on the edge of California's Desolation Wilderness, a place of extremely heavy use, but I know any number of charming, well-watered off-trail spots within an hour or two of the trailheads where I can camp in peace on virgin ground. As backcountry use continues to increase, backpackers determined to find solitude and unspoiled country will have to invest more time dreaming over their maps to find the less obvious routes that lie between the trails.

When to go is often determined by school and business vacation schedules. In California's high Sierra, spring, summer, and fall are compressed into three or four months and consequently it makes a great deal of difference whether a trip is scheduled for June or August. Often it will snow every day for a week in early June, yet the country is dusty and parched by August. The beginner should gather all the information he can about likely conditions in his area for various reasons. If there is one season to avoid, it is probably spring. Even if the weather is miraculously fair, the ground is almost certain to be wet. Indians generally avoided spring travel, preferring the middle of winter. Spring is a good time to car camp in comfort and settle for day hikes into the wilderness.

PREPARATION

Once the route has been determined, the length of the trip decided and the starting date set, it becomes possible to determine what must be taken along. Actually, I like to begin my preparations before the end of the previous trip. In camp on the last leg of a trip, or perhaps at the trailhead—after exchanging my pack for an ice cold drink—I sit down with my notebook while memories are fresh, and make pertinent notes about the trip. I criticize the food, recording both the noteworthy successes and the dishes that need never be carried again. I might write down, for instance, that breakfasts were a little skimpy so the cereal allotment should be increased from 3 ounces per meal to 4.

the trip-planner's friends:

By making notes before the memory fades, I accomplish three things: (1) I give myself the best possible chance to increase my enjoyment of future trips, (2) I avoid repeating mistakes for failure to remember them, and (3) by putting it all in writing, I avoid the mental drudgery of having to start planning each trip from scratch. Fifteen minutes spent making notes at the end of a trip will save two hours of preparation a month later; I cannot recommend this procedure too highly.

The checklist takes the place of a perfect memory, and the longer it runs the more security it provides. Every time I buy a new piece of gear, I add it to my checklist, but I rarely can bring myself to cross anything off, even the items I have not dreamed of carrying in years. Like other backpackers interested in comfort, I enjoy reading other people's lists. The abridged checklist that follows may serve as a starter for newcomers to backpacking—but only as a starter. A checklist is a highly personal thing and the beginner must eventually construct his own, updating it after every trip to make sure it contains every scrap of gear he owns.

A few of the entries on my list need further explanation. I have included gear I take most frequently on three-season trips in the California Sierra, because that's my home turf. Other areas will require vastly different choices.

FLASHLIGHTS/HEADLAMPS/LANTERNS

For safety if not convenience, you need some kind of portable battery-operated light. The choice is between the conventional hand-held flashlight and a headlamp that leaves the hands free. Headlamps have long been the choice of long-range trekkers, cooks, climbers, those who hike at night—or do anything in the dark that occupies their hands. The best-known name in headlamps is probably Petzl. Its Micro E03 provides beam adjustment and an adjustable headband.

But there are lots of other makers offering a surprising variety of styles, weights, size of batteries, etc. The buyer must sometimes make a choice between brightness (as for reading) length of beam, and number of hours of operation. Lithium batteries offer up to 20 times the life of alkaline batteries and perform even better in the cold, but initial expense is high. Since Lithium offers twice the voltage, half as many batteries are required, saving weight.

For backpackers, this means few if any spare batteries will be needed (providing 40–45 hours service will suffice) and bulbs

MY BASIC CHECKLIST

PACKS	Pounds–Ounces
External (Camp Trails)	3–12
Internal (Gregory Polaris)	7–0
Frame and packbag	3–12
Back Magic	5–2
Orange daypack	9
Fanny pack	$5\frac{1}{2}$
Belt pack(s)	2

CLOTHING—FOOTWEAR	
Hooded sweatshirt	1–3
Mesh polo shirt	3
Sportif trousers	8
Capilene zip top	13
Capilene bottoms	11
Thorlo socks	4
Hi-Tec Sierra boots	2–0
Plastic Storm Suit	1–5
Nylon Rain anorak	8
Nylon Rain pants	6
Green wind anorak	$7\frac{1}{2}$
Straw hat	3
Tennis hat	2
VB shirt	4
VB gloves	$\frac{1}{2}$
VG socks (Baggies)	$\frac{1}{2}$
Hickory shirt	10
Plastic storm suit	1–5
Zip-arm pile sweater	1–5
Down sweater	1–1
Hiking shorts	10
Running shorts	2
Lineer socks	1
Double-zip trousers	1–1
Bandana	$\frac{3}{4}$
Watch cap	2
Balaclava	3
Mittens	3
Short gaiters	4
Go-aheads (sandals)	1–0
Zip-arm rain parka	1–0

SHELTER	
Space rescue blanket	2
Stephenson tent	2–15
GT bivy sack	1–2
Ground cloth (nylon)	12
Two-man tube tent	2–4
Ground cloth (plastic)	12

BEDS	
Stephenson bag (thin)	4–2
Zip-lock (foam) bag	5–0
72-in. Camp Rest	3–5
72-in. Therm-a-Rest	2–8
72-in. Airlift	1–3
72-in. ½" EVA foam	12

KITCHEN GEAR	
Pocketknife (big)	$2\frac{1}{2}$
Two-blade Swiss army	1
Bleuet with cartridge	1–13
Extra cartridge	1–3
Peak 1 stove	2–0
Sigg pint bottle	4
Sigg quart bottle	5
Sigg pot, lid	9
Pot tongs	$1\frac{1}{2}$
Chore Girl	$\frac{1}{2}$
Salt mix shaker	2
Wooden matches	1
Emery cloth-backed sponge	$\frac{1}{2}$
Paper towels and TP	2
Plastic cup	$1\frac{1}{2}$
Aluminum measuring cup	$\frac{3}{4}$
1-Quart bottle	5
1-Quart Oasis canteen	5
Tea kettle	3
Gallon jug (plastic)	4
Tubular grill	4
Plastic tube	$\frac{3}{4}$
Lexan utensils	$1\frac{1}{2}$
Bio-suds	2

MISCELLANEOUS	
Dark glasses	$1\frac{1}{2}$
Glacier glasses w/band	2
Lip salve	$\frac{1}{2}$
Thermometer	$\frac{1}{2}$
Compass	2
Altimeter	$3\frac{1}{2}$
Maps	1?
50' 550 lb. test cord	3
Jungle (bug) Juice	3
Notebook, pencil	2
Creel (loaded)	9
Mini-MagLite flashlight	4
Petzl headlamp	6
Binoculars	12

MY BASIC CHECKLIST (continued)

MISCELLANEOUS (cont.)		#15 sunscreen	2
HP first aid kit	2	Candle lantern	1
Personal kit	3	Garbage, Ziploc bags	2
Olympus XA 35mm camera	9	Fly rod, reel, line	$7\frac{1}{2}$
Extra film	2	Paperback book	7

last longer. Seasoned travelers carry bulbs of different wattage, changing when a different level of brightness is needed.

When it comes to flashlights suitable for backpacking, it's hard to beat tough aluminum MagLites. They range in size from hefty C and D cells models down to penlights that operate on AA and AAA batteries. They variously feature adjustable beams, water resistance, dependable switches, and high-intensity bulbs. The other popular hand lights come from Tekna and offer many of the same features, but the cases are of lighter but bulkier plastic. Some are waterproof, provide battery testers, use lithium batteries and Krypton bulbs, and offer spot-to-flood adjustability. Bulbs last longer if you never touch them with salty fingers.

Lanterns get their light by burning fuel, not from batteries, and that makes them dangerous inside tents. The Lumogaz 470 uses the same propane/butane detachable canister that powers the Bleuet 470 cooking stove. It will produce like a 60-watt bulb for 13 hours and weighs a pound without the cartridge. There is a similar mantled lantern attachment for Peak 1 stoves, but it weighs nearly 2 pounds.

The alternative to gas lanterns are safer one-candlepower hanging lanterns fueled by candles or lamp oil. They usually collapse inside the glass cylinder that shields the flame, making them compact and easily packed. A single candle gives 8–9 hours of lightweight light. Windproof and dripproof, they're a great improvement over the unshielded candle.

CAMERAS AND BINOCULARS

I've had a long succession of small, lightweight 35mm cameras. My latest is the 9-ounce Olympus XA. It's semi-automatic, tough (I've dropped it on rock) and it fits easily in my front trouser pocket. It gets the pictures I want, but sometimes I take a holiday and leave it home. The choice of a camera is highly personal, being guided by your seriousness about photography and the priorities you give to cost, weight, and the type of pictures you're after.

I know serious photographers who will pay a fortune to carry the smallest, lightest, cleverest camera there is. And I know casual snapshotters who think nothing of lugging around huge cameras, extra lenses, padded bags, tripods, and all the trimmings. The selection of tiny, light cameras get better every year.

It's much the same with binoculars. Some people wouldn't dream of carrying them. Others would be lost without them. I was almost to the top of a 12,800-foot Sierra peak recently, puffing in a rocky crows' nest with dizzying drops on three sides, when my companion pointed to an eagle and handed me a huge pair of binoculars that must have weighed 3 pounds. I was glad to take a look, but I wouldn't have carried them up that mountain for anything.

If there's a particularly good opportunity to view distant wildlife, I'll grudgingly carry my old 12-ounce, 7 × 26 Bushnells. The first number in that rating represents the power of magnification; the second is the diameter of the front lens. A larger lens means more light for a better image—but also more weight. Higher magnification isn't always beneficial either since it also means a narrower field of view. Lens coatings improve color, contrast, and brightness by reducing the amount of light reflected off the surface of the lenses.

SUNGLASSES

It isn't widely known that sunglasses often do more harm than good. They trick the eyes into staying open wider than they should in bright conditions, resulting in eyestrain. And the darkened lenses block out healthful rays that are essential to the body. A wide-brimmed hat or sunshade is always preferable. "Dark glasses are a crutch," said the old prospector with whom I used to travel on the desert. "Put them on when it's bright and you'll never take them off." He taught me to squint and wear my hat low for a couple of days to acclimate my eyes, rather than develop a dependency on shades. And it works—when light conditions are bright but not extreme—because the eyes are constantly repairing minor damage.

But exposure to intense ultraviolet light, such as that reflected from water, sand, or snow, damages the eyes faster than continuous repair permits, producing severe and painful sunburn or snow-blindness. That's when top-grade sunglasses are vital. For brilliant conditions, glasses that cover the temples and block light from the sides will be important. They should be rated to absorb 99% of ultraviolet waves. Gray lenses cause the least color distortion. Plastic lenses are tougher but more likely to scratch. After a day in bright sun, beware of impaired night vision while driving.

Murl also taught me to use "Indian sunglasses" when vision was vital under extra bright conditions. Put the tips of your middle fingers together, end to end, then tuck the tips of your index fingers together tight against them, just beneath. Hold your four fingertips against your nose in the hollow beneath your brow and look through the easily adjustable slits between your fingers. Now your shaded eyes can stop squinting and open wide for maximum vision, even when looking almost into the sun.

INSECT PROTECTION

When it comes to buying insect repellent, all that counts is how much you're getting of the active ingredient, N. N-Diethyl metatoluamide, known familiarly as "deet." It comes packaged in many ways and various strengths. The choices include sprays, oils, roll-ons, creams, liquids, scented—applied by pumping, dabbing, squeezing, and aerosol sprays. A lot depends on the concentration of the bugs to be encountered and the weight priority. If it's a short easy walk on a warm day in shorts through clouds of mosquitos, I may carry a small spray bottle for quick application. If I'm walking with a group we may even share an aerosol spray can.

At the opposite extreme, if I'm climbing a mountain and may meet a few pockets of biting insects along the way, I'll probably be content with a tiny Cutters squeeze bottle partly refilled with cheap, effective Jungle Juice, the smelly oily potion devised for the troops in Vietnam. Where the bugs are really thick you may need a no-see-um headnet. And some people swear by the Moltron Bug Shield, powered by one AA battery, which uses high-frequency sound to drive away biting bugs.

If you're allergic to insect bites you may want to carry some preparation for easing pain and itching. If you need bug repellent in quantity, it makes good sense to buy the diethyl metatoluamide at the drugstore and make your own dilution. A dosage of 200 milligrams/day of vitamin B-1 taken orally will make your perspiration repellent to mosquitos and thus keep them away. So will the heavy consumption of garlic (my preference).

COLLECT YOUR GEAR

Many writers insist rather rigidly that no traveler should ever set forth into the wilderness without the security of certain (usually ten) essentials. I disagree: most people take too much, too many gadgets. I would urge people to take only what they really need, develop more self-reliance and not try to protect themselves against every possible hazard.

The properly equipped backpacker should already be carrying everything essential. He doesn't need an additional security blanket. It's a different story for the dayhiker. He needs to be prepared for getting hurt, caught in a storm or delayed past sunset, but what he actually should carry will vary too widely to be codified into a list of "essentials."

Once a new trip has been planned, I can turn to the preparation stage with much of the work already done. Having determined where, when, and for how long I am going, I get myself a pair of empty cartons, assemble my notebooks, and spread out my checklist. I read my notes from the previous trip, then I make my way down the list, considering each entry in terms of my needs for the trip in question. Each item selected is fished out of its storage box and put in the appropriate trip box. One box is for community gear (food, cooking paraphernalia, stove, first aid kit, etc.), the other is for my personal gear (sleeping bag, boots, pack, clothing, etc.).

With the equipment all assembled (or at least planned and noted) I consult old menus and the comments made at the end of previous trips. After figuring the required number of breakfasts, lunches, and dinners, I consider the appetites and preferences of party members, the likelihood of our catching trout, and the possibility of our staying out a little longer than planned. Then I compose a tentative menu that will be discussed and probably changed before the actual shopping begins.

Once the menu is set and the food acquired, most of it needs to be repackaged. Some people go so far as to separately package every meal so they need only dig out the appropriately labeled bag. In my view, this sort of packaging is excessive for short or casual trips where measurements need not be precise and where an extra ounce of cereal for breakfast for several days will not result in starvation the last day out.

My repackaging consists of stripping away all cardboard, paper, cellophane, and light plastic and replacing it with large, heavy duty polyethylene and Ziploc bags. I like to tie the long neck of

the bag into an overhand knot rather than struggle with rubber bands, twisties, paper clips, or heat sealing. Bags that will repeatedly be opened (gorp, cereal) and thus subject to more wear are usually doubled. I buy the heaviest bags I can find, rather than risk the puncture and spilling inevitable with flimsy bags that are cheap or free. After repackaging appropriately, I put fresh food in the refrigerator. Everything else goes into the food box—including a boldly written reminder to collect the refrigerated food before leaving.

On the evening before departure, I assemble the clothes I expect to put on in the morning and set them beside my bed. I also gather the clothes and food and drink that I will look forward to finding in the car at the end of the trip. As a final step, I run quickly down my checklist one last time. Everything should now be ready...hopefully.

CONDITIONING

Many a trip has been ruined—and I speak from experience—by the failure to get in halfway reasonable shape beforehand. I can remember trips that seemed to be one long nightmare of aching legs, bursting lungs, and a desperate effort to keep up with the party. It is simply impossible to turn from sedentary city life to high altitude wilderness backpacking without a certain amount of physical strain. It is however, possible to leave a lot of the discomfort at home.

At home, the conditioning can be as gradual as the hiker cares to make it, thus spreading and actually reducing the discomfort. It can be performed within easy reach of a hot shower, soft bed, and the assurance that today's blisters can be babied tomorrow. On the trip itself, there is more than enough discomfort from hiking under a load at high altitude, sleeping on the ground, wind, sweaty clothes, cold water, a noticeable lack of easy chairs and hot showers—without unnecessarily adding a lack of physical preparation.

There is no better investment of time during the several weeks prior to a demanding trip than a program of conditioning that will bridge part of the gap between city living and wilderness travel. It is far better to discover blisters while walking near home than it is at 10,000 feet in a cold, windy camp, with 10 miles to cover the following day.

It is perfectly possible for a sedentary city worker in his spare time to significantly improve the capability of his legs, lungs, shoulders, feet, and skin, depending on his condition, in anywhere from a week to a month. The program actually required will depend on many factors: age, experience, physical condition, time available, determination, rigorousness of the trip contemplated, etc.

The jogging-running boom of the eighties made us aware of the great benefits of running for getting in shape, but they also revealed the hazards of shinsplints, muscle tears, and foot injuries—not to mention stiffness, soreness, early fatigue, and pulled muscles.

It can be vital to loosen, limber up, stretch, and otherwise warm up your muscles before strenuous exercise like dayhiking— especially if you're fresh from watching TV. You need to work the rust from those hinges and oil them, slowly. It can be dangerous to subject the body to sudden stress. Sudden action can cause stiffness, soreness, early fatigue, torn tendons, and pulled muscles. The older you are or the colder it is, the more important it is to warm up.

It has been said that slow walking—half to three-quarter speed—is the best warm-up for walking. But I always stretch the backs of my legs (hamstrings) and Achilles tendons by bracing my

hands against a tree or rock, straightening my body at a 45° angle to the ground, and gingerly lowering my heels to the ground. Over the years I've added other exercises from my experience in yoga, tai chi, and dancercise and from conversations with chiropractors, runners, and physical therapists.

I start with traditional tai chi warm-ups: slowly flexing the wrist, ankles, elbows, and knees, circling the head on the neck, circling each shoulder, windmilling the arms, finishing with slow-motion bent-knee lunges with my arms outstretched. By adding conventional exercises, like touching my toes, I endeavor to gently stretch all my muscles and open all my joints.

My last stretch before hitting the trail consists of standing on one leg and pulling the foot of the free leg all the way up to my buttocks. It's also important, especially if it's cold, to freshly stretch the Achilles tendons after each stop or cool-down. Warm-ups aren't just for the overcautious, the aged, or sissies. If you're not properly warmed up, a misstep can cause a muscle pull, a slip can mean a strain, a fall can result in a sprain. And repeated injuries can lead to painful chronic problems like arthritis and bursitis when you're older.

During a hard hike—especially after a long, jarring downhill stretch—when I stop to rest I lie down on my back and elevate my feet by putting them higher than my head against a boulder or tree. And I hold my hands in the air. The object is to redistribute the blood that's been hammered down into my hands and feet, hopefully back to my heart and brain. It's a little like turning over an hourglass. Within seconds I can feel my feet begin to shrink inside my boots and the swelling in my hands subside.

It can be just as important to cool down gradually, to avoid the sudden changes that stress the body and can make you dizzy. The harder the workout, the more important the cool-down. A couple of minutes of slow walking will usually suffice, but if the hike has been grueling or my pack was heavy or I'm stiff and weary, I find it wonderfully stress relieving to systematically loosen my muscles after hiking. Five minutes of yoga stretching, culminating with a headstand, marvelously rejuvenates and refreshes me.

The transformation must be experienced to be believed. When ligaments and muscles are gently guided back into their natural state after prolonged effort, stiffness and fatigue simply dissolve. The single most rewarding exercise for me after hard hiking involves lying on my stomach, putting my hands in the push-up position, then, keeping my pelvis on the mat, gradually straightening my arms, throwing back my head, and bending my spine backward, keeping my knees locked.

After several deep breaths, I turn my head as far as possible (until I can see my feet) on one side, then the other. Then I relax my knees, lower my elbows to the pad, and lie relaxed, back still bent, breathing deeply for another minute. Other stretches of great benefit include slowly rotating the neck, rotating the shoulders, and rotating the ankles.

A SAMPLE PROGRAM

The following program is suggested for a badly out of shape, no longer young city dweller planning an ambitious two-week trip at high altitude, which will begin on a weekend. About three weeks ahead of time, our man (or woman) should, with the aid of a city map, mark out rather precise 1-, 2- and 3-mile courses that begin and end with his home. Traffic lights, crowded sidewalks, even stop signs should be avoided so there is no necessity to stop.

After work, instead of opening a beer, our man should go walking. Early risers may prefer to get up and walk at dawn; it is a marvelous time to be about. Since our man is in really rotten shape, he may have trouble the first time just getting around a 1-mile course. Nevertheless, he should time his walk in order to chart his improvement. If he is too sore after that first walk, he can take the next day off. Weight lifters and long distance runners often work out every other day, allowing the body to rest and assimilate the changes on rest days. On the third day, our man should try 2 miles and try not to stop. A brisk pace is actually more comfortable and less tiring than starting and stopping or an aimless saunter.

At the end of the first week, our man should be able to cover the mile courses in 20–30 minutes and the 2 miles in less than an hour. By the end of the second week he should be able to do 3 miles in an hour; the weekend before he leaves he ought to walk the 3 miles twice in a period of 2 hours. Walking regularly (at least every other day) and briskly (charting the times and always trying to improve) will strengthen the legs and provide endurance.

To develop the lungs and toughen the knees there is nothing like running. Once the body is used to walking, it is safe to go running. I find shorter distances (50 to 200 yards) of hard running to be more effective than a mile of slow jogging. The high school track is a good place to run. To increase my wind I run until I am gasping, then I run another 20 yards before slowing to a walk. When our man runs out of breath, he should walk slowly but not stop until his breathing returns to normal and then start running again.

By the end of two weeks, he will find his wind greatly improved and he should be able to navigate the 1-mile course, alternately running and walking. As his lung capacity grows and begins to catch up to his leg development, he will begin to feel fatigue in his knees. The ideally conditioned backpacker on a difficult stretch should feel approximately equal discomfort in his knees and lungs.

To condition the shoulders to the pull of his pack, it is only necessary for our man—probably the second or third week—to start wearing it on his walks. Books make good ballast and 10 or 15 pounds will be enough for the first tour of his routes under load. This can be increased to 25 shortly before the trip. Since backpacks are not made for running, our man will want to alternate unladen run-walk tours of his routes with pack carrying tours. So far, all of his work has probably been on flat, paved sidewalk. But backpacking usually means traversing rough, steep country, so our man should hunt out the steepest, roughest terrain in the area and work out a course or two for the final week of conditioning.

HIT THE TRAILS

Only on steep trails are the conditions in mountain wilderness closely approximated. The knees need the unique strains produced by going up and down hill and the ankles need rough and uneven

for getting in shape,
nothing beats
running
up
hills.

terrain to develop toughness and resistance to sprain. No amount of walking or running on city sidewalks can accomplish the same thing.

When I was working at a desk job and wanted to get ready for a weekend trip, I would spend an hour or two in the hills on the preceding Sunday, Tuesday, and Thursday evening running uphill until either my legs or lungs forced me to stop. Then I would slow to a walk until I was sufficiently recovered to run again. A great amount of conditioning can be compressed into a week in this manner—providing the body is in reasonably good shape beforehand.

In addition to run-walk tours in the hills, our man should carry a loaded pack on perhaps a total of 10 miles worth of walking trips through the hills. The weight of the pack will condition the shoulders, knees, ankles, and feet to the strain and jarring that rough country provides. Hiking in the hills with a pack and run-walk tours without one—this is the real conditioning. Walking and running on city sidewalks is only "pre-conditioning" for people unaccustomed to vigorous exercise.

From the beginning of this program, the feet should receive special consideration. On all excursions, our man should be wearing the boots and socks he will take on his trip. This will break in the boots and mate them to the feet before the trip begins, and it will toughen the feet sufficiently to prevent chafing and blistering in the wilds. Undoubtedly, the most overlooked and easiest part of foot conditioning is cutting the toenails.

CHECK YOUR TOENAILS

Long toenails will make boots seem too short and can be painfully crippling on downhill stretches. Cutting long toenails the night before a trip will result in pain and inflammation on the trail. Great discomfort (and holes in worn socks) can be prevented by awareness of the problem. I try to keep my toenails reasonably short with frequent cutting, but I also remind myself, sometimes in writing, to cut my toenails four or five days before a trip.

I think the best way to toughen up feet is going barefoot. Before a trip I go barefoot around the house and I like to go for short barefoot walks. Concrete sidewalks are great tougheners and callous builders. Sunlight and fresh air are healthy for feet, certainly a lot healthier than damp, constricting shoes. I spend enough time barefoot to sport a pretty fair tan on the tops of my feet by the end of the summer. Tanning can be extremely important to the comfort and pleasure of a trip. People who take lily white skin to high altitudes become horribly burned unless they keep themselves carefully and continuously covered.

A tan acquired in the city or at the beach will never fully protect the hiker against fierce high-altitude sunlight but it will enable him to travel with only normal discretion without risk of serious burning. Nothing is worse than having to hike in the heat completely shrouded from the sun—unless it is suffering with sunburned shoulders that will have to carry a pack the next day. Trying to safely tan white skin by short periods of exposure to fierce high-altitude sun is a bothersome, risky, inconvenient process on a backpacking trip.

Our man will be well advised to start cultivating a tan by getting out in the sun (in a bathing suit if he expects to hike in shorts) on weekends from the beginning of his conditioning period—taking care to use discretion and sunburn preventatives. If there is anything more vulnerable to mountain sunshine than city skin it is sunburned city skin that has freshly peeled. Special care should be taken to avoid burning the nose to prevent starting a cycle of peeling, burning, and repeeling.

Not many backpackers will need to take the full conditioning course outlined above, but most people will enjoy a more comfortable trip to the extent that they complete their conditioning at home.

SETTING FORTH

Three to five days before departure I begin to pay close attention to the weather forecast. People with set vacations can't often postpone trips, but knowing what's predicted may affect what they take. I listen on my Radio Shack Weather Radio to the forecast on the nearest NOAH National Weather Station, hoping for a 3–5 day prediction. If the outlook is fairer than normal I may decide to leave home optional clothing, while if a storm is forecast I may choose to carry more protection. I always take along extra gear and clothing in the car so it's optionally available when I make up my pack at the trailhead.

If I'm counting on crossing a snow-vulnerable pass or using a primitive dirt road for access, I may also call the Department of Transportation to determine current road and highway conditions.

With trip planning preparation and conditioning out of the way, all that remains is to pack up and go. For most people, that means taking a car to the trailhead; and sometimes that journey is

the hardest trip their car ever makes. On more than a few trips, the biggest adventure, the greatest challenge, and the hardest work is getting the car to the trailhead and back. I have slipped off the road, gotten stuck in the mud, and hung up on the rocks. I have run out of water and gas, blown out tires, smashed into rocks, and killed the motor fording creeks. Trailheads have a habit of lying deserted at the ends of unmaintained rocky roads, so it behooves the backpacker to take more than a casual interest in the condition of his car.

Backpackers are often so intent on getting their gear into the car and getting away that they forget to carry the extra food, drink, clothing, and money that is so welcome at the end of a trip. For purposes of acclimation and an early start, I like to drive from home to the trailhead on the eve of the trip in order to sleep at the highest elevation possible. To simplify matters, I usually take a car camping sleeping bag and mattress to ensure a good rest, and no matter how late I arrive I always choose my bedsite carefully and excavate for my hips and shoulders. If I have to cook, I take along a separate stove, food, and utensils rather than rummage in my backpacking gear. When possible, it is usually most convenient to eat in a restaurant or brown bag it in the car.

While driving to the trailhead, I try to get a final weather forecast on the car radio. Sometimes at the last available pay phone, I call the nearest Weather Bureau or airport or Highway Patrol office to get an extended forecast. On the basis of this information,

Dividing up the community gear.

together with weather conditions at the trailhead, I make my final selection of protective gear: tents, rain suits, ponchos, ground sheets, tarps, parkas, mittens, caps, and sweaters. My usual procedure, after deciding what to carry, is to spread out an old tarp, brought along for that purpose, and to empty on to it all the food and community gear.

Packing Up

If there are two of us, one of us divides the pile on the basis of both weight and bulk into two equal stacks; the other man gets first choice. It is probably a good idea to employ a scale to be precise, but we generally just heft comparable items at arms' length and hope that compensating errors will cancel out major differences. Sometimes one man, because of his pack size will be short on space and may request less bulky items, but both hikers still split the weight evenly, unless there's a marked difference in their size, weight, age, or sex that suggests a different division. Carrying ability is proportional to body weight. Your performance will be seriously impaired, say the physiologists, if you try to carry a pack weighting more than 20–25% of your body weight.

After combining my share of the community gear with my personal equipment, I start to make up my pack. First, I set aside anything that may be needed in a hurry—trail food, notebook, pencil, compass, first aid kit, lip and sunburn protection, bandana, insect repellent, snack food—and anything else I expect to need on the trail.

Then I make a layer of the heaviest, densest remaining gear so that the weight will lie as high and close to my back as possible.

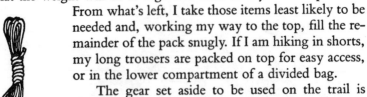

From what's left, I take those items least likely to be needed and, working my way to the top, fill the remainder of the pack snugly. If I am hiking in shorts, my long trousers are packed on top for easy access, or in the lower compartment of a divided bag.

The gear set aside to be used on the trail is then systematically divided between the pack's outside pockets. To find things fast, it helps to use the same arrangement for every trip. For instance, although I sprinkle wooden kitchen matches in every pocket, the main supply always rides in the upper right hand pocket. With the last of the small items stowed, I stuff my rolled mattress into (or onto) the top of the back pack and cinch down the flap over it. My sleeping bag is then strapped or snapped beneath the three quarter pack bag. Last to be attached is my two-piece fly rod, broken down, but with the reel still attached. The butt ends sit in a 35mm film can taped to the bottom right rail. A thong at the top crossbar lashes the rod to the rail. Finally, I check all zippers, buttons, ties, and lashings.

With the pack made up and hoisted onto the hood of the car for easy mounting, I go through my pockets, hide my wallet after extracting two or three quarters and dimes for pay phones, and lock the car. Normally, I hide the keys nearby, rather than take a chance on losing them. When all is ready, I do the warmup and stretching exercises that will prepare me for vigorous walking.

Finally, I slip into my pack and adjust the straps and buckles so the weight is borne equally by my shoulders and hips. With nothing further to detain me, I eagerly set forth up the trail into the wilds.

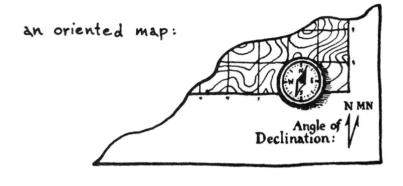

an oriented map:

N MN

Angle of
Declination:

Navigation

*It's Both Art and Science... Knowing Where You
Are... Map Reading... The Compass Game... Telling
Time by Compass... Get Off the Trail... A Navigation
Story... Finding the Trailhead... Gauging Your Speed... Getting
Lost... Four Ways to Find North... Getting Found*

R oute finding is the art of getting where you
want to go. It means knowing where you
are in the wilds, elegantly making your way
through the country, evading obstacles and barriers. It's the key to
successful cross-country travel, a substitute for blindly following
the trail. Route-finding success will help you feel at home wherever
you may be.

In the large sense, it's navigating through unfamiliar territory
to a distant goal. On a smaller scale, it means figuring out how to
get past a swamp or how to finesse a cliff with the least amount of
time and effort. On an even smaller scale, it may mean choosing the
easy way around a tree, picking the best rock to step on, ducking
a branch, sidestepping thorns, and deciding where next to plant
your foot.

IT'S BOTH ART AND SCIENCE

The exercise of route-finding ability, it will be seen, is both pleasant and practical. It can save your life. It can turn failure into success, convert a nightmare into rewarding adventure, prevent the anxiety, danger, and inconvenience of getting lost. It's the ultimate outdoor tool and challenge, problem solving at its finest, the zen of mastering the country.

For me, the most exciting, demanding, and rewarding aspect of traveling new country is pitting my ability to read the country (and use my map) against the dangers and enigmas of the natural world. Nothing is more deeply satisfying than successfully plotting a course through the wilds. I dearly love to sit on a ridge and plan my way through the country beyond, to scrutinize a map for clues to a cross-country route between two unknown watersheds, to examine the face of the mountain before me and figure out how best to get up it.

Sometimes route finding means finding the only way through a maze or around a cliff, solving the puzzle that makes the trip possible. Other times the benefits are more aesthetic: looking for the prettiest, most appealing route or staying in the shade to hike in comfort. The satisfaction comes from the success, the dominion. Route finding isn't conquering the country so much as it is becoming one with it, solving its riddles, moving through it with ease, making it yours, going with the flow instead of against it, finding its hidden secrets and delights.

An old prospector with whom I used to travel in the deserts taught me never to "cut the country," that is, not to go against the grain. "Follow the canyons and ridges," he advised. "The best footing usually makes for the easiest path, even if it is a mite longer." As we looked for gold, he showed me how to "go with" the country instead of fighting against it, to follow the ridges and the valleys and avoid "sidehilling." But valleys can turn into impassible canyons and ridges can narrow to knife-edge cliffs. Walkers must always try to conserve the elevation they have laboriously gained. A balance must be struck and that requires route-finding judgment.

The noted climber and explorer Jack Miller continued my education while we were traveling in the Andes of Bolivia and Patagonia. Studying the face of the mountain before us, he made me estimate distance, height and elevation gain, as well as projected routes and travel time. Then he'd correct my mistakes. Forced to make specific assessments and decisions, I gradually improved. Practice sharpened my judgment. Now I sometimes ask Deanne what route we should take on the slope that lies before us to make her focus on the problem instead of merely following my lead. Sometimes the route she picks is better than mine.

I feel richly content when I've cunningly made my way up a new mountain in interesting fashion—surmounting the obstacles, avoiding the pitfalls, discovering concealed treasures—and then found an even more rewarding route down. I've exercised my mind and used all my past experience to turn terra incognita into my own turf.

The pleasures of route finding are out there waiting to be discovered and enjoyed. I find them more seductive by far than mere egocentric peak bagging. As with most things, it's not just what you accomplish but how you go about it that brings the greatest contentment.

KNOWING WHERE YOU ARE

Route finding begins with knowing where you are. If you know where you are, by definition you can't be lost. The development of proficiency at route finding builds valuable confidence. It's the essential quality of outdoorsmen and women. The great explorers all have it. It will enable you to venture into strange country without getting lost. And if you become temporarily uncertain of your location, it keeps you from panicking and permits you soon to find your way again.

Even trail travelers need route-finding skills. It can be dangerous to put all your faith in the trail, blindly depending upon it to get you to your goal and home again. What if your trail inexplicably branches or disappears? What if it's wrong or a sign is missing, a junction unmarked? You're helpless if you've relied entirely on the trail. Even if you never plan to leave the well-worn, well-signed trail, you need to be able to figure out where you are.

Trail travel is fine if the path takes you exactly where you want to go, or if there's no other way through difficult country. Trails permit rapid travel, and because of the better footing they allow more attention to the scenery. But following trails can get dull. If you're a slave to trails you're going to miss the most stimulating part of traveling the natural world. The true adventure begins when you step off the trail. But you need to know where you are and be prepared to find your way.

MAP READING

The principal tool for knowing where you are is your map, though sometimes a guidebook or other written description of the terrain may adequately substitute. It seems obvious to say that a map is useless if you don't know how to use it. But a recent survey revealed that a majority of Americans today can't plot their way through a city with an ordinary street map!

Using a map means being able to read it, that is, recognize its features, understand its nomenclature, and be able to imagine and visualize what those features look like on the ground from the way they look on paper. It also means orienting the map so you're sure which way is up. If you can't line up your map with the country—or the city—it's useless. A map that's upside down is worse than useless because it gives false directions. Orienting a map means pointing its top toward true north, not magnetic north, or lining up known landmarks (like mountains) by sight.

The backpacker simply spreads out the map with the compass on top so that north points directly to the top of the sheet. The map and compass are then turned as a unit until the north needle points directly to north. When the magnetic declination (difference between true and magnetic north) is set off (it is shown on all topo maps) the map will be oriented.

When one's position is known and the map is oriented, it becomes possible to identify visible features of the countryside by

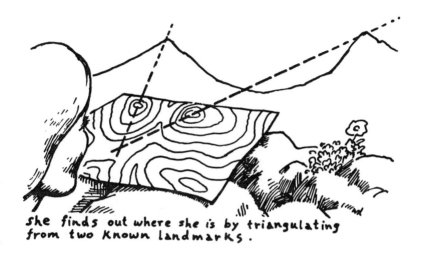

she finds out where she is by triangulating from two known landmarks.

transferring line-of-sight bearings to the map by means of a straight edge. When only one's general location is known, but several landmarks have been positively identified, it is possible to discover one's precise location by transferring line-of-sight bearings to two known landmarks onto the map. The intersecting lines reveal the compassman's exact location. This won't work, of course, where convenient landmarks can't be seen.

Reading the rise and fall of the land on a topo map is more a matter of practice than talent. The best place to begin is with solitary peaks or hills where the contour lines form concentric circles that get smaller as they go higher toward the summit circle in the center. Widely spaced lines indicate a gentle slope, while lines bunched together describe a cliff. Contour lines form arrows that point upstream as they cross water courses and downhill as they descend a ridge or bluff. As one becomes adept at reading topo maps, the actual shapes of landforms begin to materialize so that the maps become pictures of the country.

When this happens, topo maps take on a singular fascination. They also become incredibly useful. For instance, by measuring the ups and downs of a trail one can estimate with fair accuracy the time that will be required to traverse a given section of country. This, in turn, allows the trip planner to work out logical camping spots and estimate the time needed for any itinerary. Superior map-reading ability is a prime prerequisite for safely visiting the wildest of trailless country. Proficiency with map and compass has saved a great many lives.

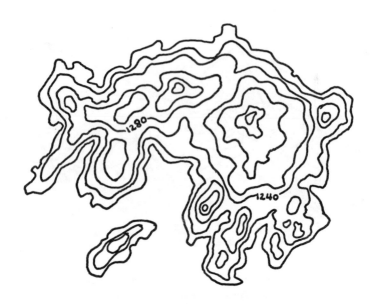

THE COMPASS GAME

The competent backpacker always tries to develop some inner orientation to make him independent of his compass. To this end, my friends and I play a game on the trail—while taking a rest—that has proven both amusing and instructive. Each of us draws a line in the dirt toward what he believes is true north. Then the compass is brought out, the declination marked off, and the winner declared. The next time the game is played the previous session's winner must draw first. It is surprising how quickly this game develops a sharp sense of direction.

TELLING TIME BY COMPASS

If I really need to know the time, my compass will give a rough approximation, provided the sun is shining. I set the compass in the sun, settle the needle on north, then set off the declination (seventeen degrees east in California). With the compass thus oriented, I stand a straight twig on the compass rim so that its shadow falls across the needle hub to the opposite rim. The position of the shadow on the opposite rim gives me a close approximation of sun time by thinking of the compass as a watch with north at noon.

To reconcile sun time to daylight saving time, I add an hour. To tell time early or late in the day one only needs to know the hours of sunrise and sunset. Of course, some allowance must be made for mountains that rise high to either the east or west. Time

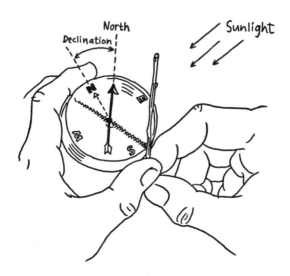

is still important, but it is suntime, not clock time, that counts. How long before sunset, when it starts to grow cool? How long before dark? These are the pertinent questions in the wilds.

GET OFF THE TRAIL

Some backpackers find a greater sense of adventure in deliberately planning no itinerary, going where and when the spirit moves them. Others, similarly motivated, spurn trails altogether in favor of cross-country travel, finding pleasure in avoiding people and the beaten path. Since true wilderness does not begin until the trail has been left behind, it should probably be the goal of most walkers to travel cross-country. Wilderness travel means getting off the trail, even if only for a dayhike from base camp.

I like to start thinking about future trips while I am still in the mountains. I find myself wondering, for instance, whether the rocky, trailless canyon I am passing could be ascended under load to the lake that lies above. As I move along, I try to estimate the difficulty of reaching passes, following ridges, and crossing slopes, with an eye toward future trips. I study the topo map to learn what lies on the other side of the mountain and to compare the bunching of contour lines with those on slopes I can see or have already climbed.

This type of on-the-spot research becomes invaluable for plotting feasible cross-country routes in trailless country. A glance up a canyon shows the gentle slope suggested by the topo map turns out to be a series of ledges and cliffs. Or I confidently plan a route down a forbidding steep slope because I know it to be an easy sand and scree slide.

A NAVIGATION STORY

Careful trip planning, I've found, generally yields the most memorable trips and prevents the small disasters that can ruin a fine outing. Prospector Murl defined adventure as "the result of poor planning." Time has proved him correct. Successful trip planning requires route-finding skills. To plan a trip you must somehow picture it. After choosing your goal(s) you must estimate the distance to be walked and the elevation gain. To compute likely speed, you must consider the weather and terrain. Only then can you judge the time and energy required to make the trip.

These abstract considerations might be clarified by looking at a trip that Deanne, Grant, and I took while I was writing this chapter. It was the end of October in the California Sierra, and we hoped to squeeze in one last high trip before winter. We wanted to climb 10,400-foot Round Top Mountain just south of Carson Pass. None of us had been there but we'd seen the north side of the peak from a nearby summit, so we knew the type of terrain, the landmarks to the north, and the driving time required.

The 15-minute USGS topo map showed three trails that might be used to approach the mountain. Two of them started at opposite ends of Woods Lake at 8200 feet, passed mountain lakes and joined near the mountain's west ridge. There the contour lines were well spaced, suggesting a feasible route up. We decided to ascend by one trail and return by the other, making a loop. The trail distance looked to be about 6 miles, with a climb of 1200 feet. The ascent of Round Top would require another mile each way, cross country, with another 1000-foot elevation gain.

We judged we could cover the 8 miles, with a total 4400-foot elevation change, fairly comfortably in 5 hours. We wouldn't have to leave early and we'd be home in time for planned Saturday night socializing.

The weather forecast warned that a storm was moving in from Alaska on Sunday. Snowfall could be heavy and close the area for the winter, so we set forth on Saturday morning, leaving at a civilized 9:00 A.M. Although we planned to hike in shorts, we took long pants, watch caps, and mittens in the car, just in case. And I brought my vapor barrier shirt. Less than an hour's drive from our home in Pollock Pines, we reached Woods Lake.

We were mildly surprised to find that a dusting of snow from a storm two weeks before still covered the shady north side of the peak, down to about 9000 feet. But the sky was clear and sunny and the temperatures comparatively mild, so we didn't hesitate. We had come prepared. The mittens, long pants, and watch caps went into our daypacks. Since the creeks would be flowing with snowmelt, we left all but a pint of water in the car. We set forth up the trail about 11:00 A.M.

When we emerged from the trees at timberline and started dodging snowbanks, it was windy—advance disturbance from the approaching storm—but the air remained mild and we walked in shorts. We made fast time on a good trial, passing choppy Winnemucca Lake and climbing to where the trail crosses the mountain's north ridge at 9400 feet. The flat sunny ridge offered a largely snow-free corridor that led us to the high west ridge, where 50-mile-an-hour winds filled our eyes with tears, spun us around like staggering drunks, and made us put on mittens, watch caps, and wind shells—but not long pants.

Gaining the sunny south slope behind the ridge, we left the snow behind and made our way to the windy summit, taking shelter wherever we could. After climbing all morning on fruit power alone, we ate lunch in a crow's nest behind sunny sheltered rocks just under the crest while the wind roared inches above our heads. Then we swiftly descended on loose scree to the trail, drank snowmelt from a stream, and took the homeward trail, via Round Top Lake, back to our car at Woods Lake. We were back home by 5:00 P.M. in plenty of time for the Saturday night festivities. Careful planning and route finding had made the trip a success. The following day it snowed.

FINDING THE TRAILHEAD

Sometimes the toughest part of route finding is finding the trailhead. I've wasted a lot of time trying to get off a freeway, driving up and down dirt roads, thrashing through underbrush—all in search of some elusive trail. Sometimes I merely hoped to find a trial, even a game trail, heading in the direction I wanted to go. At other times, the directions I'd obtained were bad or vague. I've learned that I've got to allow time to find a strange trail. If I can, in new country I scout the trailhead beforehand—the day or night before—so I don't waste precious time on the day of my hike.

Expert help finding trailheads is available from DeLorme Mapping Co., which offers detailed atlases for 14 states—one to a state—for $12–13 each. They specialize in presenting the kind of frontier backroad data you need to find elusive trailheads. (See Sources.)

GAUGING YOUR SPEED

The question inevitably asked by strangers to the wilderness is how fast will I travel? Or, how far should I plan to go in a day? There are no answers, only generalities. On relatively level trails at moderate elevations, a long-legged, lightly burdened well-conditioned man may manage four miles per hour. At elevations over 6000 feet in rolling country, a well-acclimated backpacker is moving extremely well if he can cover three miles per hour. The average hiker, fresh from the city, heading up into the mountains wearing a full pack will be lucky to average two miles per hour. These speeds are for people who keep moving and should probably be cut in half for those who want to poke along, smell the flowers, take pictures, and enjoy the view.

Cross-country walkers may average only one mile per hour. Children, the elderly, and hikers strongly affected by the altitude may manage as little as half a mile an hour. A friend of mine has devised a useful formula for predicting his speed. He plans every hour to cover two miles if the trail is flat or mildly descending. For each thousand feet of rise he adds another hour. For steeply descending trail he adds a half hour per thousand feet, increasing that to a full hour for extremely steep downhill trails. By plotting a rough profile of the trail from the topo map and applying his formula, he can estimate quite accurately the time needed to walk it with a moderate—under 30-pound—load.

There is no particular virtue in covering great distances. I have received more pleasure, solitude, and sense of wilderness from hiking less than two miles cross-country into a neglected corner than I have from following 60 miles of well-traveled trail and camping in battered, over-used campsites.

Survival should not be a problem for the backpacker unless he is hurt or lost. A first aid kit and the ability to use it should enable him to cope with all but the worst accidents and health failures. His equipment, experience, and trip preparation should enable him to survive whatever bad weather or minor mishaps befall him with no more than discomfort. It simply isn't possible to protect against all the hazards of wilderness travel. Develop self-reliance, build your experience, and don't make the same mistake twice.

GETTING LOST

Getting lost—or thoroughly confused—is not uncommon in the wilds and rarely leads to tragedy if sensible procedures are followed. I have been unsure of my location a good many times without suffering unduly. The lost backpacker's ability to regain his sense of direction and rediscover his location (or make himself easy to find) depends largely on his ability to control panic and fear so that logic and reason can prevail.

The best insurance I know against getting lost in strange country is to study it as I move along. I consult the map and reorient myself with each new turning of the trail. I identify and study the configuration of new landmarks as they appear. I frequently look backward over the country just traversed to see how it looks going the other way. If I am traveling cross-country or on an unmapped trail, I stop several times each mile to draw the route on my map. And at critical points (stream crossings, trail branchings, confusing turns), I make appropriate entries in my notebook or on my map.

A compass is the easiest means of orientation, but the sun, the stars, and the time can also be used to determine direction and to act as a check on the compass. More than a few disasters result when lost travelers refuse to accept what their compasses tell them. Unaware that they are lost and convinced they have their bearings, they assume the compass is broken or being unnaturally influenced.

Incidentally, precision compasses rarely are needed in wild country simply because it's impossible for the hiker to measure distance accurately and maintain precise bearings. One degree of error in a mile amounts to only 92 feet, so compasses that can be read to the nearest 5 degrees will be accurate enough for most purposes. In strange country where landmarks are unfamiliar, a compass is no less than indispensable. Many times I have worked out my true location or avoided a wrong turn by referring to a dollar-sized compass that weighs a fraction of an ounce and cost less than a dollar. But don't forget to allow for the declination. A compass will be useful in well-known terrain if sudden fog cuts visibility. So will an altimeter.

FOUR WAYS TO FIND NORTH

1. A roughly accurate watch will function as a compass on any day that the sun is out. If one turns the watch so that the hour hand points toward the sun, true south will lie halfway between the hour hand and the number twelve. An allowance must be made if the watch is set on daylight saving time, which is generally an hour earlier than standard (or sun) time.
2. If the time is known generally, even if within only two hours, a rough but very useful idea of direction can be obtained simply

by knowing that (in western America) the summer sun rises a little north of due east, stands due south at noon (standard time), and sets a little north of due west. In the winter the sun's path lies considerably to the south, rising south of east and setting south of west. Early and late in the day, we can easily determine directions with sufficient accuracy for most purposes.

3. Another useful strategy involves pushing a stick vertically in the ground, marking the end of its shadow, waiting about 15 minutes, then marking the shadow again. A line between the two marks will run east-west (the first mark is the west end). A line drawn at right angles will run north-south.

4. If the night is reasonably clear (in the northern hemisphere), it is relatively easy to find the North Star (Polaris), which is never more than one degree from true north. Its location is determined from the Big Dipper (or Big Bear), a bright and easily identifiable constellation nearly always visible in the northern sky. A line drawn upward from the outermost stars at the bottom and lip of the cup will point to Polaris. In the south-

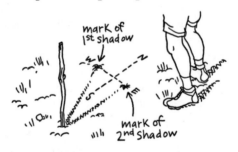

mark of 1st shadow

mark of 2nd shadow

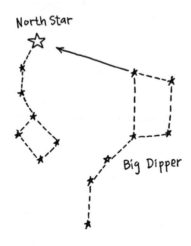

North Star

Big Dipper

ern hemisphere, the long axis of the Southern Cross points toward a starless region that lies due south. The prominent constellation Orion lies in a nearly north–south plane, and the uppermost of the three stars in the belt rises due east and sets due west from any point on the face of the earth.

GETTING FOUND

There are so many variables in every situation that it is difficult to advise the walker who has managed to get lost. However, a few general rules nearly always apply. The novice hiker has a tendency to plunge on through country that has gradually grown unfamiliar in hopes of reaching a familiar landmark. The veteran will resist this impulse, stop, admit to himself that he is at least temporarily lost, and sit down to review the situation. When he has overcome the anxiety that often accompanies such an admission, he will rationally review the situation, carefully considering all the information available.

After studying the map and thinking carefully, he may find a landmark he can identify that will reveal his approximate position. Or thinking back over the country he has traversed he may feel that by retracing his steps he can return to a known point in a comparatively short time. After all the evidence has been sifted, the important decision is whether to try and return to a known point, whether to stay put and await rescue, or whether to head hopefully toward civilization. Only full consideration of the situation in a rational, panic-free manner will reveal the best course of action.

But prevention, of course, always beats cure. To avoid getting lost, hone your route-finding skills. Learn to read and orient maps. Play the compass game until you can always point to north. Practice navigating your way through the unfamiliar areas of country you know close to home. Develop an awareness of distance by making an association between map miles and hiking miles. Test your estimates of altitude and elevation gain against your map. Plot routes through and around local obstacles. Study topo maps until you can "see" the country they depict at a glance, and memorize your declination. As your route-finding proficiency begins to grow, you'll enjoy the deep satisfaction that comes with feeling at home in the wilds.

Walking

There is nothing much to be said about walking... on a sidewalk at sea level for short distances, carrying nothing. But walking long distances on rough ground through high-altitude wilderness, under sizeable loads, is something else. Luckily there are a few stratagems and techniques that can add considerable pleasure to walking in the wilds.

There is a myth that one should find a comfortable pace and then stick to it. Nothing could be farther from the truth. The most common error among hikers is trying doggedly to maintain a set pace despite changes in the grade. Constant speed is an impossible goal. Comfortable, efficient walking depends on maintaining one's energy output—not one's speed—at a level that will not produce excessive fatigue. This simply means slowing down when the trail climbs, then speeding up when it levels off.

The length of one's stride should also be variable. When the trail suddenly grows steeper, I not only slow down, I take shorter steps. When the trail levels off, my stride gradually lengthens. Walking in this manner, i.e., trying to maintain an even and comfortable output of energy rather than trying to maintain a constant speed, I am never forced to stop from exhaustion, and I log more miles per day in greater comfort.

There's a scientific basis for my "variable speed" philosophy. Specialists have determined that for every individual and set of walking conditions there is an *ideal* pace, an optimal speed that requires minimal energy per step. Our internal computer instinctively tries to conserve energy and it will govern our speed for maximum efficiency—if we let it! Ignoring the clockwork within ourselves—by hurrying and even by moving too slowly—will be far more tiring than the optimal pace because it's using more energy than necessary.

Since every individual will have a different ideal speed, group travel presents certain problems. A 5'2" lady complained, "My 6'3" boyfriend, who is normally very thoughtful, spent a lot of time on our backpacking trip bawling me out for being slow, clumsy, and lazy—none of which I am if I'm accepted at my size and weight. It took me three steps for every two of his." Her boyfriend complained about his 40-pound pack, though it was only 20% of his weight, while she struggled to keep up carrying 25 pounds, fully 25% of her 100-pound weight. This couple was trapped into a mutually unhappy situation by his failure to understand their different physical capacities and by the less obvious but more common assumption that they had to travel together—which means at the same speed.

Because of their construction and chemical makeup, women are at a disadvantage carrying a pack in the wilds—quite apart from their lesser size and weight. Couples determined to hike together can best equalize the situation by adjusting their loads. In the case above, I would recommend the lady carry 15 pounds while her boyfriend lugs 50.

Where togetherness isn't vital I urge people to travel at their own pace, the tortoises starting earlier and meeting the hares at the halfway point for lunch. I also advise people to savor the joys of solo travel or pick companions with similar capabilities. Increasingly on the trail I meet carefree groups of women happily poking along together, free of the strain of performing or keeping up.

DYNAMICS OF WALKING

The experts have learned some interesting facts that can help us walk more functionally. Walking involves about a hundred different muscles, but *all* the walker's propulsive thrust is delivered by the terminal bone off the big toe. Our computer propels us by converting potential energy to kinetic energy with almost 50% efficiency. Walking is a state of carefully controlled falling, using the acceleration of gravity for the purpose.

There is an advantage, it turns out, to a certain amount of bobbing as we walk. The extra work of raising the body increases the help we get from gravity by permitting us to fall further with each step. Walking downhill is easier because the body can fall further. Freely swinging arms help walking efficiency by stabilizing the shoulders and pelvis with the thrust of their counter rotation.

Hurrying, especially uphill, can be counterproductive in another way. Superexertion produces lactic acid in the blood, which hampers muscle performance, causes great discomfort, and requires more than an hour for recovery, during which the walker suffers from exhaustion. So the clever backpacker's strategy requires keeping his activity level below the lactic acid formation stage. On difficult grades that means slowing the pace to a comfortable level or stopping frequently to rest and allow oxidation to flush the blood of acid buildup. By experimentation I have discovered that on the steepest trails under heavy load I drop below the level of painful lactic acid buildup by shortening each step from 18 inches to 14. That four inches makes a huge difference in my comfort.

It is important to react immediately to changes in grade. Failure to cut speed instantly when the trail turns abruptly upward places a demand on the body for extra exertion. And extra exertion consumes a disproportionately large part of one's store of energy. For instance, with the energy required to run 50 yards uphill one can easily hike a quarter mile up the same grade—in far greater comfort. Large expenditures of energy—running, lunging, jumping, taking huge steps, even hiking too fast—must be avoided.

On a really steep slope, at high altitude under load, or where the footing is bad (sand, scree, or loose snow), I adjust my pace even more precisely by controlling my step-to-breath ratio. I may, for instance, take two steps to the breath, inhaling as I plant my right foot and exhaling as I plant my left. If that proves hard to maintain, I may slow to a breath for every step or even two breaths per step, with a greatly shortened stride.

On exceptionally difficult slopes it is better to slow to a crawl, taking 6-inch steps, then to make the frequent stops a faster pace would require. Starting and stopping consume extra energy. A dependable rule of thumb is that where the going is hard it is better to slow down and keep going than it is to make frequent stops. An unlooked for dividend of step-to-breath counting is the welcome distraction the counting provides.

Every experienced backpacker at some time or other has experienced a sinking feeling when, coming around a bend, he discovers a long, shadeless trail switchbacking endlessly upward toward a high and distant pass. When I find myself faced with a prospect of this sort, I often distract myself from the ordeal with the self-induced euphoria that comes of concentrated daydreaming. In a state of mild self-hypnosis, my daydreams so totally absorb my conscious mind that the discomfort of the grind goes mercifully dim.

As I start upward toward the pass I rummage about in my memory for some event or scene that is so thoroughly pleasant and engrossing that I recall it with consummate relish. Then I unhurriedly embellish my recollection with the endless details that enable it vividly to fill my conscious mind. At first, it may be hard to escape into the past, but as the details pile up my awareness

daydream
dis-
comfort
away.

of present time and distance almost ceases. I climb automatically, sufficiently aware of my surroundings to make the necessary adjustments, but too engrossed with my dream to feel the discomfort. In fact, I'm sometimes reluctant, when the pass has been reached, to abandon my dream and shift my attention to the country ahead.

While I find daydreaming dependable and easily sustained, some people prefer the more companionable distraction of conversation. One of my regular walking companions, when we face a demanding stretch of trail, will say "Well, what shall we talk about?" We may very well get rid of a quarter of a mile before we settle on a suitable topic. Often we trade accounts of movies, dreams, books, trout we have caught, or mountains we have climbed. Sometimes we may be driven to simple word games (especially useful with children) like Twenty Questions or Animal-Mineral-Vegetable. If we have been out in the country awhile, we may get rid of half an hour concocting menus for fantastic meals. Talking as we move upward tends to slow the pace, but that, in turn, further reduces the discomfort.

TAKE A BREAK

Despite my advice "to slow down and keep going," rest stops are a vital part of walking. Unless the trail is like a sidewalk, one has little opportunity for looking around; the footing requires almost undivided attention. The walking itself is usually the least memorable part of any trip. So rest stops offer a means of savoring the country as well as restoring the body. One school holds that rests ought to be ruled by the clock, i.e., so many minutes of resting following by so many minutes of hiking. This arbitrary arrangement makes no allowance for the difficulty of the terrain or the allure of the country.

But what's worse is the notion that one needs to be ruled by the clock, even in the wilderness. The tyranny of time, it seems to me, is one of the things that people go to the woods to escape. I am willing to admit the usefulness of a wristwatch in the woods for arranging a rendezvous with other watch-wearing members of the party—but I find clock time as dispensable in the wilds as doorbells, radios, telephones, and cars, and I refuse to carry a watch, with only minor inconvenience.

Getting back to rest stops, most walkers, provided they have a modicum of self-discipline and know how far they have to go, will find it more satisfactory to rest when they want to or need to. I like to stop, if I can manage it, beside a stream, at the top of a slope,

rest stops are a vital part of walking.

in the first shade after a treeless stretch, where a log or rock forms a natural seat, or at any point where the view is unusually fine. I also favor mossy dells, waterfalls, brilliant patches of wildflowers, and fords where I can wash my feet or set up my rod and take a few casts.

When it comes to a real rest, I like to imagine I have earned it. On a particularly difficult slope, for instance, I might promise myself a rest after another 100 steps. Sometimes 100 is impossible and I have to settle for 50 or even 25. But if I get to 35 and think I can squeeze out another 15—I try it. For variety, and to add to the distraction, I sometimes count my steps backwards.

When I am ready to rest I take some pains to enjoy it. I slip out of my pack (leaving it propped against a rock or tree to make it easy to put back on) and sit or lie down. If my boots are the least bit uncomfortable or my feet are damp, I take off both boots and socks and set them to air in the sun or breeze. If there is water running nearby, I give my feet a soapless washing and a rub and let them dry in the sun. If I am feeling faint or tired I lie down with my feet propped high against a tree so the blood can drain from my legs back into my body. Once my fatigue has drained away and my breathing has returned to normal, I usually have something to eat.

Sometimes the greatest benefit of a rest stop—especially if there are children along—is having some fun, doing a little exploring. I like to stroll away from the trail to have a look at country I would otherwise miss. Often enough, I discover something unsuspected—an abandoned prospect hole, a bed of mushrooms, a hidden view, the remains of a lean-to, a tiny spring, or a wild sheep horn.

A rest may last anywhere from 30 seconds to overnight! When the time comes to move on, it is vital to start out at a moderate pace. There is a tendency, especially with children, to rocket up the trail after a refreshing rest. I have often seen eager children start off at a run, slow to a walk, then sink into a panting, dispirited trudge—all within 60 seconds.

FLUSH AWAY FATIGUE

The single most valuable (and spectacular) walking technique I know of, one that literally flushes away fatigue, is variously called the "rest step" or "limp step." Though little known among backpackers, this mountaineer's trick is based on the simplest of principles. When a hiker climbs steeply or carries great weights, the strain on the muscles around the knee is excessive and these muscles quickly fill with lactic and carbonic acids, the products of fatigue. This buildup of acids in overworked muscles, in turn, produces the painful ache that makes terrific slopes or heavy loads so uncomfortable.

The rest step is designed to flush away the acids of fatigue, thus relieving the ache they create. In the course of normal walking knee muscles never quite relax. But if at some point in the step the leg is allowed to go entirely limp, even for only a fraction of a second, the excess acids are carried away and the pain miraculously disappears.

The necessary relaxation can be managed in either of two ways. The leading leg can be allowed to go limp for an instant just after the foot is placed for a new step and just before the weight is shifted to it. Or the trailing leg can be relaxed just after the weight is transferred to the lead leg and just before the trailing leg is lifted. I have gotten in the habit of relaxing the lead leg, but most people seem to find it easier to let the trailing leg go limp. The trailing leg method is also easier to learn and easier to teach. My daughter learned it when she was eight.

We were dayhiking up a relentlessly climbing trail that gains 1200 feet in less than a mile. When she complained that she was tired and her legs hurt, I had her stop and shift all her weight first to one leg then the other, explaining that the pain would go away from a leg allowed to go limp. After she had stopped to flush her legs in this manner several times, I suggested that she take a small step forward with the leg that was relaxed, explaining that it was less tiring to keep going, even very slowly, when you rested your

Limp-stepping brings amazing relief:

legs. Before we reached the top she was able to flush the fatigue from her legs whenever she needed to, without stopping.

As few as two or three limp steps in succession will usually bring amazing relief. Of course, the acids of fatigue continue to collect as long as the knees continue to work hard, and it soon becomes necessary to flush them again. But I find that after half a dozen limp steps I can return to my normal stride for anywhere from ten to a hundred yards. Besides offering relief from aching muscles, limp-stepping also provides comic relief by causing its practitioners to look a little like staggering drunks.

WALK LIKE AN INDIAN

A technique of somewhat narrower application is the Indian Step, a style of walking long used by cross-country skiers and European gymnasts as well as American Indians. Modern Americans tend to walk without swinging their hips. The Indian travels more efficiently. At the end of each step he swings the hip forward as well as the leg, pivoting at the waist. And he leans forward slightly as he walks. This forward lean and turning of the hips lengthens the stride, positions the feet directly in front of one another, and minimizes the wasteful up and down movement. The result is a more fluid, floating walk, with less wasted motion. And on easy ground the longer stride produces more speed. The chief disadvantages of the Indian Step are that it is difficult to master, requiring agility and balance; and the advantages are greatest for the unburdened walker.

I occasionally use the Indian Step if I am lightly burdened and wish to travel rapidly across level terrain that offers good footing. I also employ its principles to minimize my up and down motion on a steep climb. The easiest way to get the feel of the step is consciously to stretch the stride, thrusting the hip forward, aiming the foot for the center of the trail, swinging the shoulders counter to the hip thrust. Once the rhythm is established the shoulder swing can be reduced. Walking on narrow city curbs is a good way to practice.

Having dealt with uphill and level trail hiking, it is time to go down. It is common to feel relief when the trail starts down because it is so much easier on the lungs. But downhill travel is twice as hard on the legs as going up. When descending a steep trail I try to cushion the shock of each downward step by rolling my hip forward (not unlike the Indian Step movement) and placing my foot with the knee slightly bent. As I transfer my weight I allow my knee to flex so that it functions in much the same fashion as an automobile shock absorber, reducing the jarring that downhill travel inevitably produces.

When I'm walking with my wife, I find it difficult not to keep in step with her. There's something about the rhythm and cadence—and the compulsory marching when I was in school—that drives me to match my step to hers. When I unconsciously fall into step, I soon regret it. To keep abreast of her and keep in step I have to shorten my stride uncomfortably. Deanne is five inches shorter than I am, so her legs are at least two inches shorter. As a result, she has a natural stride that's a few inches shorter than mine.

So, if we're going to walk together, she has to speed up or I have to slow down. Since I strongly believe that everyone should be free to travel at his or her own speed, sometimes we part. I may walk ahead, then stop to wait for her. She likes to walk energetically, and she's 20 years younger than I am, so we travel uphill at close to the same speed. I'm a bit faster downhill, so we often separate if the way down is difficult, reuniting at the bottom.

GROUP WALKING

The fact that people walk at different speeds is neither bad nor good. Don't feel guilty if you're slow and don't brag, judge, or blame if you happen to be fast. For happy carefree walking that doesn't tire you out, protect the integrity of your own individual stride. Walking with the brake on can be tiring because it's unnatural. Trying desperately to keep up with longer-legged companions is even worse. I'm intimately familiar with both positions.

The best compromise involves stopping periodically if you're fast to let your partner(s) catch up. And don't dash off the moment they get close. Being acutely aware that they're holding you up, they're probably pushing themselves a little, so they could use a companionable moment or two to blow and visit before you take off and they fall behind again.

On group hikes the slowpokes often get left far behind. If they're also inexperienced walkers and don't know the country—very often the case—an assistant leader content to poke along should be detailed as "rear guard" or "sweep" to be sure no one gets lost or left behind. Larger groups will often sort themselves out into a fast section and slow one, allowing the members of each to stay comfortably and companionably in sight of one another.

Of course social considerations may dictate considerably more togetherness. Walking with a partner or a group can be the very best form of companionship. The miles slip away when you're talking to a friend. And there's something about walking together that invites intimacy. Maybe it's the stimulation of motion and the relative freedom from interruption. There isn't any awkwardness because you're doing something together. The country rolls by like a slow moving picture. There's no doorbell, phone, or TV to interrupt. If you want to really get acquainted with someone, take them for a two-hour walk in the country.

CROSS-COUNTRY TRAVEL

Trails provide a measure of dependability and security. Cross-country walking is altogether different. Instead of relying on an established course, one must find his own way; instead of the improved footing of a prepared trail, there are obstacles to contend with. Carrying a pack cross-country can be serious business and requires much greater experience, balance, strength, adventurousness, and caution than does backpacking by trail.

In the California Sierra in the space of a mile, one may have to contend with brush, bog, loose sand, boulder slopes, snow, deadfalls, mud, streams, and cliffs. And one of the most treacherous steep slopes I ever descended was covered with innocent-looking tufts of extremely slippery grass. Just as slippery are glacially polished slabs that are wet, mossy, or invisibly dusted with sand.

Footing of this sort demands caution. I often take some trouble to climb around a wet or mossy slab, and when traction is vital I test the slope for sand by listening for the telltale grating sound. When I must cross slippery terrain, I often twist my foot slightly as I put my weight upon it to determine how well my boot soles are gripping.

TEST YOUR TRACTION

When climbing a sandy slope it is important to plant the foot as flatly as possible; the greater the surface area of boot on sand the shorter the distance one is likely to slip backward. If there are rocks or patches of grass or low brush, I think of them as stepping stones and zig-zag from one to the other. Sometimes steep sand is best treated like snow and the easiest way up is a series of switchbacking traverses or a herringbone step in which the toes are turned outward.

Spring travel in the Sierra is often over old snow; sometimes I walk all day and scarcely touch dry ground. Hard and hummocky slopes of spring snow can be extremely tiring, and nothing short of wading tests the waterproofing of boots so severely. It is virtually impossible to keep feet dry. All one can do is carry several pairs of dry socks for a single day's travel. Since wet boots are extremely slow to dry, the Indians of northern Canada carry four pairs of sturdy moccasins or mukluks instead. By the time the fourth pair is soaked through the first pair has dried. My own solution, if I am rushing the season, is to content myself with dayhikes and keep dry boots waiting at the trailhead.

In the spring there is the constant danger of falling through a thin crust of snow with painful, even serious, results. There is hardly an easier way to bark shins, twist ankles, and even break legs. Whenever I cross a rock-studded spring snowfield I am reminded of a trip I made with my father when I was twelve. I was walking a little ahead and we were talking. When he failed to answer a question I turned around, and he was gone. There was nothing but a vast snowfield broken only by an occasional rock. As I followed his footprints back toward one of these, I heard what sounded like muffled shouting. Close beside the rock, which turned out to be a boulder, I came to a hole 10 feet deep. In the bottom stood my father, uninjured, calling for help. It took half an hour to get him out. The cavern had been hollowed by heat from the sun transmitted through the boulder despite the fact that only a few square feet of rock actually rose above the snowfield.

spring snow by a rock is often undermined....

so step over such areas.

The margins of spring snowfields should always be treated with suspicion. So should snow-covered logs and snow from which issues the muffled sound of gurgling water. The best strategy I know for testing suspect snow is to kick it without actually committing any weight to it. If it withstands the kicking it can probably support my weight. Sometimes a big step or jump will avoid the necessity of stepping on what looks like rotten or undermined snow.

FORDING STREAMS

In the spring it can be dangerous to ford creeks and streams, never mind rivers. If you can't find a log or a series of stepping stones, you'll have to wade. The first decision is whether to protect your feet but soak your boots, or take a chance on injuring your feet (and increasing the likelihood of falling) by going barefoot. If you choose the latter, be sure your socks and boots are tied securely to your pack or around your neck as you wade, so that they can't possibly be lost if you fall or go under—unless you're prepared to walk barefoot to the car! When wearing a pack on a dangerous crossing, always release the hipbelt and loosen the shoulder straps so you can jettison it instantly to protect yourself from drowning.

If conditions warrant, send the strongest man in the party across first with a rope but no pack. A fixed rope tied tightly between trees will provide a great deal of security and peace of mind. So will poles to probe for holes and brace like a third leg against the current. Choose a wide shallow ford over a short but swift or deep one. The job will be easier if you start on the

the arms can help
on a long step up.

upstream side of a good fording site and plan to angle downstream, because that's where you'll end up. If you can help it, don't cross immediately above a falls, cataract, or other substantial hazard. Organize your party for the safest possible crossing. And remember that risks are enormously magnified when you're traveling alone. It's better to change your plans or make any detour than it is to take a chance when there's no one to help if you get in trouble.

Nothing consumes energy in such big gulps as maneuvers that require extra effort, like taking a giant step up onto a rock or log. If I cannot easily make my way around such obstacles, I transfer most of the extra effort to my shoulders and arms by placing both hands on top of the knee that is making the step and pushing down hard as I step upward.

SAFETY TIPS

Don't flirt with hypothermia. It's the number one outdoor killer. Take along enough clothing to keep warm under all conceivable conditions. I learned that the hard way on my closest brush with hypothermia. When I headed into Desolation Wilderness alone, it was an unusually warm summer day, without a cloud in the sky. So all I wore besides my boots was shorts and a thin T–shirt. But waiting just out of sight behind a peak was a storm. I didn't see it until I reached the high country.

Suddenly clouds blocked the sun. Then it started to rain, so I turned back. When the rain turned to snow, I started to run. Teeth chattering, soaked, losing body heat fast, shaking with cold and fatigue, I ran for miles. I didn't dare stop until I reached the warmth and shelter of a cabin. Even then it took hours by the fire to bring my thoroughly chilled body back to normal.

Safety also means guarding against lightning, falls, snakes, poison oak, biting and stinging insects, and so forth. Lightning kills nearly fifty hikers every year. On an easy climb of Silver Peak, I again was surprised by a hidden storm. Winds were high, but rain was light. Thunder was booming, but the lightning was striking more than a mile away. I felt I could safely make the last thousand yards to the summit, though my companion refused to come with me.

When I reached the top, lightning began to strike all around me. Boom and flash were simultaneous. I felt naked beneath a furious artillery barrage. There was no place to hide, but I didn't dare descend. I wedged myself half under a small boulder and waited, heart pounding, for the strike that would explode both me and the boulder. For 20 minutes I crouched there, soaked and shivering in the rain, until the bombardment shifted and I was able to run to where my partner was safely waiting.

I also learned the hard way why authorities admonish "don't climb alone." When I first went hiking above beautiful Zermatt, Switzerland, on my twenty-first birthday, I exuberantly began climbing an innocent-looking crag called the Gornergratt, planning to eat lunch at the restaurant I knew was on top. It seemed like the perfect dayhike. I didn't think of danger. It didn't occur to me that the restaurant might only be reachable by cable tramway. Climbing steadily, I expected to find a good trail at any moment, so I didn't pay close attention to my route. After scrambling up a 20-foot cliff, I found my way conclusively blocked. But when I looked down, I found myself 2000 feet directly above the Rhone Glacier!

If I fell while descending there was a fifty-fifty chance that I'd fall all the way to the glacier! Sweating, I started down, remembering too late that it's far harder and more dangerous to go down than come up. Halfway down the pitch I found myself blocked again. I couldn't find a needed foothold, hidden somewhere below me. There was nothing to do but jump. With all my strength I threw myself away from the abyss, clawing as I fell in the direction of safety. I landed two feet from the brink, bruised and scratched but intact. Since then, whenever I'm tempted to attempt a solo scramble, I remind myself of what might have happened the day I came of age on the Gornergratt.

If the trail divides with no sign when we're exploring new country, my partner and I split up, each taking a branch, calling to maintain contact until we decide which one to follow. Often the split is only a brief detour and the trails soon rejoin. Other times we discover in a few hundred yards where the branch is headed, making a note to follow it another day.

Before starting out, be aware of likely hazards to be encountered en route—like poison oak and nettles, poisonous snakes, dope growers, mean dogs, angry property owners, livestock, hunters, dirt bikers, snowmobilers, fog, rednecks, private armies, shooting ranges, barbed wire, electric fences, swamps, rising tides, armed farmers—and take appropriate precautions.

Swing your arms when walking for added stability on treacherous terrain or when trying to make fast time. They'll help you balance as you dance past obstructions. When the trail takes a sudden dip, then climbs steeply, I often run through the dip so my momentum carries me up the far side, conserving energy and refreshing me with the use of a different set of muscles.

USE THOSE ARMS

Most walkers don't use their arms enough. A vigorous arm swing functions like a gyroscope to help the walker maintain balance. The rougher the country the more valuable it is to swing those arms. If I'm boulder hopping or moving fast through rough country, my arms are going like crazy. I quite literally dance my way through the obstacles. And if I'm descending a steep loose slope through forest, I often swing from tree to tree like Tarzan. I safely descend a slope that would otherwise be dangerous by counting on catching branches or saplings to slow myself down.

Beware hiking across slick surfaces with your hands jammed in your pockets. I was walking one day in snow that hid the ice just beneath, my cold hands jammed in the bottom of my trouser pockets. My feet went out from under me so fast that I hit the ground with my hands still stuck in my pockets. I landed on one arm, cracking three ribs, and was sore for a month. Now I automatically take my hands from my pockets, no matter how cold the day, if I suspect the slickness could cause a sudden fall.

If the trail turns steeply uphill or down or I'm picking my way across a sidehill, I stamp my feet very slightly with each step, especially in damp duff or loose rock, to gain extra traction by getting maximum shoe sole against the trail.

BABY YOUR TOOTSIES

Clean feet are happy feet. When you get dirt in your boots, your socks don't cushion as well and the dirt can cause chafing. Gravel can be infinitely worse. If a rock in your shoe is causing pain, stop immediately. Don't put it off. A rock will not only abrade the skin, it can make you favor the foot by walking unnaturally. And walking unnaturally can cause cramps, muscular aches, even injury. I generally pull the top of my socks down over my boots to keep out rocks, dirt, and sand.

And at every opportunity I take off my boots, turn my socks inside out to air in the sun and breeze, and wash my feet if I'm eating lunch by a lake or stream. I dry them with my bandana, letting the air complete the job. By the time I'm ready to go, my socks are much drier, my feet are dry and refreshed, and I'm ready to set forth in greater comfort—after emptying out my boots and knocking off the dust.

When I encounter loose sand, deep dust, fine gravel, or soft dirt, I remind myself to turn my toes inward. I know that my normal "toes out" style of walking will dependably shovel loose material into the back of my boots, where it trickles down to grate painfully on the back of my Achilles tendons. Consciously turning my toes in keeps my boots from shoveling, so I needn't stop as often to empty them out.

Nothing is more important to a dayhiker than his feet, the wheels that have to get him home. At the first hint of distress from somewhere inside your footwear, stop and attack the problem. Find the fold in your sock or the pebble in your instep. Loosen or tighten laces. You want your boots as tight as is comfortable. The tougher the terrain, the tighter they should be to give you maximum support. But it's better to have the boot or shoe top comfortable and loose than tight and chafing.

If there is soreness, take off both shoe and sock to find the problem. Inspect the skin carefully. The slightest pinkness demands attention. If you can't stop the chafing that's causing your foot to redden, put on adhesive tape, Moleskin or Molefoam, a bandage, or extra socks. Failure to deal with irritated skin will soon lead to blisters.

On exceptionally steep rocky slopes, it sometimes becomes necessary to step forward onto the toe of the foot instead of the heel. Toe stepping adds power and balance on steep grades, but soon tires calf muscles. I find it helps to alternate heel and toe steps to prevent the cramping the latter produce. By following ten toe steps with twenty heel steps, I spread the work over two sets of muscles. The necessity of counting helps distract me from the rigours of the climb. If this arrangement continues to produce excessive fatigue, I sheer off from the fall-line and climb in longer but easier switchbacking traverses.

When climbing cross-country it is sometimes necessary to remind oneself that the easiest route up may not be the easiest way down. Going up, I generally go out of my way to avoid sand, snow, and scree; coming down I go out of my way to make use of them. Nothing is so pleasant after a hard climb up a mountain as glissading down a slanting snowfield or gliding with giant, sliding steps down slopes of sand or gravel.

THE JOYS OF CLIMBING

One of the greatest sources of joy I know is climbing to some attractive summit. It has been a long time since I called myself a mountain climber, but I enjoy getting to the top as much as ever. And I get just as much pleasure from walking up a little granite dome after dinner to watch the sun go down as I do spending all day working my way up a big mountain. The important thing to

"Getting to the top" can be a joy.

remember is that anyone can (and should) make his or her way to the top of an appropriate hill, ridge, or peak. I know of no better way to savor the wilderness.

Climbs are classed roughly as follows. Class I means following a trail or the easiest of terrain to the top, in any kind of footwear. Class II requires good boots and perhaps the use of hands on more difficult terrain. Class III requires route-finding skills, the use of hands and the possible use of ropes to protect the climber during exposure to very steep slopes or cliffs. Class IV means continuous exposure requiring ropes and perhaps pitons to protect the climber. Class V and above is technical climbing demanding constant aid on the most difficult slopes.

Scrambling—Class II or III climbing that requires the use of hands, but not ropes—demands agility, good balance, endurance, and desire. Success may depend on the scrambler's ability to discover a feasible route by studying the slope during the approach and by consulting a large-scale topographic map. The basic rules for beginning climbers include never climb alone; never go up a pitch you cannot get down; never climb on your knees; lean out from, not in toward, the slope when exposure is great; and never take chances or attempt maneuvers that are beyond your skill.

Despite the need for caution, climbing can be enjoyed by most walkers, including women and children. Both my wife and daughter have climbed a number of peaks with me; my daughter made her first ascent when she was six. It is unfortunate that so many people think climbing means inching up sheer cliffs by means of ropes, pitons, and limitless willpower. There is immense satisfaction to be gained in scrambling up peaks that demand little more than determination and offer no disconcerting exposure.

Climbing can be as safe as the climber cares to make it. As I come down a mountain late in the day, I remind myself that the majority of mountaineering accidents occur after three in the afternoon, and that twice as many falls happen on the way down as on the way up. The most expert climbers force themselves to descend with caution, thinking out difficult steps in advance to keep down the chance of injury.

Rock-hopping—crossing a boulder field by stepping or jumping from rock to rock—is probably the most demanding and dangerous way to travel in the mountains, but it is often unavoidable. I mentally try to keep a step ahead of my feet so when I run out of rocks I will be able to stop. I also treat every boulder, no matter how large, as though the addition of my weight will cause it to move. To slow myself down on a dangerous slope, I sometimes think back to a cross-country backpacking descent on which a companion, when forced to leap from a rolling boulder, opened 6 inches of his leg to the bone. Whenever I am forced to make a sudden or awkward jump, I try to land simultaneously on both feet with knees bent, to cushion the shock and minimize the danger of injury.

GET OFF THE TRAIL

With more and more people heading for the wilds, the complaints grow louder and more frequent: "You can't get away from people anymore." "There's nowhere decent left to go."

Nevertheless, I manage, with very little effort, to find plenty of places to camp, dayhike routes, peaks to climb, even trout water to fish, where the country is handsome and wild and I see more wildlife than people. Others who find their wilderness getting crowded may be interested in some of the stratagems I use to get away from the mob and get closer to the country.

A majority of hikers, or so it seems to me, are slaves to the trails. Many newcomers to walking are perhaps not aware that trails are the means, not the ends. The trail, however faint, is merely an extension of civilization. Wilderness does not begin until the trail is left behind. Trip planners, without thinking, plot their routes exclusively from existing trail systems. And many squander a whole vacation on wilderness travel that never leaves the beaten path. But the solitude—the true wilderness experience—does not materialize until the traveler is finding his own way through wild country, rather than following a route marked by others.

By far the easiest way to escape the trail is to dayhike, carrying only sweater, lunch, and first aid kit. More country can be covered in a day without pack than on a weekend under load. Hikers who want to spend a maximum amount of time in truly wild country may find it more fruitful to car camp close to the trailhead and spend the time dayhiking. I sometimes begin a wilderness weekend by backpacking cross-country for less than a mile to some unsuspected campsite by a spring or small creek; I then spend the bulk of my time dayhiking unencumbered.

The most heavily populated wilderness areas are those where fish are (theoretically) to be caught. It is my experience that most trail networks link fish-bearing waters. A great many people who have little or no interest in fishing regularly camp in noisy overused areas beside lakes, simply because that is where the trails take them. In heavily used country, the trails and the campsites along them are generally the poorest and certainly the least wild places. By planning routes that avoid well-known trout waters, I escape the mobs, find beautiful virgin camping areas with ample water, and occasionally I find exceptional fishing.

A good many trips have been ruined in the planning by the seemingly harmless assumption: "We ought to be able to make ten miles a day." On some days 50 feet would be too far. People have a habit of committing themselves to rigid goals: making 11.2 miles, fishing Lockjaw Lake, climbing Indian Peak. Somehow these achievements become substituted for the original or underlying reason for going—to enjoy roaming wild country. When people become so achievement oriented that they measure the success of a trip in terms of miles tramped, elevation gained, or speed records, they often find themselves losing interest in wilderness travel. Working toward ambitious goals becomes too much like the rat-race at home.

When peak bagging becomes obsessive or competitive, when each summit conquered becomes a mere achievement, the joy of reaching new heights disappears.

I do not reject all goals when planning a trip, but I try to plan routes with maximum flexibility and minimum strain, thinking in terms of options and possibilities rather than achievement. I try to arrange for the possibility that I will find a place so perfect that I lose all ambition to travel farther.

When I was a boy I had the good fortune to belong to a small group led by the well-known author-naturalist, Vinson Brown. Vince used to take us into wild places he knew in the hills and station us, out of sight of one another, perhaps a hundred feet apart, on conveniently located rocks and logs. After wiggling into comfortable positions, we would be instructed to sit absolutely still for five minutes, not moving anything but our eyes.

If we were quiet enough, Vince told us, the birds and insects and small animals in the area would come gradually to accept us as part of the environment, just as they accepted the rocks or logs on which we were sitting. It was truly remarkable how well it worked. I don't know a better way to get close to the country, and often when I am walking alone in wild country I will seat myself in some fruitful looking place and let myself once again become part of the country.

In most parts of the country summer-style backpacking and wilderness travel have to be modified for mid-winter climates. Many people don't bother. The majority of those who like to hike in the summer give it up with a sigh when the weather turns cold and begin the long wait for the following summer.

But one needs contact with the earth just as much in the winter as during the summer. Maybe more. In the winter we spend most of our time confined to the cities and the insides of buildings. A majority of people, in the depth of winter, go to work in the dark and come home in the dark, seeing the sun dimly through the window or only on weekends. We lose contact with the real world, the natural order of things. And our retreat indoors from the cold and the dark contributes, I am convinced, to sagging spirits, and a liability to illness. Over the years I have discovered that I am happier, healthier, more vitally alive if I get outside often to work up a sweat and immerse myself in the natural landscape.

TRAIL MANNERS

With more and more people walking in the wilds, trail manners have become more important. In most states discharging firearms, even during hunting season, is illegal across or in the vicinity of a trail. Equally objectionable is the boom of gunfire that invades privacy and solitude, and shatters the wilderness experience of other travelers for miles around. Guns are not needed as protection against wildlife and they have no place in today's crowded wildlands.

Horses and pack stock, once necessary to reach remote country, are now less common. But since stock can be unpredictable and difficult to control, it retains the right-of-way on trails. Walkers should move several yards off the trail, preferably downslope, and stand quietly while animals pass. Since walkers inevitably travel at different speeds, slower-moving parties should be considerate enough of faster walkers to let them move by. And fast hikers ought to politely ask permission to pass when the trail is narrow.

Overriding the backpacker's concern for his comfort should be a sense of responsibility toward the country through which he passes. Increased travel in diminished wild areas makes it necessary for all of us, consciously, to protect the environment and keep it clean. On the trail this means throwing away nothing, not even a cigarette butt, broken shoelace, or match. In camp it means burn-ing, then bagging, but never burying, garbage. Leftover edibles, not including egg shells and orange peels, can be scattered for the birds and animals. Everything else should go in heavy plastic garbage bags to be packed out. The thoughtful walker takes pride in leaving no trace of his passing.

TWELVE

Camping

Choosing Your Campsite... Bedsite Enhancement... Setting Up Camp... Foiling Hungry Bears... Organizing Dinner... Kick Back by the Fire... Toilet Training... The Joys of Cleanup... Disposing of Trash... Secure Your Camp... Reading the Weather... Thunder and Lightning... Erase Your Camp

A richly satisfying camping experience depends on the perfect mix of the gear you brought with you and your choice and development of the best available campsite.

The backpacker with no mattress, stove, or tent travels comfortably light. He can go faster and farther than heavily laden hikers, and he is free to leave the trails and travel cross-country. But when the sun goes down he becomes increasingly vulnerable and must find comparatively ideal conditions in order to make a comfortable camp. The party carrying a floored tent equipped with mosquito netting and rainfly, stove, mattresses, and all the trimmings is practically invulnerable to camping conditions, but its range and speed and traveling comfort are more limited, and it is more dependent upon trails.

The dilemma can never be completely resolved, but as a backpacker's experience, technique, and equipment improve, the cost (in pounds) of camping comfort can be considerably reduced.

The question of what to take must be reconsidered afresh for every trip. The likely weather, season, and type of trip will influence the decision regarding tents, tarps, ponchos, and storm gear—so will the route, the type of outing, length of stay, and familiarity with the country. There is no convenient way to avoid decisions, though some hikers persist in carrying the same gear on every trip. On a two-mile trail haul to a family base camp I might seriously consider carrying the kitchen sink. On a 30-mile cross-country ridgewalk I pare my equipment to Spartan proportions.

No amount of mountaineering equipment, of course, can ensure camping comfort in a steep, waterless, windy rockpile. There is simply no substitute for a wise choice of campsite. No skill is of greater value to the comfort-oriented backpacker than the ability to select the best possible spot to camp, and then to develop it for optimum comfort.

A persistent wind, damp ground, sloping bedsites, a lack of fuel or shelter, noisy neighbors, clouds of mosquitos, lack of water, etc., will rob the best equipped party of a pleasant night. There are times, of course, when bad weather, poor planning, inhospitable country, or just plain bad luck make a terrible location unavoidable. The veteran backpacker will choose the least terrible site and devise the most ingenious development in order to make it yield minimal comfort.

CHOOSING YOUR CAMPSITE

A veteran backpacker will instinctively pick the best possible spot to camp, based on long experience. The novice may need a checklist. The ultimate choice is based on two decisions. First, pick your general location. Let's say you're exhausted and the sun is going down. There's water and level places to sleep. Shelter and firewood seem to be ample. Maybe it's the only such camping place for miles. Or maybe it's a long planned destination.

Whatever the reasons, having decided to make camp in the general vicinity, the first thing to do is take off your pack, relax, take a drink, stretch some muscles—maybe take off your boots and put on camp shoes or sandals. Now you're ready to go looking for the best possible specific campsite. There are several immediate considerations. You want to be near your water supply, but not on top of it. To minimize impact and avoid contamination, camp 200 feet from any lake or stream. If insects are swarming, prefer higher ground where a breeze will help thin out the bugs.

Your choice of a campsite must consider shelter for both cooking and sleeping. A lot depends on whether you'll be sleeping in a tent or in the open. In the friendly summer Sierra, I prefer to sleep beneath the stars unless I need a tent for protection from bugs, wind, rain, or cold—or maybe for privacy. Sleeping outdoors is

what camping is all about. A tent walls off the wilderness. Don't automatically seal yourself in a nylon cocoon if there's no reason to. If you belong to the new tentbound generation and have never slept in the open or under a tree, try it. It might make your trip. Here's how to go about it.

First priority in site selection must go to bedsites since nothing is more important than a good night's sleep. Damp and sloping ground should be avoided—so should roots and rocks that cannot be removed. Spare clothing and equipment should not be forgotten in the struggle to make a poor bedsite passable. Shelter from wind, unwelcome sun, evening downdrafts, or intense cold may be essential to restful sleep.

As many a beginning camper has learned the hard way, there's more to a good bed than sleeping bag, mattress, and ground cloth. A well-chosen, well-prepared bedsite may be even more important. Practiced backpackers will recognize a good place. Beginners will need to consider various criteria. The chief enemies of a good night's sleep are cold, dampness, wind, insects, running water, flying sparks, falling widowmakers, avalanche, and the snoring of one's companion.

The most common mistake is to select a depression, dry ravine, streambank, or dried up snow pool because it is sheltered from the afternoon wind. But winds have a habit of disappearing around dusk, turning an unfriendly promontory into an admirable camp. As the evening advances, a gentle but persistent night wind commonly rises to pour cold heavy air down the streambeds and ravines and into those inviting depressions, leaving them as much as 10 degrees colder than higher ground only a few feet away.

Dry ravines and snow pools, besides collecting cold air at night, also collect running water quickly in a cloudburst. Meadows tend to be damp and attract heavy dew. Dew results when moist air cools, causing a fallout of condensation. Dew will be heavier near a lake, stream or meadow, and just after a storm. Heavy dew is capable of severely wetting an unprotected sleeping bag in just a few hours. Woe to the weary backpacker who, late on a night of heavy dew, has to climb inside a drenched bag left open or inside out.

There are enough advantages to sleeping beneath a tree to more than compensate for the filtered view of the stars. Trees serve as an umbrella to shield the sleeper from heavy dew and light rain. On a bitterly cold, clear night sheltering branches serve as insulation from solar radiation. The air temperature beneath a tree may be 10 degrees warmer than a bedsite exposed to the chill night sky. Since I rarely want to be wakened at dawn, I regularly position my bed to the west of a good-sized tree so that it can shade me from the early morning sun. The shade allows me to sleep an hour or so past sunrise without being cooked in my mummy bag. Trees frequently serve as windbreaks, clothes hangers, pack supports, tarp tie-downs, and a source of cushioning pine-needle mattresses. (The cutting of living boughs for a mattress can no longer be justified.)

It is generally important to know the direction of the prevailing wind in camp and to use this information in locating a bedsite, especially if the weather is unsettled or threatening. Even on a still night it is a bad idea to sleep directly downwind of the campfire. A wind in the night can fan the coals and bombard the bed with glowing sparks, each of which will burn a neat round hole in the nylon fabric. If the fire is utterly dead the sleeper will instead receive a shower of ashes.

Badly placed beds are rarely forgotten. One sultry night, making camp after dark, I placed my bed on the crumbled and cushiony remains of a thoroughly decayed log—usually an excellent location. I awoke after an hour, in the rain, crawling with big black ants whose home I had disturbed. Another time I was awakened by cold feet sloshing in a wet bag; a light rain had come up and though I was covered by a tarp a stream had materialized in the shallow gully containing my feet, soaking the bottom of my bag. The wakeful nights that followed both incidents were so grimly memorable that I now scrutinize prospective bedsites for disguised watercourses and concealed inhabitants.

Unusually good beds can be memorable, too. At a windy timberline camp on a rocky exposed mountain, I found a cleft in the rock beneath a prostrate whitebark pine that was just the right size and deeply filled with needles. All night the wind howled a few inches above my head while I lay snug and warm under the fragrant pine. On another windy high country night, I lay on a deep bed of needles in front of the fire in the mouth of a shelter made by roofing the space between two big fallen trees. Though the night outside was freezing, I was snug and warm in my little cabin.

BEDSITE ENHANCEMENT

Bedsites need to be very nearly level. If there must be a slope, it should run downhill from head to feet. Sleeping on a hillside is nothing short of torture. One is generally better off with an inferior level site than a sloping bed that is otherwise perfect. It is not uncommon for the sleeper who made his bed on a slope to wake up in the morning 10 feet away with the distinct impression of not having slept at all. I believe strongly that a bedsite's most important characteristic is its susceptibility to temporary alteration, and I have yet to encounter one I could not improve.

As I view potential sites, bare earth is fine, deep pine needles or duff are perfect, decayed tree trunks are excellent—when not inhabited—sand and gravel are satisfactory, provided I am carrying a cushioning foam mattress. Grass is poor because it cannot be contoured without removing the roots and permanently scarring the ground.

When I have selected the best available bedsite in all respects and decided where my head is to be, I dig a rectangular hip and shoulder hole. It measures about 18 inches wide, 28 inches long, and $2\frac{1}{2}$ inches deep with sloping sides and a slightly concave bottom. All of the excavated earth or sand is heaped into a pillow about 3 inches thick. From the bottom of the hip hole to the bottom of the foot area, I smooth the ground, removing sticks, rocks, pine cones and twigs. If the ground is sloping, I often use the earth excavated from the hip hole to build up the area that supports the legs, finding some other way to make a pillow. For maximum comfort, the feet should be a little higher than the hips and I find it well worth the trouble to make sure that they are. In seriously sloping or less than level ground it is sometimes easier to dig the hip hole deeper rather than pad the leg area. Like the highway builder, I try to balance my cut and fill.

Once the preliminary shaping is complete, I lie down on the bedsite on my back to test the contours. If the shoulder section needs widening and the hip hole deepening, I scratch some kind of a pattern with a twig, then get up to make alterations. When I lie down a second time, if everything feels comfortable (nothing pressing or cramped) I roll over on my side. This will generally feel less comfortable and additional excavating will be needed at the point of the hip and thigh. But I dig with restraint, knowing that no hole can fit perfectly both ways. The results must be a compromise which favors the position in which one usually sleeps.

In an attempt to make a perfectly contoured hip hole, the novice will often build up an area to support the small of the back. This is a grave mistake and is guaranteed to produce an aching back before dawn. Women, because of their broader hips, usually are less comfortable on the ground than men; they will want a deeper hiphole that tapers to a shallower shoulder hole.

My contouring operation may seem a waste of time to some, but I can think of no better investment of time than the five minutes it takes me to transform a small strip of earth into a comfortable bed that will assure me eight hours of restful sleep.

If the wind is blowing and cannot be avoided I take pains to point my feet to windward, and if the night promises to be cold I build a small earth and rock windbreak at my feet. Even on a warm night a persistent wind can chill exposed limbs; the noise, the twitching of the bag, and the breeze in one's face will rob even—perhaps especially—the most exhausted camper of hours of sleep. On an evening when the wind promises to blow, an extra 15 minutes spent hunting for or constructing shelter from the wind will be time well spent.

The old prospector with whom I used to camp in the desert considered me too finicky about my bed. After throwing his 50-pound bedroll (including mattress) from the truck, he was guided by just one consideration: his bed must be lined up north-south—with the head in the north—to ensure a refreshing sleep. He believed that the magnetic lines of force must pass through him properly (head to toe) in order to recharge him with energy for the following day.

Most of the above applies whether you're using a tent or sleeping in the open. When the bedsite is sculpted to your requirements, simply set the tent down over it—after first putting down a visqueen subfloor. Tent doors, of course, need to be oriented with regard to the rising sun, kitchen access, the view—and sometimes privacy.

SETTING UP CAMP

When my bed is ready to sleep in, I sort through my pack and dig out everything I am liable to need in the night: personal kit, watch cap, bandana, flashlight, down sweater, and socks for the following day. All of these are tucked in appropriate spots beside my sleeping bag inside the bivouac cover; a rock on top of my pillow assures that nothing will be dampened by the dew that will fall before I finally go to bed. The only exception is the small flashlight, which for the time being goes in my pocket. In the process of digging through my pack, I collect everything needed for preparing dinner: packets of soup and stew, herbs, condiments, pots, cups, stove, etc.

Since even a small breeze disturbs the flame and reduces the efficiency of most stoves, it's advisable to locate the kitchen in the most sheltered, protected part of camp. The alternative, especially if preparation requires a low flame, is to build a windscreen of some sort.

One morning I awoke with my family in a heavy breeze. My wife needed a cup of tea before facing the world, but the Bleuet would not light in the most sheltered spot available. I pulled the 6-foot foam pad from my bed, bent it into a circle around the stove and got my daughter to hold it in place while I made Sherpa tea and hot cinnamon oatmeal.

Once the stove is set up, water drawn from the lake, and the soup packet emptied in the pot, I know I am no more than 15 minutes away from enjoying the first course of dinner. If hunger and approaching darkness do not urge me to start cooking, I usually

see what can be done about preparing a campfire to cheer up the evening. A good many people like to get up early in the mountains and consequently they are ready for bed soon after dinner. I carry my city habits into the wilds, rising at a comfortable hour and sitting up rather late. Without a campfire, I can't indulge myself so easily. Nowadays, of course, wood fires are prohibited in an increasing number of areas.

FOILING HUNGRY BEARS

Hungry bears present mammoth headaches to backpackers in many regions, and the problem is growing worse. Because they are protected in parks and have no enemies, bears have multiplied unnaturally to become formidable predators, preying on unprotected food supplies. While preparing this revision, Deanne and I backpacked to Young Lakes in Yosemite. Though the alpine landscape was barren, distinctly not bear habitat, we were harassed by marauding bears every night. And on returning to the trailhead we found a bear had bashed in a window in our car, then climbed in and wreaked havoc in the search for food.

Yosemite backpackers know that they must hang every bit of their food out of reach every night—or it won't be there in the morning. It's a sizable hassle, especially if there aren't any trees. I was fishing at a lovely timberline lake when a backpacker walked up, holding a long stick, and asked if I knew of any "bear trees" nearby. I didn't. The few trees along the shore grew prostrate like hedges—not high enough to offer any protection. He told me he had already lost half his food to a bear and couldn't spare any more or he'd have to go home before his vacation ended. So he sadly turned around and headed down the trail toward timberline, so he could hang his food out of reach.

There are several strategies for hanging food—and everything else that might smell like it—from trees. First, find a slender tree branch 20 feet above the ground that's close to but not directly above your bed/tent. Next, divide your edibles into two bags of about equal weight. Toss a weighted rope over the limb and tie one sack to its end, along with a retrieval loop.

Now pull the sack up to the limb and tie on the second sack as high as you can, along with another loop. Stick the excess rope in the bag and toss it gently up toward the limb. Finally, using a long stick like the one my sad friend carried, nudge the sacks until they hang 10–12 feet above the ground and well away from the tree trunk. And hope it works! Be ready in the night to take action if it doesn't.

A more dependable bagging system involves somehow throwing your weighted rope over high limbs on two trees spaced about 20 feet apart, tying your food bag in the middle. Then reel in the rope until the bag is suspended at least 12 feet above the ground. In popular backcountry camping areas, the park service has strung "bear cables" 20 feet above the ground between two trees. Every evening after dinner, backpackers congregate from every direction

to hang their food bags on the cable and trade tales of the day's adventures beneath the assortment of dangling food bags, stuffsacks, and daypacks.

When planning a trip in bear country, first contact park forest or wilderness rangers to learn recommended procedures and what you need to bring with you. And plan on losing a little sleep when the bears arrive each night to try for your food. Most rangers now counsel aggressive defense, like yelling and shining lights in the eyes of your tormentors as you pelt them with rocks. Before the sun goes down, organize your defense with your companions to avoid mishaps. One night my partner drove a bear toward where I lay dozing in my mummy bag. It stepped on my legs as it galloped out of camp.

In timberline camps where fires aren't permitted, bears often provide the evening's entertainment.

Even if there aren't any bears where you camp, you'll probably have to protect your food every night from whatever hungry wildlife lives in the vicinity, most often raccoons, deer, porcupines, squirrels, mice, and other rodents. Hanging food out of reach is still the best defense. If you merely zip it in your pack, you may find that something has chewed its way through the fabric while you slept. To protect empty pack pockets from being drilled in the night, leave them unzipped. Most animals are drawn to foods containing salt, sugar, fat, and beguiling odors. Don't take the wildlife lightly just because you don't see any. Many a long-awaited trip has been ruined when the food supply was stolen the first night out!

If my campsite has been used before, I use or rebuild the existing firepit, taking care to turn the blackened sides of the rocks inward so I do not add to their discoloring. If I am on virgin ground, I try to dig a shallow pit in sand or mineralized earth (never duff, meadow, decayed wood, or vegetation) so that I can safely build a fire without blackening anything.

If firewood isn't plentiful, I make my small campfire using rotten wood that another winter will render unburnable, chunks of bark, smashed pine cones, and other junk wood. Since chunks of charcoal are unsightly in the wilderness, I try to burn all that I find in a campsite, as well as all the fuel I use, down to an ash that will blow away and convert quickly to soil.

ORGANIZING DINNER

At sunset or thereabouts, I light the stove beneath my soup, put on warm clothes for the evening, zip extra food securely into my pack, take in the wash and stow it also in the pack, stir the soup to make sure it is not sticking, adding whatever butter, milk or garlic, onion or herbs I can spare. If it's going to be dark before dinner is ready, I light and nurse my campfire past the critical stage. The best single rule I know for successful firebuilding is for the fire builder to be supplied with twice the tinder, matches, twigs, paper, etc., that should be needed.

A great many fires die while the builder is out looking frantically for more of something that burns well. Other common mistakes are packing the paper too tightly and smothering it with tinder: any kind of fuel needs plenty of oxygen to burn properly. At the other extreme, spreading the fuel so loosely that it fails to concentrate its heat is a familiar cause of failure.

Before the soup is ready, I arrange all the components of dinner—opened packet of freeze-dried food, sumptuous supplements and condiments and water so that as soon as the last of the soup has been poured the main course can be started. In parties of three or more, this usually means that the stove need not be shut down in order to conserve fuel—extremely desirable in gasoline and kerosene stove cooking—and the pot neither cools down nor scorches. Simplicity of meal preparation, of course, is essential to such exquisite timing.

Before the main course is ready, I lay out the makings for tea, and the stewed fruit or pudding that will very likely be eaten in the dark. If my craving for sweets and liquids promises to be hard to satisfy, I may also select a packet of lemonade. Since I tend to spend a good deal of time beside the fire in the evening, it is often worthwhile to drag or roll a boulder or log before the fire to serve alternately as a seat or back rest—providing, of course, that the dislocation does not disfigure the immediate landscape.

It is generally advisable to schedule dinner so that the meal is over—except for dessert, snacks, and drinks—well before dark. I like to go fishing or walking between dinner and dark. These excursions, I have discovered, often turn out to provide the most pleasant experiences of the trip. After a long day, of course, it is easy to lie in camp, feeling comfortably weary, and often I do exactly that. If fires aren't permitted, my companions and I may do some stargazing while we talk. Sometimes we sing or someone plays a harmonica. Or we light a lantern and read or play cards. The great advantage of a wearing a headlamp instead of carrying a flashlight, is that your hands are free for all these evening activities.

If there won't be cheerful firelight, I make sure I bring extra batteries, candles or lanterns, and after-dinner entertainment—like deck of cards, books, and Deanne's songbooks. And a sponge bath helps pass the evening if I haven't had time to warm water in a black plastic showerbag. After unaccustomed hiking under load, I find I sleep much better if I'm not gritty or sticky. A couple of cups of warm water and a washcloth can make a big difference.

But the wildness I have come to see does not really begin until camp and trail are left behind. Campsites and paths are simply extensions, however faint, of civilization. To experience wildness one must wander away from all travelers' routes to see what lies in the country beyond. It never seems hard, even if I know the immediate area quite well, to find someplace intriguing to go walking after dinner. Since my jaunts have a way of running longer than planned, I always carry matches, pocketknife, jacket, and flashlight.

Unless I am leaving early in the morning, I give the soup-stew pot only a brisk, brief cleaning after dinner, planning to wait for better light to finish the job. But quick attention after dinner—even before the pan cools (and food congeals)—will save considerable work in the long run. I scrape the pot with a big spoon to loosen all excess food and empty the contents in thick brush, for the nourishment of small animals, well away from camp and water. (There is nothing quite so grim as stepping down to the shore of a pretty pool, only to see the remains of someone's spaghetti dinner strewn across the bottom.) Then I add a little water (hot if the tea kettle has been on the fire), scrub briefly with the Chore Girl or abrasive pad and empty the scourings in the brush again. The pot, filled with water, is easily cleaned later.

KICK BACK BY THE FIRE

When the campfire is really burning and the coals are hot, I toss in not only the paper and plastic refuse, but foil packages as well. If the fire is hot enough these are largely consumed; at the very least they are cleaned and much reduced in volume for the trip home. I usually drink tea in the evening, keeping the teapot warm in the fire even though the water is usually heated on the stove. In the city, I take nothing in my tea, but camp tea often suffers from boiling, debris, weakness, or bitterness and I find I prefer it in the English manner well laced with milk powder and honey.

When the time approaches to go to bed, I customarily brush my teeth in my last cup of tea and stir up the fire to coax as complete combustion as possible; partially burned sticks make unrewarding scenery. If the night is cold I put on a watch cap to ward off the cold (body heat is rapidly lost from the head). If I

dismantling a poorly-located fireplace.

am putting on long johns or other clothes to sleep in, I warm them first over the fire and change quickly. I tend the fire until it has burned down to a safe bed of ash and coals. If there is a breeze or danger of traveling sparks, I spread the ashes to reduce heat and cover with sand or water.

There are easier jobs than getting undressed in the cold and dark and wriggling into a mummy bag without getting cold or wet. I generally sit on my pillow, take off my shoes and turn them upside down; then I take off my socks and trousers and slip into bed in a sitting position in my shoulder hole. From this point it is comparatively easy to peel off the rest of my clothes and tuck them under the tarp or bivouac cover before sliding the rest of the way into bed. After pulling the drawstring that converts the top of my bag into a hood, and locking it, I zip up the bag, leaving my flashlight by the top of the zipper.

In the morning the first thing I do—after rising and getting on my clothes—is to dismantle my bed and set it to dry. Even if the dew seems already to have dried, there is liable to be ground dampness and condensation from my body. Weather has a way of changing fast in the wilderness, and it is nice to have one's bed bone dry and securely packed; the same goes for tents and tarps; anyone who has had to pack and carry a wet tent will go to some lengths to avoid repeating the experience.

I spread my foam pad, bivouac cover, and sleeping bag out flat on sunny rocks or breezy bushes until they are warm and absolutely dry, then I turn them over. When the outsides are nicely toasted, I turn them inside out and repeat the process. In the dry air of a high Sierra, the whole process rarely takes more than half an hour, even after a heavy dew or drizzle.

Since I am more likely to wake up feeling sticky than hungry I usually wash, or possibly swim, before thinking of food. On most

relaxing after breakfast

summer days my breakfast consists of cold cereal or fruit, along with Sherpa tea, so I am not obliged to clean the stew pot before eating. But if the morning is cold and blustery, and cold breakfast is unappealing, I clean the pots sufficiently (often by merely wiping it out carefully with a paper towel) to avoid unduly flavoring the hot spicy applesauce and oatmeal I customarily make.

After a bad night, a very hard yesterday, or just for fun if there is no great hurry—I like to lie down and take a rest after breakfast on my foam pad. I sometimes read, make notes, study the map and make plans for the day, while lying comfortably on my back. Often I just examine the treetops, and sometimes I accidentally fall asleep.

TOILET TRAINING

When it comes time to relieve myself I play a kind of game; I pretend to be a trapper who is traveling in the country of the sharp-eyed, sharp-nosed Sioux, and I hunt for a concealed spot unlikely to be visited by scouting parties—under a deadfall, in a thicket of brush, behind a boulder. I roll away a rock or kick a hole in loose soil, and slip the rubber band from the toilet paper roll around my wrist. When I have made my contribution, I burn the paper, cover the hole and jump on it once or twice to pack down the soil; then I roll back the rock, kick back a covering of leaves, duff, or pine needles and branches, artfully landscaping the site until an Indian scout would never give it a second look.

I am careful to avoid any place that might serve as a campsite or trail. Running water, dry streambeds, empty snowmelt pools and any location within a hundred feet of a camp are also shunned. There is nothing more discouraging than finding that the second best campsite in an area has been used as a latrine by the people from the number one camp—unless it is streamers of used toilet paper fluttering in the trees.

In recent years I have increasingly become interested in cleaning up the country. Restoring a quality of wildness to the wilds by erasing the blighting marks of man has become one of my chief pleasures in the areas I travel. It seems the least I can do to repay the joy that wilderness has given me—and the one thing I can do to help make it last a little while longer.

Like many backpackers, I used to try to leave a camp as clean as I found it; it did not occur to me to try to leave it any cleaner, much less to go looking for other people's trash. I shook my head sadly at badly littered camps and passed them by in hopes of finding something cleaner. Then some years ago I spent several days on a cleanup party into Desolation Wilderness behind my cabin in Echo Lake. Carrying burlap sacks, we systematically scoured the trails, circled the lakes, and worked our way through commonly visited areas, picking up litter, tearing down fireplaces, filling latrines, restoring battered campsites, hiding blackened rocks, scattering firewood, and so forth. By the end of the trip I found myself hooked on cleaning up the country.

THE JOYS OF CLEANUP

When I say cleaning up other peoples' trash can become addictive, I expect to raise a few eyebrows. How can picking old toilet paper out of the trees or broken glass from the ashes in a ruined fireplace possibly be fun? My answer is that the pleasure comes from the sense of accomplishment, from the restoration of an ugly site to its previous condition of natural beauty. For instance, a handsome little alpine lake may be marred by a sheet of glittering aluminum foil lying on the bottom. The act of fishing out the foil, crumpling it up, and packing it into a corner of the knapsack restores the beauty and naturalness of the setting. Simple acts of this sort, surprisingly enough, can provide immense satisfaction.

Sometimes I carry a burlap sack or plastic garbage can liner with me on these excursions. If I gather more than I can carry, I leave the partially filled bag on the edge of the prominent trailside campsite, then on my return I mention its location to the ranger. When I am backpacking, it is no longer possible to bend over and pick litter from the trail while wearing a full pack. And there is a limit, of course, to what I am willing to add to my load. My scavenging activities are necessarily limited to forays from wherever I am camped.

If the area is near a pack stock trail, I consolidate the trash, bag it if I can, and notify the authorities of its specific location, estimating the number of sacks and pack animals that will be needed. If the area is remote and cannot be reached by stock, and if carrying everything out is simply beyond feasibility, I set about trying to hide my collection so well that the likelihood of its being found again is exceptionally small. In an area of boulders and talus, for instance, quite large objects can often to be stuffed out of sight into cracks and then covered again by a minor avalanche of loose rock, hopefully never to be seen again by anything larger than a Cony.

DISPOSING OF TRASH

Both the weight and the volume of trash I collect must be greatly reduced for optimum carrying purposes. Raw garbage or spoiled food left in a campsite can often be scattered well back in the brush where animals, ants, and decay can dispose of it. Egg shells and other indigestibles must be treated like foil, unless they will burn. Orange peels, plastic, and discarded clothing can usually be burned, along with waste paper, if the fire is sufficiently hot. I save the more difficult items for the evening campfire, and I am careful not to breathe the often poisonous fumes of burning plastics.

I shake or rinse the dirt from ancient rusty tin cans before crushing them flat beneath the heel of my boot. Foil and new tin cans can be cleaned and partially consumed in a hot fire, before being crushed. Bottles can be shattered for reduction in bulk, but only if a suitable (heavy) container is available for safe breaking. Broken glass is best collected in an uncrushed tin can that should then be packed upright in its own plastic bag.

Often enough I have circled a small remote lake, visiting all the campsites, cleaning up several messes, collecting an empty six-pack of beer, hiding blackened rocks after carefully dismantling inferior camps—all in less than an hour. And I have left, with less than 2 pounds of junk in my pack, well satisfied at having largely restored the area to a natural and inviting condition. Of course when I find such large or heavy items as skillets, life rafts, or sleeping bags, disposal becomes something of a problem.

A friend of mine carries cleaning up one step farther. He carries with him a spray can of powerful oven cleaner with which to remove the names and comments of that strange breed of traveler who goes hiking with a spray can of paint. Oven cleaner also removes the soot from unfortunately blackened prominent slabs and boulders. By getting rid of the black and rearranging the rocks it is possible to discourage future use of an inappropriate spot.

The fact that "trash begets trash" is as true in the wilds as it is in the city. Let litter accumulate and travelers will feel free to help swell the accumulation. But when a public place has been freshly cleaned people become reluctant to scatter their trash. And if containers are provided most people will use them. After the cleanup trips in Desolation Wilderness it was found that extra burlap sacks left behind in popular campsites were generally filled by the parties that followed.

Enthusiasm for cleaning up the country is not peculiar to me; it is shared by nearly all of my friends who have tried it. I have found that people who endlessly procrastinate about cleaning out their cellars will conscientiously clean up other people's campsites. And children whose rooms at home stand knee deep in litter will patiently pick the broken glass from someone else's fireplace. Our cleanup trips in Desolation have actually become popular. The companionship, sense of accomplishment, and the beautiful country combine to make these trips highly memorable.

Every hiking club, summer community, or group of backpacking friends owes it to itself—and to the country it enjoys—to try a cleanup trip. The Forest Service stands ready to encourage serious groups by providing empty sacks and hauling collected debris.

SECURE YOUR CAMP

Before leaving camp on short excursions—cleanup, fishing, an after-dinner stroll—I always take a look around to make sure it is secure against the incursions of small animals, near neighbors, sudden weather change, and fire. Brazen chipmunks, mice, bluejays, and squirrels have more than once escaped with significant portions of my larder without even waiting for me to walk away

he wasn't ready for rain.

... now he's ruining his boots!

from camp. Enticing food should always be stowed in a pack, preferably in a zippered compartment that can be tightly closed, before leaving camp, and the pack should be hung from a tree or rope—depending on the type and voracity of predators.

One spring, I followed the snowplow into the mountains and made camp with a friend in an alpine meadow—after a long and heavy winter. Either the wildlife in the region was starving, or our food had unusual appeal. The first night, despite a fire that burned continuously, we spent half the night yelling and throwing pine cones at a bear who refused to leave us alone. We moved our camp the next day and that night we built a bigger fire, but the snuffling and stomping of the pacing animals that circled us all night gave us little rest. In the morning we found a ring of bear, coyote, and deer tracks just beyond the firelight. After two sleepless nights fending off the wildlife, we gave up and returned home.

There was a time when one could leave money lying around camp in perfect safety—provided one was beyond the range of day-hikers. Nowadays, it is a good idea not to leave anything valuable in camp. A camp that will be seen by a large number of hikers is far too vulnerable to leave. More than one group of hikers in recent summers has come back from a hike to find their camp entirely vanished. And backpackers in roadhead camps have awakened to find that everything but the bags they were sleeping in was gone. Packs, boots, down bags, parkas and the like have significant resale value and are easily sold, so it pays to protect expensive gear—and to camp well away from the boulevards whenever possible.

It should be a matter of common sense never to leave camp for even a few minutes if a fire is burning. A gust of wind can carry flaming embers into the woodpile, dry pine needles, or a $300 sleeping bag and cause substantial damage in a matter of moments. The fire should be absolutely stone-cold dead whenever camp is left untended. Every summer I pass empty camps in which a fire still burns or smolders. The incidence of man-made fires is climbing every year.

READING THE WEATHER

Long excurions from camp require more precautions because weather must also be taken into account. Consider my recent experience. We had left our high Sierra camp close under a mountain on a clear summer day without any thought of a possible storm. Our mistake was in forgetting that we really had no idea of weather conditions on the other side of the mountain.

By the time we reached the ridge the storm that had been hidden was almost upon us. By the time we returned to camp, late that afternoon, it had been raining steadily for several hours. Fortunately, our clothes and food were safe in our waterproof packs and our sleeping bags, though damp in places, were under tarps. The Bleuet stove was soaked and would not light, but we managed to build a big fire and stood before it in the wind and rain for another long hour before the sun came out a few minutes before sunset.

There was just barely time to halfway dry out our beds and get them back under tarps before a drenching dew began to fall. Even without seeing the sky behind the mountain that morning, I should have been suspicious because the breeze, though faint, was blowing from the south. Wind blowing from the south, east, or northeast is liable to bring a storm. Wind blowing from the north, northwest, or southwest generally heralds fair weather; the major exceptions are mountain thunderstorms which often come from the west.

Clouds offer the backpacker another aid to weather forecasting. Big fluffy cumulus clouds are harbingers of fair weather—so long as they do not join together and begin to billow upward. When they cease to exsist as individual clouds and the bottoms darken and the tops form columns and flattened anvil heads—a thunderstorm is on the way. High, thin cirrus clouds are generally filled with ice particles; when they whiten the sky or their mare's tails reach upward, a storm can generally be expected within 24 hours.

Stratus clouds, as the name implies, come in waves or layers or bands; when they are smooth and regular and rolling the weather should be fair, but probably cool; when stratus clouds are mottled or fragmented into a buttermilk sky, it will usually storm.

The astute wilderness traveler learns to recognize a number of signs of impending weather change. Sun dogs or halos around the sun forecast rain or snow; so does a ring around the moon. A red sky at dawn or an early morning rainbow or the absence of dew on the grass—all of these should warn the traveler that bad weather is brewing. So should yellow sunsets and still, ominously quiet moist air.

Sensitivity to the signs should influence the backpacker's choice of camps and trip itinerary. If the signs are bad, he should erect the tent, lay in a good supply of firewood beneath a tarp, and schedule close-to-home amusement rather than exposed activities like climbing. On the other hand, a careful reading of the weather may enable him to set out on a climb, confident of good weather, even before the rain has stopped. For instance, clearing can be expected despite heavy clouds, providing "there's enough blue to make a Dutchman a pair of pants."

THUNDER AND LIGHTNING

Thunderstorms, those exciting, dramatic, generally short-lived phenomena, are nevertheless frightening to a good many people. I have seen tall trees virtually explode when struck by a bolt of lightning, sending huge limbs flying in every direction. But the danger is negligible for anyone willing to take the necessary precaution— leaving vulnerable locations before the storm begins. The places to avoid are high, open exposed slopes, hills, ridges and peaks, isolated or unusually tall trees, lakes, meadows, or open flats. The safest places are in caves, canyon bottoms, and a part of the forest where the trees are comparatively short.

The hiker or climber anxious about lightning usually has considerable warning. When cumulus clouds have darkened and fused and still air has been replaced by sudden erratic winds, the storm is about to break and backpackers should already be snugly sheltered. Lightning usually appears to be striking closer than it is, especially at night. The distance can be accurately gauged by counting the seconds between flash and boom.

Every five seconds in time means a mile in distance. Thirteen seconds between flash and boom means the lightning is striking

lightning strikes prominent exposed places.

two and a half miles away. No matter how fierce the storm may seem, summer afternoon thunderstorms characteristically are short, and the chances are good that the sun will be out before sunset. If my camp is battened down and I can watch in some comfort, I enjoy the noisy melodrama of an afternoon storm.

ERASE YOUR CAMP

When the time comes to pack up and move camp, I like to see how wild I can make my campsite look. If I have camped on virgin ground, I take pains to restore it to its natural conditions so that a passerby would not guess it had ever been used. There are far too many campsites already in existence; my aim is to decrease, not increase the number. After collecting all the unburned foil and metal from the ashes and packing it in a garbage bag, I bury charcoal, ashes, and partially burned twigs or scatter them well back in thick brush.

The firepit is filled in, blackened rocks are hidden and turned black side down in the brush, and the hip and shoulder hole from my bed are filled in and smoothed over. Pine needles, sand, soil, duff, pine cones, and branches are scattered naturally about and if the area still faintly resembles a camp I sometimes roll in a few rocks and large limbs or small logs to fill up the bare spots. After firewood is scattered, all that remains are a few footprints. Once rain has fallen it would be difficult to tell that the area ever had been disturbed.

The extra effort I would invest in disguising a virgin camp, I am likely to spend destroying surplus or inappropriate camps in the neighborhood. Campers who arrive late at night or on crowded holidays often camp in gullies, or boggy meadow and even in the middle of the trail. These camps, which are rarely used a second time, can often be entirely obliterated with a little work, greatly improving the wilderness character of the area.

Even a dayhike no longer seems to me complete unless I have dismantled a few fireplaces, disguised a few old camps, and stuffed a little debris in my pack. The blackening on granite from a single evening's fire will withstand erasure by the elements for as long as 50 years. Though I cannot hasten the process I can at least enjoy hiding some of the evidence.

THIRTEEN

First Aid

*Foot Care ... Sprains and Broken Bones ... Shock ...
Minor Wounds ... Altitude Sickness ... Sunburn and Tan ...
Burns ... Heat Exhaustion and Heat Stroke ... Hypothermia ...
Snakebite ... Insect Bites ... Poison Oak and Ivy ...
Cardiopulmonary Resuscitation*

The best First Aid, all authorities agree, is Prevention. Walking in the wilds can be distinctly dangerous to your health. So don't take foolish chances. Veteran backpackers make it a rule to exercise substantially more caution in the backcountry than they do at home. So, emulate the pros and be more careful on the trail—and *much* more careful climbing and traveling cross-country.

"Keep it short and simple," advised the doctor who counseled me on this chapter, "and hope people will read it." So here's a quick course in the basics. For a more comprehensive treatment of wilderness first aid, see my book *Dayhiker, Walking for Fitness, Fun & Adventure*, also from Ten Speed. And take a Red Cross First Aid Course next winter, so you'll be confident and adept at dealing with emergencies, administering CPR, and so forth. The life you save, as they say, could be your own!

The greatest danger in wild country is traveling alone. Trail hiking is bad enough, but cross-country travel is infinitely worse,

and climbing alone is idiotic. Unfortunately, some of the joys of wilderness travel are only to be discovered traveling alone. When I hike by myself, I tell someone responsible where I am going, what route I plan to follow in both directions, when I expect to be back, and the time to start worrying. I usually draw the route on a map and mark the places where I expect to spend the night.

While out in the wilds, I pay close attention to what my body tells me, make proper use of my clothing, and take precautions against injury. By doing likewise, you too can double your chances of enjoying a safe, happy trip.

A selection of adequate first aid kits is available on the market, but it isn't hard to make a better one from scratch. Your kit might consist of a dozen adhesive bandages in assorted sizes, four butterfly bandages, four individually wrapped gauze pads (2×2 and 3×3 inches), 3-inch roller gauze, a roll of 1-inch adhesive tape, a small bar of soap, a sheet of Molefoam or a lump of foam rubber, a small pair of scissors, a needle, a backed razor blade, a clean washcloth, half a dozen matches, and any medicines you might want.

Everything should fit snuggly into a screw-topped plastic ice-box jar three inches deep and four inches in diameter. I like to carry a carved bar of soap in 35mm film can (marked "S"). I tape the needle and razor to the lid of the ice-box jar and mark the top and bottom of the jar with big red crosses to distinguish it from the other containers. The entire kit only weighs about 6 ounces.

For more extensive trips your kit should also include a good pair of tweezers for splinters, a 3-inch Ace bandage for sprains, several extra needles, and 6 safety pins. Sprain-prone hikers should carry an ankle brace. Extra soap, a washrag, and a towel would be useful in poison oak country, and salt pills are a good idea in the desert.

In a separate toilet kit for everyday use, you might include vaseline, athelete's foot powder, sunburn ointment, glacier cream, dental floss, a toothbrush, and any special medicines. If the water is mildly suspect, include a 2% Tincture of Iodine for purification. Use 5–10 drops per quart of water.

FOOT CARE

"At the first hint of discomfort, stop, take off the boot, and have a look," a backpacking doctor once told me. "Wash and dry a place that is getting red; then tape a thin sheet of rubber foam over the spot."

I had always relied on moleskin for covering blisters and inflamed places on my feet. Moleskin's disadvantage is that once it is stuck directly to the injured or tender area it cannot safely be removed (without removing the skin) until the end of the trip. In the meantime, of course, the moleskin is certain to get damp and dirty, encouraging bacteria growth. On the doctor's advice, I have switched to either molefoam or foam rubber and find both perfectly satisfactory.

Often as important as bandaging an inflamed foot is attacking the cause of the inflammation. On occasion I have had to hammer down a nail with a piece of granite or whittle away a protruding ridge of leather. More often the problem is solved by kneading new boots that pinch, removing a pebble, loosening laces, removing the wrinkle from a sock, adding an extra pair of socks, or changing to a dry pair.

Dry socks are vital to happy feet. Wet, clean socks are far harder on feet than dirty, dry ones. Experienced hikers tend to do far more sock washing and sock changing than beginners, and they take off their boots and air (and wash) their feet at every opportunity. People unaccustomed to walking are likely to suffer from tender feet. Foot powders, Benzoin skin toughener, and alcohol rubs may help, but there is no substitute for adequate conditioning.

Sometimes the best solution to aching feet is a change in footwear. If those newish boots deliver agony with every step, stop and switch to the comfortable old cross trainers you cleverly brought along for day hiking and lounging around camp. Whenever I stop by water, I take off my boots, clean them out, rub my feet in the water, turn my socks inside out to dry in the sun, and air-dry my feet. I find this ritual wonderfully refreshing.

As soon as I get to camp, my boots come off and I wash my socks and hang them out to dry. Then I wash my feet and switch to sandals. I love to go barefoot, but it's dangerous when I'm many miles from the car and the only way to get there is to walk.

SPRAINS AND BROKEN BONES

Nothing is more common among dayhikers accustomed to doing their walking on sidewalks than turned or sprained ankles. Severity

sprained ankles can be chilled in icy streams or with snow-filled plastic bags →

varies greatly. Some sprains amount to nothing more than a momentary twinge. Others require the victim to be immobilized immediately. Often the wisest course for the person who has suffered a bad sprain (with the ankle immediately turning black and blue) is to apply a tape cast and head for the car before the ankle can swell and stiffen.

Braces are likely to be carried only by people with weak ankles who have come to rely on them. Ace bandages have the advantage of being usable on other parts of the body. In either case, it may be necessary to remove all (or at least the outer) socks to make room for the bandage in the boots. And people who have sensitive Achilles tendons may find it impossible to wear an elastic bandage very long. Bandages need only be worn while walking. They should be removed at night and at any other time that the ankle can be elevated.

All of the swelling that is going to take place will happen on the day of the sprain or the day that follows. On the third day, with the swelling stopped, the treatment changes from the application of cold to the application of heat. The intent now is to stimulate blood flow through the injured area in order to reduce swelling. Hot compresses made from bandannas, towels, diapers, or washrags dipped in heated water are excellent, or the ankle can be baked before an open fire.

Hot water bottles can sometimes be fashioned from large plastic bags, but care must be taken not to burn the patient. The exception to heat treatment is for the ankle that is immediately encased in a cast of tape. Such casts should be left undisturbed for two or three days and heat applied only after removal.

Although splint protection is part of first aid, amateurs should not attempt to set broken bones. Either the patient should be moved to a doctor, or a doctor should be brought to the patient.

SHOCK

Shock is a state produced by injury or fright. The victim feels cold and clammy and weak. The treatment is to lay the patient down on level ground and make him as comfortable as possible, usually by loosening constricting clothing and covering him if it is cold until a feeling of well-being returns. Except in cases of severe head injury, difficulty breathing, a broken leg, or neck injury, elevate the legs about 30 degrees.

MINOR WOUNDS

Slight bleeding from a small wound usually stops soon after the wound is elevated so it lies higher than the heart and pressure is applied with a gauze pad. For a cut foot or leg, the patient lies down and props his leg against a tree; a cut hand should be held above the head. Closing the wound to stop the bleeding is vital. A puncture can be firmly blocked by the palm or a finger. On a slice or cut it may be necessary to draw the edges together with the fingers before applying pressure. A large or heavily bleeding wound may have to be closed by hand pressure, or it may be necessary to tape the edges of the wound together with a butterfly bandage in order to stop the bleeding. Once bleeding has been controlled, the wound should be kept elevated to reduce the blood flow and aid clotting.

Never attempt to substitute a tourniquet for these procedures. Tourniquets are dangerous and rarely necessary since pressure and elevation will stop all but the most serious bleeding.

As soon as bleeding is under control, the wound should be washed with soap and water or irrigated with water to carry away bacteria and dirt. It may be necessary during the washing to keep the wound elevated to lessen bleeding. Do not apply antiseptics (Mercurochrome, iodine, methiolate and the like); they tend to

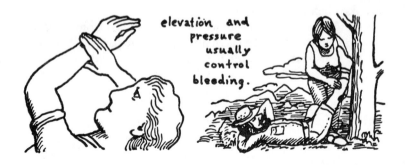

elevation and pressure usually control bleeding.

do more harm then good—inhibiting scab formation and trapping bacteria that cause infection. Soap and plenty of water are all that's needed. Once cleaned, it may be gently blotted dry with a clean cloth or towel (not to mention toilet paper or clean socks).

Minor cuts and scratches, especially on protected parts of the body, are better left unbandaged. Protected but uncovered wounds are more easily kept clean and dry; healing is faster and the chances of infection are lower. Small wounds need only Band-Aids. Larger ones will require a gauze pad held in place by narrow strips of adhesive tape. The largest may require wrapping the limb or body with roll gauze. Gauze and adhesive bandages should be applied directly on top of a wound held closed by a butterfly bandage.

butterfly bandage

The greatest enemy of wounds is dampness. A wet bandage inhibits healing by providing a favorable environment for the growth of bacteria. Once a bandage has become wet, whether from blood, perspiration, or water, it is a menace to health and should be replaced. No bandage at all is far superior to a wet one. The drier the wound, the less the chance of infection.

ALTITUDE SICKNESS

As altitude increases, the oxygen content of the air decreases. In order to adjust, the body strives to process more air by means of faster and deeper breaths, to better extract oxygen from the air. Adjustment begins at only slight elevation, but shortness of breath and dizziness do not usually appear until about 7000 feet. The more gradual the change in altitude, the easier the acclimatization. Individual tolerance to altitude varies widely. The well-rested, vigorous, healthy individual usually acclimatizes easily. Smoking, drinking, and heavy eating before or during a climb make acclimatization difficult.

Failure of the body to adjust to reduced oxygen intake results in altitude or mountain sickness. Mild symptoms include headache, lassitude, shortness of breath, and a vague feeling of illness—all of which usually disappear after a day of rest. Acute mountain sickness is marked by severe headache, nausea, vomiting, insomnia, irritability, and muddled thinking. The victim must descend to a lower elevation. Mountain sickness can usually be avoided by beginning a trip in good condition, spending a night at the trailhead before starting out and choosing modest goals for the first day's walk. Most acclimatization occurs in the first two or three days. The rule is "climb high but sleep low."

People who acclimatize poorly are susceptible to high altitude pulmonary edema (HAPE; fluid accumulation in the lungs) when they reach elevations in excess of 8000 feet. The first symptoms include a dry, persistent, irritating cough; anxiety; an ache beneath the breast bone; and shortness of breath. If the victim is not evacuated promptly to lower elevation or given oxygen, breathing may become rapid, noisy, and difficult; the skin often takes on a bluish tinge; and death may occur quickly.

SUNBURN AND TAN

Sunburn is a constant threat, especially at higher altitudes, to city dwellers who are not deeply tanned. At 6000 feet the skin burns twice as fast as at sea level, and the liability continues to increase with altitude. Sunburn often ruins a trip when a pale backpacker tries for a fast tan. Few people ever acquire a deep enough tan to expose themselves all day at high altitude without burning; precautions should be taken to cover—or at least shade—all parts of the body for most of the day. Take special care to avoid burning the nose to prevent starting a cycle of peeling, burning, and repeeling—and don't forget protection for your lips.

Potent sunscreen/blocks are essential on most trips, but beware toxicity and allergic reactions to preparations with ratings higher than 15. A friend of mine was temporarily blinded by sunblock rated at 36 that found its way down from her forehead into her eyes.

BURNS

For first- and second-degree burns, apply cold water for five minutes or until the pain stops. Apply a loose dressing to a second-degree burn; do not break the blister. Check for shock. Keep all burns dry and avoid oils and greases.

HEAT EXHAUSTION AND HEAT STROKE

Hikers on any length trip can be prone to heat illness. To protect yourself, drink plenty of water (at least four to five quarts per day), even if you don't feel thirsty. Avoid coffee, tea, and alcohol, which lead to excess urination and dehydration. Wear clothing in layers so you can add or shed as necessary, and wear a broad-brimmed hat.

Salt pills (five grains) are not required by most people unless the perspiration is literally pouring off the body. The usual dosage in such cases is one pill every 4–8 hours, but only with a quart of water per 1 or 2 pills. Overdosing on salt is dangerous!

Heat exhaustion and heat stroke, both caused by excessive heat, have distinct symptoms and are very different in severity. A person with heat exhaustion, the less serious of the two, has not consumed enough water to compensate for loss of fluids through sweating. The person sweats profusely, is fatigued and weak, and may collapse, but the body temperature is normal and there is no real immediate danger. Sip salt water, lie down, and apply a cool, wet washcloth. If fainting occurs, lowering the head will probably bring back conciousness.

In heat stroke, the body temperature is high, up to 106°F, and the sweating mechanism fails. The skin is hot, red, and dry, and there is no sweating; the pulse is rapid and strong; and the victim may be unconscious. Sponge the bare skin with a cool washcloth, and fan, being careful to prevent overchilling once the temperature gets below 102°F. Heat stroke is life-threatening and requires immediate care.

HYPOTHERMIA

The number one killer of outdoor travelers is hypothermia, defined as "rapid mental and physical collapse due to chilling of the body's core." When the body loses heat faster than it can be produced, you instinctively exercise to keep warm while the body cuts back blood supply to the extremities. Both drain your energy reserves. If chilling and exposure continue, cold will reach the brain, depriving you of judgment and reasoning power without your awareness. As chilling progresses, you lose control of your hands and body. When your body can no longer summon reserves to prevent the drop in core temperature, stupor, collapse, and death await.

The first line of defense is awareness that most hypothermia cases occur during mild temperatures, 30 to 50°F. The greater hazards are wind and water. Wind drives away the skin's cushion of warm air, and it refrigerates wet clothing. Remember that 50°F water is unbearably cold, and the wet body can lose heat two hundred times as fast as one protected by dry clothing. Get out of wet clothes, get dry, and put on vapor barriers to stop heat loss; there is no better clothing to protect against heat loss. If you can't stay dry and warm, do whatever is necessary to stop exposure. Turn back, give up, get out—before exhaustion can complicate your plight.

Don't shrug off shivering. If you have to exercise continuously to prevent it, you're in danger.

Don't use alcohol to warm a dangerously chilled or hypothermic person. Liquor causes blood vessels to dilate (enlarge), increasing heat loss through the skin, which threatens a severely chilled person. It also impairs judgement and reduces coordination, which can be dangerous.

A modest amount of alcohol will produce a beneficial warming sensation in the extremities of a warm and healthy individual with cold hands and feet. Drink will also cool the torso in the summer by directing more blood to the extremities. Just remember that alcohol moves the blood (and thus the heat) from the core and torso towards the hands and feet.

SNAKEBITE

The prerequisites in prevention are caution and the ability to recognize poisonous snakes and the sort of terrain they like. I have spent a good deal of time in heavily infested areas and have encountered a great many rattlers. But by never extending any part of my body into a concealed place that could contain a snake, I have avoided being bitten.

While fatalities from snakebite are rare, travelers in poison snake country need to be prepared. Since the old "cut, suck, tie" formula has been discarded as dangerous for the sucker and ineffective for the suckee, there has been no agreement on first aid treatment. Carrying antivenom is impractical. Some say get the patient to a hospital, pronto. Others stress immobilization with a splint and keeping the bitten extremity below the level of the heart, but all are opposed to using tourniquets. If symptoms are severe, see a doctor.

INSECT BITES

Biting insects are everywhere and threaten the enjoyment of many a hiker. Mosquitos, spiders, gnats, blackflies, no-see-ums, sand flies, etc., are hard to defend against. Heavy clothes, headnets, and a coating of repellent aren't always sufficient or convenient.

POISON OAK AND IVY

Poison oak, like rattlesnakes, is a hazard that can usually be avoided by caution and the ability to recognize the danger. Poison oak in the west and poison ivy in the east have oily looking, distinctive three-lobed leaves that are easily remembered once they have been identified. Tolerance to the oil, which remains potent for some time on clothes and on the fur of pets, varies widely.

Persons exposed have a second chance to avoid the itching, easily spread rash by scrubbing exposed skin vigorously with soap and hot water on the same day. Skin irritation generally begins four to five hours after exposure. In the west, poison oak rarely grows above 6000 feet.

CARDIOPULMONARY RESUSCITATION

Victims of lightning strikes may appear to be dead because the heart and breathing have stopped. But they can often be brought back to life through cardiopulmonary resuscitation (CPR). The same is true for drownings. Persist with CPR even though the victim appears dead and doesn't seem to be responding. Remember, the colder the water, the longer the victim can survive it, because cold reduces the brain's need for oxygen. So don't give up. And resolve to learn more about wilderness first aid by taking a course before your next trip.

FOURTEEN

Family Trips

Make it Easy and Fun ... Children's Packs ... Kids on the Trail ... Camping with Infants ... Watch Kid's Feet ... Fun versus Discipline ... Kids in Camp ... Teach Trail Manners

All parents who love the outdoors would doubtless like to instill the same feeling in their children. But many parents who badly want their children to enjoy the wilderness either cram it down their throats or fail to make sure those first trips are enjoyable. The world is full of people whose first experience in the wilds was unpleasant—and who therefore never went back.

So considerable effort should be invested in seeing that those first experiences are happy ones. This doesn't mean dragging children along on a short adult trip. It means carefully planning an easy trip into pretty, familiar country and tailoring all aspects to maximize the enjoyment of the children. The same principle applies to anyone who is a stranger to the mountains, whether girlfriends, boyfriends, children, parents, brides, or even inexperienced friends.

In my view, there are a great many parents who are not ready to take children into the wilderness—and a great many children who are not ready to go. Every summer I see miserable families struggling up the trail or bickering in camp. The parents are bitterly disappointed because the children are spoiling their trip, and the children are tired of being hurried, picked on, and yelled at. The parents vow never to take those "ungrateful brats" again, and the children are equally determined not to go.

Generally speaking, I feel parents should not take their children backpacking until: (1) they themselves can travel in the wilds with some degree of comfort and competence; (2) the children have been taken on several successful dayhikes; (3) parents are willing to tailor an overnight trip to country they know, expressly for the pleasure of their children; (4) the children want (or are at least willing) to go; and (5) the parents genuinely want them along. Families able to meet these criteria have a fighting chance for a pleasant trip.

The most common cause of disastrous family trips, it seems to me, is the failure of parents to see the trip through their children's eyes. Any child will ask "If it isn't fun, why do it?" He does not insist every minute be fun, but he will expect that, taken as a whole, the trip should be pleasant, After all, what good is a vacation if it isn't fun? The honest adult will find no satisfactory objection to this reasoning. If parents are not willing and able to make the trip fun—for themselves as well as for the children—there is little point in going.

Parents with little experience in backpacking generally have difficulty enough without the added burden of children. People who cannot go into the woods with confidence are not likely to have the patience or the skill to provide children a happy time. There is rarely a good reason why children cannot be taken on a considerable number of dayhikes before taking them overnight. I first took my daughter backpacking when she was eight. Because she had made many day trips with me, had walked up a few peaks, and had slept overnight in the forest by our cabin, she took the trip in stride. Very little was strange to her and she required very little persuasion.

That first trip was simple and short. With another family, we walked no more than a mile and a half from our cabin. Though we traveled cross-country rather than on a trail, and climbed perhaps 800 feet, walking conditions were good and I knew every inch of the way. The campsite I had chosen offered a spring, a marvelous view, a cozy dell for sleeping, wildflowers, and small caves. The children got to arrange their beds together, apart from the adults, before gathering wood and water for dinner. There were songs and marshmallows by the campfire before bed. Everything was planned with the children in mind. We were back at the cabin before lunchtime the following day.

MAKE IT EASY AND FUN

Once it has been decided to take children backpacking, the trip should be planned with the tenderest, most timid member in mind. Backpacking parents might normally scorn camping at the first lake or stream on the trail, but if the children are young (under ten) that may be the wisest plan. Chances are that the country will be more than wild enough to excite them. Being relatively close to civilization (telephone, campground, motel, grocery) has its advantages. If the weather turns bad, the children get sick, the mosquitos are unbearable, or something else goes wrong, the car is a mercifully short dash away. And the shortness of the trail may seem a blessing to parents who find themselves carrying twice their normal loads.

I do not believe children should be taken backpacking for the first time to an area that has not been thoroughly reconnoitered by their parents. The campsite should be known in advance and selected on the basis of its appeal to a child. Adults often arrange their itinerary for the photography, fly fishing, and rock climbing afforded, but a small child will be interested in none of these. Trips should be planned for the warmest weather and fewest bugs. In the Sierra, that means August. The fact that the traffic is heavy, the wildflowers past their prime, and the fishing slow will not bother your children in the least. For a child's first trip, one or two nights will be long enough. If camp is to be moved it should be moved in the morning, with lunch and a leisurely afternoon planned in the new campsite.

As on any backpacking trip, there is a limit to what can be carried. But parents should not expect children to be voluntarily spartan—or even to be impressed with the size of dad's pack. Emphasizing sacrifice only makes it harder for them to understand where the fun comes in. Clothes must be carried to protect children from extremes of heat and cold. Sunburn must be guarded against with long-sleeved shirts, long trousers—and, if possible, hats. Extra quantities of sunburn cream should be provided so that children can carry individual tubes. The same goes for lip salve.

Extra aerosol cans of mosquito repellent (kept away from small children) are important for quick relief from a sudden invasion, and nylon netting and head nets may be required if the bugs are likely to be fierce. Too much protection is better than too little—even though it swells the pack. Rattlesnake country should be avoided if possible.

The first aid kit should be enlarged by the addition of extra bandaids and spare soap, and wash cloths and towels are certain to be needed. Petroleum jelly will be invaluable to ease chafing. Since children have an unfailing affinity for water, three pairs of extra socks will be needed, the heavier the better. Wool and synthetics are best because cotton tends to stretch and sag, producing first wrinkles then blisters.

CHILDREN'S PACKS

In recent years, a great many cheap, small knapsacks and packs have appeared on the market, many of which are suitable for children. Flimsy plastic knapsacks that roll up into their own pockets cost as little as $5. Of course, canvas or nylon packs are preferable. For older children who can carry larger loads, a small aluminum pack frame (available from surplus stores, Kelty, Jansport, Camp Trails, and others) will be a better investment.

My daughter likes to carry a fannypack, which gives her greater freedom of movement than any shoulder pack. She often wears it with a knapsack that will just hold her sleeping bag. All but the youngest children should be encouraged to carry at least a token pack—of course, if the trail is too long or the load too large it may end up being carried by dad.

Extra sleeping bags tend to make dad's pack unwieldy, so children should carry their own bags, if possible. Since even an adult warm-weather sleeping bag should not weigh more than $5\frac{1}{2}$ pounds, most children old enough to backpack should be able to carry their own. If suitable bags cannot be bought, rented, or borrowed, an adequate cocoon can usually be fashioned from cotton sheet blankets and old wool blankets or a quilted comforter fastened together with large safety pins.

Kids love tube tents

Tarp tents keep the kids happy

For small children, a tube tent can be important, even if there seems no chance of rain. The small cozy space tends to be reassuring. Tents are extremely useful for afternoon napping and changing clothes out of the wind. And children fearful of the dark may insist on sleeping inside no matter what the weather. Children are usually intrigued by tents, and parents can often generate enthusiasm for camping by pitching one on the lawn at home before a trip, putting in sleeping bags, and serving a picnic lunch.

A tarp tent, though more difficult to pitch, is also a good low-cost family shelter where insects and wind are not great problems. In addition to the tent, a sizable extra tarp can serve as picnic blanket and dining table. When children are along, there is generally a need for something on which gear can be spread out.

Food that meets the adult backpacker's demands may or may not satisfy your children. Special emphasis should be put on snack foods and liquids. To maintain energy and prevent dehydration, children will need plenty of both. To encourage the between-meal eating so necessary in the wilds, plenty of goodies are needed, especially gorp, cheese, salami, nuts, and dried fruit. Children should be urged to drink small amounts of water often while traveling, and quantities of lemonade, Koolaid, Fizzies, and reconstituted milk should be available in camp. Since kids will immediately notice that camp milk tastes "funny," powdered flavorings should be carried to transform it into chocolate milk, cocoa, and milkshakes.

Young children will probably want to take along toys from home and since these will promote security and supply entertainment, parents ought to indulge at least one, so long as it is light and appropriate. Generous parents can sometimes be recognized on the trail by the teddybears and Raggedy Anns riding on top of their packs.

family camping means carrying a little more.

KIDS ON THE TRAIL

When the trailhead has been reached and the loads handed out, the real work begins. Getting children up the trail and into camp demands patience, a strong back, and considerable psychology. Parents unwilling or unable to keep the children amused and moving—without losing their own sense of humor—will wish they had left them home. And so will the children. Without supervision, children tend to start out fast, which means they will soon want to rest. It is hard to curb the enthusiasm and effervescence that eats up their energy without curtailing the fun of the trip; it is also hard to keep them going when they feel tired and want to rest: and children fatigue quickly.

It is unfair to expect children to have the self-discipline necessary to conserve energy for the climb ahead. Instead, one has to supply incentives, distractions, goals, and just plain entertainment— with the minimum necessary discipline mixed in.

CAMPING WITH INFANTS

Taking infants camping presents a different set of problems altogether. But for many it easily beats staying home. And people who love the wilds often want to share it with their children as soon as possible. Your baby is ready to go camping as soon as her neck is strong enough to hold her head up—and hang on while swaying and bouncing in a Kiddie Carrier. By the age of 4–6 months your baby should be old enough, and before she starts crawling she's much easier to look after in camp. Crawlers must be constantly watched.

Single parents will find baby camping almost impossible. You need another strong-backed adult companion to share the considerable weight and bulk of all you need to bring for the three of you—and to share the job of looking after a delicate, sensitive, highly vulnerable young camper. You won't enjoy the trip if you can't escape the nursery for a few hours every day. Couples camping with infants find they don't want to hike very far, just far enough to escape civilization. A short hike to a base camp a little off the beaten track—but not too far from the car—works best.

To get ready for a happy trip, you may need to practice. Try to get your baby used to backpacking by carry her around the house or the neighborhood in your Kiddie Carrier. Put up the tent in the backyard and sleep overnight with her in your sleeping bag. This kind of dress rehearsal will help you plan the trip—and make it go more smoothly. Dayhikes are also good conditioning—for both of you. When it comes time to pack up, you'll have a better idea of what you need to carry. Plenty!

Diapers in the wilds are a huge hassle. If you rely on disposables you'll pay for the convenience by having to pack all the used ones in plastic bags and carry them out—a significant amount of weight and bulk. If you choose cloth diapers, you'll have to figure out how to wash and dry them—without polluting streams or lakes or campsites. Folding plastic wash basins are good for laundering. You may need a clothesline, or you can hang drying diapers on your pack if you're dayhiking or ambitiously moving camp.

Ideally, your first trip should be short and easy, to a campsite you've scouted, where you won't disturb other campers (a crying baby could destroy your neighbors' long planned vacation). You should be a very competent camper yourself, able to deal with difficulty and danger in a safe, responsible, cautious manner. The weather should be mild. You should be strong and in good shape and mentally ready for a less than carefree adventure.

On the trail you may need to protect your baby from sun and glare, mosquitos, dehydration, hunger, discomfort, drafts and so forth. She'll need to eat and drink often. Dress her warmly, but don't smother her. The secret of a happy walk is frequent "babychecks," stops and rests to feed her, give her water, check her diaper, and let her out of the carrier. She may need a hat or a mini umbrella. A pair of your socks will protect her legs nicely. Be sure in advance that your sunscreen and inspect repellent won't be toxic for her sensitive skin.

The most useful baby garments are overalls, T-shirts, rompers, knitted caps, balaclavas, sleepers in several weights, and turtlenecks. To transport your baby on your back you'll need some kind of Kiddie Carrier. Two that come recommended by *Backpacker* are the Kelty Child Carrier and the Tough Traveler (or L.L. Bean) Stallion Kid Carrier. Both are recommended for babies of at least 15 pounds or 6 months of age. Both have padded safety harnesses and carry extra gear in zippered bags, and costs of the two are roughly comparable.

The Kelty will take very small babies. Because it carries them high, they can see more country and may therefore stay happier. The Kelty appears to have been made for women, so men may find it too narrow. But it's easy to lash on extra food sacks, diaper bags and spare pockets. The Tough Traveler is built for larger babies. They sit lower and see less. Side pads wrap around the child's head, which restricts vision but makes it easy for your baby to sleep. The Tough Traveler fits men as well as women and is comfortable, adjustable, and carries more gear. There's even an optional sun/rain awning that will fit either pack.

The rest of this chapter comes from notebooks carried on a number of trips with my daughter, other people's children, and other families. Since, like kids, it seems to defy organization, I offer it more or less as collected.

Call the trip a "walk"; "walking" is fun but "hiking" is work. Making the trip a lark for the kids means getting into the spirit of *their* adventure rather than fretting about the slowness of the pace.

Keep children moving but don't try to make them hurry; it will only slow them down and rob them of their cheerfulness. Make sure they get away from the trail occasionally. Let them put down their packs and go investigate something they've discovered.

Take them off the trail to see mossy glens, snowbanks, waterfalls, a tree that looks like a witch. If they've been trudging along wearily for awhile, don't wait for them to ask for a rest or simply sit down. Stop voluntarily, give them something to eat and show them something interesting. If they're happy they'll recover from their fatigue with amazing swiftness. Keep in mind the fact that the long-range goal is to just to get them to camp before lunch—it's to make the trip so much fun that they'll want to come again.

WATCH KID'S FEET

It's always a good idea to keep watch on children's feet. By putting a stop to chafing in the early stage you may avoid having to carry a child to the car! I have more than once discovered my daughter hiking happily along despite the fact one sock had worked so far down her foot that it had disappeared entirely into her boot. Fortunately, children's feet take the abuse of rough country much better than their parents' and do not easily blister.

I find it important on the trail to talk to children a good part of the time. I give them progress reports "We're more than half-way. . . . It's only fifteen minutes until lunch. . . . There's a spring where we can get a drink behind that big tree. . . . It's all downhill to camp." Whenever I can, I praise their achievements. I try to distract them from the drudgery of the trail, and in doing so I find I have distracted myself.

When they grow weary of such temporal phenomena as birds' nests, rills, and rock rabbits, I try to stir their imagination by pointing out a cloud formation that looks like a ship, a leaning tree that resembles a poised runner, or patch of lichen that looks like a lion. Finding strange likenesses can be made into a contest in which children point out their own discoveries. The reward for the most imaginative can be a specially prized piece of candy.

I carry a considerable stock of snacks in wide variety, and I keep them concealed to add mystery and anticipation. It's less important that kids eat well at mealtime than it is to feed them snacks between meals to keep their energy and spirits up. I pass out food with the smallest provocation and often with none at all.

FUN VERSUS DISCIPLINE

It's always important to keep the kids happy, but there's still the problem of getting them up the trail. A minimal amount of discipline, and self-discipline, is indispensable. So is a certain amount of desire on the child's part to please his parents and do his part. I explain at the outset that while we're going to stop and rest, play games, explore and generally have fun, we still have to make it to camp before lunch, so we'll have time to set up camp and spend the afternoon playing without our packs. And that means we have to keep moving. As we move along, I show kids easier ways to get around obstacles, help foot draggers, readjust packs, show how the Indians walk, and if the trail grows steep, I demonstrate the rest step, which I represent variously as the "polar bear shuffle," "kangaroo limp," "dromedary drag," etc.

If there are several children, I work most with the slowest ones. Sometimes the slowest becomes the fastest if you put them in the lead, explaining that they now have the responsibility for keeping the group on the trail, showing them how to recognize blazes and ducks and the footworn groove. It is usually best to bring up the rear when hiking with children, so you can help the ones who fall behind and so you'll know if a child quietly sits down on the rock or wanders off while the rest of the party marches by.

The hardest part of handling a group of kids is keeping them together and controlling the rest stops. Energetic older boys will want to keep going while younger girls will frequently want to rest. It's not difficult to spread your party all over the mountain.

don't panic
at every danger

I urge the stoppers to keep going, and as a last resort I take their packs. If other kids get too far ahead, I may saddle them with the unwanted packs. When we stop for a rest I encourage the energetic ones to explore the immediate area while the tired ones sit and puff.

When the weariest seem to be somewhat restored, I simultaneously announce we must be off and pass out lemondrops all around. It is important after a rest not to let children dash up the trail with recharged enthusiasm or they'll burn themselves out after only a few yards and plead for another rest. If they fail to restrain themselves, after you've explained the reason for starting off slowly, there is nothing to do but nag. Chronic fast starters are best reminded at the end of the rest instead of after they take off.

Even with all these strategems, the trail can become monotonous, and when the group becomes dull or dispirited I call an early rest. Everyone takes off his pack and we make a little side trip to some interesting spot out of sight of the trail—usually a waterfall or a cool glade or a lookout point, and we have a drink of lemonade (powder and plastic bottle must be handy) or lie in the cool grass or throw snowballs off the cliff. This side trip is likely to refresh the group and the time spent seems a worthwhile investment. Progress, in this fashion, will be anywhere from a quarter mile to one mile per hour.

KIDS IN CAMP

When camp is reached (and by now it should be evident why it needs to be close and the trail well known) some kids will want to flop down and rest, others will want to explore. No one will want to unpack, lay out beds, or gather wood. The best strategy is to let everyone squander at least half an hour before assigning chores. Everyone should have something useful to do; if the tasks are thoughtfully assigned and described, previously exhausted children will go to work with surprising enthusiasm.

Limit the amount that thirsty children drink, but allow them—in fact invite them—to drink frequently from unpolluted streams and rills and your water bottle or canteen. Snowball fights and singing make good diversions. So do yodeling and echoing. Give kids the sense of helping you and finding the way. Don't communicate anxiety about reaching camp, snakes, storms, or mosquitos. You must be relaxed and at home in the woods if you want your children to feel the same way. Don't panic if they step near the edge of a cliff; their natural caution should protect them. Don't yell at them. Be alert for excessive fatigue, dizziness, blisters, chafing clothes, sunburn, and chapped lips.

Explain in advance that you want to keep them comfortable and therefore they must let you know what's bothering them. They'll tell you all right! When you come to sand on smooth slab, wet slippery surfaces, loose gravel, mud, etc., calmly demonstrate how to cross safely. Celebrate all achievement; be liberal with praise and rewards. Teach your kids not to litter and get them to help you pick up gum wrappers and trash—if the going is not too difficult—to be deposited in one of your spare plastic bags.

TEACH TRAIL MANNERS

Impress your kids that nothing must be left behind to mar the wilderness, especially used toilet paper! Children at all times should carry about three feet of TP folded up in a pocket. Teach them when traveling to choose a place that won't be found; supervise if necessary. Show them how to fold the used paper inward for easy handling and put it in a plastic bag for later burning. In camp, build a latrine and furnish it with TP and a collection bag for used paper. Unless you provide instruction there are sure to be toilet paper streamers decorating the trees, and the responsibility will be yours.

It's a poor idea to plan to take children cross-country on rough terrain unless they are large, strong, proven hikers. Being closer to

Kids are good at finding firewood...
... and mud!

the ground, children see relatively small objects as real obstacles. A rock that's just a knee-high step to you will be a waist-high roadblock to a six-year-old; a good scramble for you may be a nightmare for them. Forget boulder-hopping altogether. Be wary of fussy eaters. Explain before the trip that the food—in order to give everyone more energy—will be a little different. Then serve them sample dishes or meals at home, making the change of diet an adventure.

In camp, find them rocks to climb, rills to dam, a snowpatch to slide on; define the bathroom area boundaries, explain camp rules regarding fire, food, muddy feet in the tent, and the sanctity of the kitchen during meal preparation. Alert them to the continued need for wood and water. Explain that, like Indians, you plan to leave this camp so no one will know you've been there.

Taking children into the wilderness can be demanding, even maddening, but by allowing yourself to see the trip through their eyes you can share their wonder, joy, and adventure. You can remember what it feels like to be a kid in the woods when everything is new and mysterious and exciting. And when the trip is over and you're homeward bound there is deep satisfaction in hearing your youngest ask "Daddy, when can we go again?"

Trout Fishing

It has always seemed to me that many more people would enjoy catching and eating trout ... if only they knew how to go about it. Of course, catching trout is not the only measure of fishing success. The pursuit of trout, even when unsuccessful, is the best way I know to become intimately acquainted with a part of the wilderness. Whether following the rocky shore of a mountain tarn, watching trout feeding in a crystal pool or making my way cautiously among the bank of a brook, angling has shown me many more wonders than all the trails I ever traveled.

The hunt for solitude and challenging country often leads the backpacker past trout waters that would fill a fisherman with envy. More than once I have caught so many trout (and put them back unharmed) that the feathers were totally stripped from my fly. Of course, I also have been skunked on good trout water. I do not consider myself first of all a fisherman. I sometimes pass good trout water without setting up my rod. Sometimes I even fail to take a rod along. But I am fond of eating freshly caught, wild trout. And I rely upon trout fishing, cross-country and climbing to get me off the trails and into corners of the country that I otherwise never would see.

Several years ago I developed the clear, cold, year-round rill that flows through the forest below my house by building low dams and excavating behind them to form deep pools. A neighbor contributed several dozen brook trout that he brought home in a cooler from Yosemite, and I bought 50 pounds of hatchery rainbows to supplement the few small, scared native rainbows I inherited.

The fish have grown (some to nearly 20 inches) and become pets, and now they come to be fed when they see us approach. We watch the brookies spawn in the fall and find deep satisfaction in the resulting thousands of fingerlings that range upstream and down, restoring the fishery. Having sizeable trout to watch has taught me a lot—and reduced my need to go fishing. When Deanne wants trout for dinner, I could probably catch my own, but so far I haven't been able to do it.

Some writers insist that it is enough for the backpacker to carry a few yards of line, a few feet of leader, and a couple of hooks. The idea is to cut a willow rod, catch grasshoppers or grubs for bait and then go blithely forth to catch fish with this clumsy rig. An expert might catch unsophisticated trout on virgin waters, and a hard-working angler might land starved fish, but this kind of outfit is utterly worthless for the beginner who would like the best possible chance of eating trout for supper.

Trout fishing gear, luckily, is neither expensive nor heavy. Basic outfits (rod, reel, and line) for both fly casting and spinning are commonly offered for as little as $50. Neither pleasure nor fish-taking ability are much sacrificed in modestly priced gear. Of course, high-quality backpacking outfits can easily cost $400. The fly fishing outfit I generally take backpacking weighs anywhere from 9 to 24 ounces. The cheapest equipment may weigh a little more, but the beginner should not have to carry more than a pound and a half for fly fishing or 2 pounds for spinning.

trout on willow stringer

"natural" fishing rods mean frustration -not fish.

Trout fishing tackle is designed for maximum lightness, because the lighter the gear the more sensitive it will be to the antics of the trout. Fighting an 8-inch rainbow on a 3-ounce fly rod is three times as exciting as playing the same fish on a 5-ounce rod.

SPIN VERSUS FLY FISHING

Trout fishing gear sharply divides itself into two different types: fly-casting and spin fishing. In traditional fly casting, it is the weight of the comparatively heavy line that carries the nearly weightless fly out across the water. The angler must lift the line into the air and keep it suspended there with alternate forward and backward casts until he is ready to place the fly on the water. Most people find fly casting harder to learn and more demanding than spinning.

In spin fishing, the comparatively heavy weight of the lure propels the almost weightless nylon line out over the water. There is no back cast to tangle and no necessity to keep the line suspended in the air. While the fly fisherman is largely restricted to flies the spin fisherman an cast spinners, plugs and bait, as well as flies.

Of course, the angler who has mastered both types of fishing and is prepared to use whichever seems most likely to be effective, will double his chances of catching trout. He need not carry two complete outfits since the fly-spin combination rod will suffice for both techniques. In recognition of the backpacking boom, tackle manufacturers are designing more and more gear for lightness, durability, and easy carrying.

For years I carried a three-piece, split-bamboo, 8-foot fly rod weighing $5\frac{1}{2}$ ounces and fastened together with metal furrules. And I held my breath every time the fragile tip caught on a branch. Today, I carry a four-piece slipjointed Browning Waterton Backpacker weighing 3.5 ounces and using a #5 line. I couldn't resist buying it while researching this revision. Matched with a light graphite reel, it enabled me to release more than a hundred Rainbow, Brook, and Golden trout in a pair of week-long High Sierra trips. For many years in between those two rods, like everybody else I carried fiberglass rods, but now Graphite is the standard for strong, tough, trouble-free, lightweight rods of all kinds.

The beginning trout fisherman in search of an outfit can choose from several outfitting philosophies. He can buy the cheapest drugstore/discount house spinning outfit, including a big heavy reel, probably from Zebco, for under $20, pick up some lures, weights, and bait—and go spin fishing. Or, if he wants the capability to fly and spin fish both, he can buy an inexpensive combination spin-fly (combo) rod. But it won't be much good for fly fishing—especially if he's just learning how.

My friend Sam Ragent, to whom fly fishing is the most important thing in life, believes a better approach is to buy a good fly rod and equip it with both ultralight spinning and fly reels. His theory is that fly fishing capability will be undiminished with such an outfit, while spinning (much easier to learn) will be little affected. The smaller guides will cost you very little distance. It makes good sense to me. Combo rods *are* terrible as fly rods.

CHOOSING A FLY OUTFIT

When it comes to choosing fly fishing gear, you can opt for a complete pre-packaged outfit (rod, case, reel, line, maybe even leader, flies and instruction manual) that are pre-balanced and matched—even if some assembly is required. When you buy a package, you're trusting the maker because you don't usually get a chance to try the action of either the rod or the reel, encased as they are in cardboard and plastic. You'll find most of these kits in discount and backpacking stores, where the clerks are scarce or know nothing whatever about fishing.

Or you can go to a sporting goods or tackle shop, spend some time talking to the salesman and heft and whip back and forth the rods he recommends, assemble and dismantle them, crank and adjust the reels, finger the lines, and ask a lot of questions. You'll learn a lot about trout gear while purchasing a rig that feels right to you. You may even be able to dicker with the dealer on overstocked or out of fashion gear, perhaps getting a discount on a complete package. You'll be relying on the salesman and yourself, instead of the manufacturer.

Once you know what you want, you may even be able to save a bundle by mail ordering from a catalog.

The next decision that must be made is whether to buy a standard two-piece fly rod of 7–9 feet, which means it won't come close to fitting in your pack, or a 4–5 piece pack rod that, because of its many joints, might be heavier and have poorer "action." Action refers to the rod's stiffness (how it feels when you whip it). "Stiff" is for long casts in big rivers or lakes; "soft" is for short, accurate stream casting; "medium" is for everything else. But even more important is how the rod feels to you.

The most widely available kits are the Eagle Claw Trailmaster four-piece, 8' rod; the Berkley three-piece, 7'9" Graphite; my four-piece Browning; the Cabela four-piece pack rod; and the Sage four-piece package. There are doubtless other good pack rods, and too many good two-piece kits to mention, but some of the best come from Orvis, Martin, Cortland, Fenwick, L.L. Bean, Daiwa, and G. Loomis.

When it comes to reels, Phlueger and Martin are standouts, but any sturdy single-action reel will do. The beginner should avoid wind-up automatic reels.

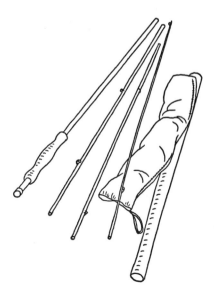

Sam's priorities—if you're putting together your own package in a tackle shop—are to put your money into a good rod, one you won't soon outgrow, followed next by a good line. It's a common mistake, says Sam, to buy a fancy reel and any old fly line. A good tapered line is almost as important as the rod. It must shoot through the guides well, float high, never kink, and exhibit no memory when knotted. You can save money on a simple reel without sacrificing performance, but a crummy line will hurt your ability to catch fish.

TAPERED LINES AND LEADERS

Fly line is classified as either "level" or "tapered." The tapering in the last few yards at the end (tippet) avoids an abrupt change in diameter between the line and the leader while retaining the line weight necessary for casting. Efficiency of casting and smoothness and naturalness of fly presentation are greatly increased by the use of a tapered line— especially for the novice.

Conventional tapered lines are tapered at both ends ("double tapers"), so when one tippet wears out the line can be taken off the reel and reversed to make use of the other taper. Level fly lines, though less than half the price of tapered, are not worthwhile investments for anglers interested in assembling competent fly casting outfits.

spliced
loop

Depending on the water to be fished and the angler's experience, it may be necessary to back the tapered fly line with a length of level line. The junction of the two should be spliced and whipfinished, rather than simply knotted. The fly line tippet should have a whip-finished, spliced loop for easy knot-free attachment of the leader. A knot both catches the air to obstruct smooth casting and catches the water to disturb shy trout. A nail knot coated with Duco cement will substitute for a spliced loop. And there are all manner of other

ordinary
knot

metal and plastic gadgets designed to make a streamlined connection between your line and leader.

Leaders are also either tapered or level, and the tapered leader is much to be preferred. The stiffer butt section helps transmit the thrust of the line while the delicate tippet allows the fly to settle lightly on the water after the leader has straightened out. The biggest benefit for the beginner—especially in brush—is that when the fly is caught on an obstruction the tapered leader always breaks at the weakest point—next to the fly, so the leader is rarely lost.

The rule of thumb for leader length is slightly less than the length of the rod, which avoids the necessity of drawing the leader-line junction through the guides. In murky water, spring fishing under cut banks, or lowering a fly through brush, as little as 2 feet of leader may suffice, while 9 to 12 feet may be needed when casting in the fall over clear, glassy pools. Tapered leaders are rated according to tippet diameter (1X for heavy bass bugs down to 6X for the smallest flies on the clearest water) and also by breaking strength (from perhaps 5 pounds down to a pound and a half).

SELECTING TROUT FLIES

Trout flies come in four basic types: dry, wet, nymph, and streamer, but wet flies are scarce since they can only be fished wet, while dry flies can be fished either wet or dry. Dry flies are designed to resemble flying insects; streamer flies and bucktails imitate minnows and large bugs; nymphs are tied to look like grubs, aquatic stage insects, worms, caterpillars, larvae, and other fish foods.

Most of the time, flies must closely resemble the insects on which trout are feeding in order to be effective. But a majority of fishermen find that trout are more sensitive to size than shape or color. Rarely will they make any noticeable distinction between patterns, so the angler can choose the flies he likes best—as long as they are comparable in size to those on which trout are feeding. Even size is less important, some experts say, than the manner in which the fly is presented and fished. The most common mistake is to fish flies that are too large. For mountain trout, sizes 14 to 16 are more appropriate than the 10s and 12s that are most often available. It is a myth that "it takes big hooks to catch big trout."

A beginning fly fisherman on a three-day trip should have at least a dozen flies, divided into three or four patterns. For variety I would choose a Royal Coachman because its white wings make it easy to follow, a grey hackle peacock with a thick body, and a mosquito, because these are among the commonest of summer insects. The cheapest flies, imported from Japan, often are not glued securely to the hook, have clogged eyes, and tend to break easily, but

I have used dozens of them and most were satisfactory. More than anything else, the price of the fly reflects the quality of its hook.

TIE YOUR OWN FLIES

Another source of reasonable flies—in the long run—is fly tying, a common hobby among fly fishermen. Kits start at about $20. There is real satisfaction in devising and typing flies—and then taking trout on them. Since I pay nearly as much for fly tying hooks as I do for Japanese flies, dollar savings tend to be negligible.

On a long trip where I'll do a lot of fishing, I carry 50–100 flies tucked in the springloaded clips of a 2.5 ounce Perrine aluminum fly box. On short or casual trips I pack a dozen likely flies in a small compartmented, weightless, plastic transparent box that fits into any pocket.

A creel is a considerable luxury for a backpacker, and the traditional woven willow basket is out of the question. On easy trips I sometimes carry a canvas creel if I plan to bring home fish to eat, but usually I rely on a V-shaped willow stringer or use a short length of nylon cord tied around a stick. Either can easily be threaded through the trout's gills and mouth for easy carrying.

Since it is necessary to be able to control the floating or sinking of the leader and fly, I often carry a small tin of Mucilin with Silicone and a plastic vial of Orvis Leader Sink. When it is vital to keep a fly floating on choppy water, Mucilin is invaluable. Of course, a fly can also be dried by vigorous false casting. A film of mud, mosquito repellent, or sunburn cream rubbed on the leader will cause it to sink, but Leader Sink is more convenient. In the swiftest water, split shot clamped directly on the hook can be used to sink a fly—but casting becomes difficult.

A necessity in any angler's kit is a sharp knife, with a sharp point, but this the backpacker already should have.

CHOOSING SPIN GEAR

Spinning equipment is not quite so light as fly casting tackle, but it, too, has been developed during the past few years with the backpacker in mind. Spinning rods measure only 6–7 feet in length, so a two-piecer is easy enough to mount beside a pack. The old telescoping rods were horrible, but the new ones are so improved and so marvelously convenient and inexpensive that they're the first choice of the casual weekend backpacker/fisherman I meet on the trail.

Probably the best of the backpacking spinning rod packages comes from Daiwa, a rod that breaks down into 15-inch sections and, with a tiny 6-ounce reel, weighs only 10 ounces. Unlike cheap fly reels, cheap spinning reels tend to be big, heavy, angular and lacking in durability—especially closed-face plastic reels. Of course, since spinning outfits (rod, reel, line) are cheap, the beginner can afford to try spinning very reasonably before making a larger investment.

Backpacking spin fishermen commonly use either 2- or 4-pound test monofilament which serves as both line and leader. The lighter the line the lighter the lure it will cast. Backpackers need only 100–150 yards of line, which costs little more than a dollar per 100 yards if bought in bulk and wound on the spool at a sporting goods store. Several spare loaded spools should be carried.

The principal use of spinning gear is to cast hardware: metal spinners, spoons, and other lures. These commonly weigh from $\frac{1}{16}$ to $\frac{3}{8}$ ounces. Most of the price of the more expensive lures pays for fine quality treble hooks. The Super Duper, Mepps, and Panther Martin are favorites. There is evidence that trout in heavily fished waters may actually grow wary of familiar-looking lures, while accepting new ones with a different action. But most veteran anglers believe the lure or fly that the fisherman uses with the greatest persistence and confidence will catch him the most fish.

Beginners are advised to buy as great a variety of lures as possible—probably half a dozen to start—in the smallest sizes available. Considering the advice of the salesman is a good way to begin, provided he knows the type of water to be fished. Most accomplished spin fishermen use tiny swivels to reduce line twisting. Perrine makes a good aluminum lure box, but plastic boxes are much lighter.

To make light lures cast farther and sink deeper, the spin fisherman should carry a small selection of various-sized split shot or sinker putty, which can be clamped onto or next to the lure. Even more useful are plastic bubbles that can be filled with shot and fastened to the leader to make lures run deep. The same bubbles, partly filled with water, serve as floats and provide the necessary weight for spin-casting flies. Many bubbles accept water but not shot, so the angler must shop carefully to assure versatility. Bubbles are inexpensive and almost weightless, so three or four can easily be carried. Bubbles should be fastened 2 feet from the fly for beginners and 3 feet for more experienced casters.

BAIT SELECTION

The most popular bait for trout is the salmon egg. Small bottles of identical-looking pink eggs may range in price from 50¢ to $3. The difference lies in the quality (firmness, toughness) of the egg and the appeal of the ingredients used to treat it. Trout rely principally on the smell of an egg rather than its appearance. Eggs are soaked in chemicals that toughen the skin and impart a flavor to the milk within. When the egg is punctured by the hook, the milk oozes out to flavor the surrounding water and attract the trout.

Pautzke's Balls O'Fire stay together, stay on the hook, and do a good job of attracting trout. Despite their high price, they are the choice of regular egg fishermen. Salmon eggs are the most popular bait because they are neat, easy to use, and do not wiggle. But they are generally much less effective than such natural baits as worms, grubs, helgramites, and grasshoppers; and heavily fished trout tend to ignore them. Size No. 14 egg hooks, either snelled or unsnelled, or required to completely hide the hook. There are various other beguiling patent baits; mostly they rely on the aroma of their sauces. The most tempting is Powerbait, said to be so lethal that it will tempt any living thing that swims. Many a fly fisherman believes it should be banned!

The most successful bait fishermen go prepared to catch whatever wild creatures the trout are feeding on. They roll rocks to collect ants and beetles. They dig in rotten logs for grubs. They catch grasshoppers with their hats in the early morning before insects become active. And they prowl the margins of a stream or lakeshore for whatever insect life is plentiful, digging in the mud beneath hovering dragonflies to capture their larvae and turning over rocks to uncover helgramites.

Serious bait fishermen work in pairs, one holding a sheet of nylon mosquito netting in the water while his partner turns over rocks just upstream. The same netting will produce a variety of wildlife when spread beneath violently shaken shrubbery. Worms, which should be brought from home to save digging up the meadow, require worm hooks that have two or three barbs on the back of the shank.

Trout, for the most part, are not very smart, i.e., they learn very little from experience or association. But their instincts and senses are often acute and serve to protect them. Trout see well underwater, but distinguish only movement, not shapes, above the surface. And their field of vision does not extend to the area behind their eyes—which is why knowledgeable fishermen work

stalking grasshoppers gets harder once they're warm & awake.

their way upstream in order to approach the fish from behind. (Trout generally face the current in moving water.) Trout have demonstrated a preference for red, but probably distinguish other colors as well.

Trout do not actually hear, but are extremely sensitive to vibrations. They will often be frightened by the tread of a heavy-footed angler they do not see. As demonstrated by the makers of various salmon egg sauces, trout have a well-developed sense of smell. This tends to explain why natural live bait is successful while exact rubber imitations are not. Taste is closely related to smell and since trout are able to discriminate between food and non-food, a good bait must satisfy both the trout's taste and smell.

TROUT FEEDING HABITS

Trout feed most actively at dawn or dusk. Poor light early and late conceals the angler and the artificiality of his offerings, and trout are apt to venture farther from shelter to feed when protected by shadow.

It's long been known that wildlife, like the ocean tides, is affected by the pull of the sun and moon. Four times in each 24 hours, wild creatures—including your dog and cat—are stimulated to activity, and that activity includes feeding. You can buy a print-out of the major and minor feeding times for every day of the year for less than a penny a day.

This little booklet is called the Solunar Tables (see Sources). Over the years I've often enjoyed spectacular fishing by using it to decide when to fish. If you're already on trout water and can fish when you want, it makes sense to take advantage of the forecasted feeding times. Of course they're often over-ridden by more powerful changes in barometric pressure. When the glass is falling the fish usually stop biting. With rising pressure they start to feed again. I see a correlation between feeding activity and both Solunar Tables and barometric changes in my own pet trout.

Fishing will generally be better in the dark of the moon, because the brighter the moonlight the better the fish can see to feed at night—and the less avidly it will feed during the day. If I am making a trip primarily to fish, the phase of the moon will be a factor in scheduling the trip.

More important than the time of day or the phase of the moon is the angler's technique, and passable technique comes most readily from practice. The scarcity of fly fishermen stems from the fact that it takes a little time and patience to learn—and instructors are not easily found. An expert fisherman and tournament fly-caster friend suggests the following to beginners.

LEARN TO FLY CAST

Using a 7 to 8 foot fly rod, matching reel, tapered line and leader and a fly from which the barb has been filed, the student should measure his fly line and wind it with different colored strips of tape at 25, 30, and 35 feet. On a stretch of lawn with plenty of back casting room, he should lay out a sheet of newspaper for a target. Fly casting demands a relatively stiff wrist and the student will benefit by fastening his wrist to the rod handle with a big rubber band to remind him to use his elbow instead. A book held in the armpit will discourage excess movement of the shoulder and promote good form.

Starting with about 15 feet of line stretched out on the grass in front of him, the student, holding the rod in one hand and the line in the other, should lift the rod tip quickly from the 10 o'clock position—as viewed in profile against a giant imaginary clock—stopping at the 1 o'clock position. The motion's suddenness must lift the line into the air and into the backcast. The student must wait until the line is stretched out tight behind him before bringing the rod forward with enough force to carry the line out straight in front of him when the rod is returned to the 10 o'clock position.

False casting should be continued until the student can keep the line suspended in the air with a minimum of effort without exceeding the 10–1 o'clock range with the rod. To make the cast, it is only necessary to aim the forward cast to a point 3 feet above the newspaper and then drop the rod tip to 9 o'clock and allow the fly to quietly settle.

The student should become adept at dropping the fly accurately with 15–20 feet of line before trying longer casts. It will be helpful to use a highly visible white winged fly and to watch the path of fly, line, and rod continuously at first to become acquainted with the paths they travel and to discover the necessary rhythm. When the fly can be placed gently on the newspaper every time at a distance of 30 feet the caster will be ready to catch fish.

Long casts are not essential to catching trout. The uncle who taught me to fly cast regularly outfished me on a stream with casts no longer than 20 feet. The most important factor in his success, it seems to me, was his knowledge of where trout lie. Nearly as important was his ability to present the fly in a natural manner without frightening the fish. Trout will choose protected feeding places during the day and will not venture more than a few inches away from that protection to take fly, lure, or bait. Random casts into open water will only serve to scare them.

TROUT STALKING STRATEGIES

Placing the fly so that it floats on the current without drag past the likely lie, or casting quickly to a rise in a lake comes with experience. But approaching carefully so as not to spook the fish is largely a matter of patience and self discipline. The difference between scared trout and a full creel is often the angler's willingness to crawl slowly to the protection of a tree and then carefully cast

stealth & concealment are important in fly fishing

from behind it. Concealment is far more important to the fly caster than to the spin fisherman because he is operating at closer range with trout on or near the surface, and will often be within the trout's field of view or vibrations.

Two other essentials for fly casting success are keeping a tight line and setting the hook. Only a small percentage of trout will hook themselves, and nearly all trout, given the chance, will reject artificial flies and try to spit them out. It is up to the angler to strike back when a trout takes the fly, before it can throw the hook. The angler's strike—lifting the rod tip with a snap—must be an instantaneous reaction. With a slack line, obviously, it will be virtually impossible to strike back in time. So the angler must balance the need to let the fly float naturally without drag, against the need to keep the line tight enough for setting the hook with a single jerk.

Since excessive casting tends to spook the fish, the fly caster must exercise restraint and emphasize accuracy. Whether in a lake or stream the closest lies should be explored first before working out toward the casting limit. Various retrieves can be tried to intrigue trout: leaving the fly motionless, twitching it, skittering it, or dunking it—until a strike is forthcoming. If fishing it dry fails, it should be allowed to sink below the surface. For wet fly fishing, only a single backcast should be used. If rising fish ignore the fly, either: (1) it is too large, (2) it is being presented unconvincingly, or (3) the fish are too small.

It is nearly always worthwhile to immediately examine the food in the mouth, throat, and stomach of the first fish caught for a hint in the choice or modification of flies. For instance, finding a stomach full of small beetles, I might trim the hackles very short to make my fly more beetle-like—or go catch the real thing.

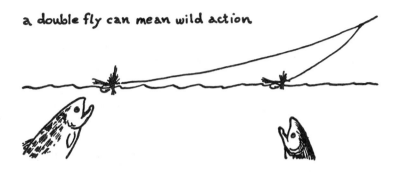

a double fly can mean wild action

CAST AND MOVE ON

Once a stretch of water has been well prospected, even if unsuccessfully, it is a good idea to move on. If I get a good strike, but miss the fish, and several further casts bring no response, I immediately move away to rest the water, making a mental note to return later. When the water is still and well lighted it is next to impossible to catch trout on flies and casting will only frighten the fish. But the turbulence of current, the shadows of trees or clouds, the swirl of rising fish, or a wind-ruffled surface will hide the angler, disguise his offering, and give the trout an illusion of protection, which will reduce its inhibitious.

Fly rod fishing, though more limited in variety than spinning, offers several variations. When the trout are numerous and receptive, but not overly large, and casting room is ample, I often attach a dropper fly to the middle of my leader by means of an 8-inch length of monofilament. It more than doubles the chance of a strike and provides wild action when two fish are hooked. Early in the year, I sometimes crimp a split shot to the curve of the hook and, fishing off a ledge, jig for bottom-feeding trout. And in desperation, I have even stripped the fly off my hook to impale an ant or ladybug or grub when there seemed no other way to catch my dinner.

SPINNING IS EASIER

Spin fishing is a good deal easier to learn for the beginning angler. Spinning covers more water, offers less risk of frightening fish and permits a greater variety of lures and baits, especially in lakes. The elements of spin casting can be learned in 15 minutes. All that is required is the synchronization of the release of the line with the forward thrust of the rod. Backcasting room is not required;

neither is false casting, nor the stealthful approach. The greater the weight of the lure or lead or water-filled bubble, the greater the range of the caster. The beginner is not limited to short casts; in fact he will easily cast farther than the experienced fly caster. Of course spinning's advantage lies in fishing big water: lakes and big rivers. In small or brushy creeks, spinning is virtually impossible.

Spin fishing divides neatly into three categories: lures, bait, and flies. Lure casting, being easier, is naturally the most popular. It also produces the most fish. The beginner should purchase spinners with both wide and thin blades, wobbling spoons that are thick, thin, heavy, and light. Several sizes of split shot will also be needed. The angler's imagination will suggest various combinations of lures and lead, fished with various kinds of retrieves at varying depths. There is no end to the possibilities. I have taken trout by skittering an unweighted spinner-fly rapidly across the surface—and by bouncing a weighted spoon along a gravel bottom. Most fish, of course, are caught somewhere in between. The angler needs to be conscious of the depth at which a trout strikes in order to determine where fish are feeding.

The great advantage of spinning is the increased water that can be covered by longer casts that can be retrieved at any depth, but the advantage demands that the spin fisherman keep moving and experimenting in order to show his wares to a maximum number of fish. When trout follow a lure peacefully at a respectful distance they are only mildly curious, or well fed, and a change in lures is indicated. If trout follow closely or dart around the lure in an agitated manner they can sometimes be induced to strike by changing the action, or the depth, or the size of the lure, or perhaps by baiting the hook to add appeal. Lures should be connected to the monofilament by a swivel to prevent excessive twisting. Lure casting in streams or shallow water or weedy areas can be a very expensive sport!

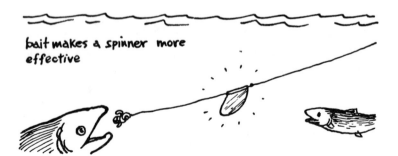

bait makes a spinner more effective

Bait fishing looks deceptively simple, but it requires consider-able art to make bait impaled on a hook attached to a line behave in a convincingly natural manner. There are two types of bait fishing: still fishing and casting. The still fisherman hopes he has a likely spot, hopes the fish are feeding on the bottom, and hopes the fish will hook himself. The bait caster at a lake generally attempts slow deep retrieves, tumbling his bait along the bottom, but also exper-iments with different depths. In some cases he is a still fisherman who occasionally moves.

DEADLY BAIT TECHNIQUE

In streams and rivers, the bait fisherman who can drift a bait along the bottom through likely lies with a tight enough line to feel a strike, but without tell-tale drag is an artist who will never lack for fish. The beginner who wishes to use bait will do bet-ter using a bubble for a bobber, attaching it at a point that will allow the lightly weighted bait to bob a few inches above the bottom.

Spin fishing with flies is much the same. A partially water-filled bubble is fastened $2\frac{1}{2}$ or 3 feet from the fly and cast. Flies can be fished either wet or dry. Despite the splash of the bubble and its wake during the retrieve, the fish are not much bothered by relatively long casts on a wind-ruffled lake.

There are certain techniques applicable to both spinning and fly casting. The most important is to keep moving. Ninety percent of the water contains no fish. The angler's objective is to eliminate much of it on the basis of experience, knowledge, and inspec-tion and to prospect the rest with diligence and imagination. The greater the area effectively fished the greater the chances of fill-ing the creel. Beginners are apt to cast endlessly to water that has yielded a fish or a strike or a rise. The veteran angler will generally move after playing a fish, knowing the water is too disturbed to produce.

Trout lie facing upstream in running water and will gener-ally hold in the same positions all day unless badly frightened. Under cover of dusk or darkness, however, they will move out into shallow or still or unprotected water to feed on morsels they would not have dared to pursue during the bright part of the day. The water that can be safely eliminated without a second glance during the day often yields the most fish in the evening. (Trout fishing is commonly permitted for an hour after sunset.)

WHERE TROUT HIDE

Though difficult to reach and maddening to fish, the most productive water—even in heavily fished areas—will often be in brushy, swampy, heavily wooded country. Fishermen endowed with great patience—and some skill—often seek out just such hard-to-fish spots when they are determined to catch fish. The backpacker should not scorn accessible water because it is regularly fished, any more than he should depend on remote water to produce sensational results.

Trout are a roaming species in lakes and they tend to follow the shores near the bottom, patrolling the area they know. The best place to find them is where a stream feeds the lake. The second-best place is off a point of land jutting into the lake. Coves are often good, especially if there is drainage into the lake. The foot of a dry watercourse is often attractive to trout, as are undercut banks and willow and alder thickets that overhang the water. Boulders, ledges, blankets of moss, and submerged brush and logs all are favored by feeding trout.

Once the trout is hooked, two things become vital: to keep a tight-line, and to keep from reaching underwater obstructions. Slack in the line helps the fish throw the hook and invites knots and snags. Brook and brown trout instinctively bore for the bottom when hooked and must be turned before they can rub the hook free or cut the leader. Rainbow and golden usually jump in hope of throwing the hook, so relatively little pressure is required to keep the line tight.

Beginning anglers tend to drag in their fish in great haste, often jerking them so violently from the water that the fish sails over the fisherman's head. This technique not only risks breaking the leader and pulling out the hook, it eliminates the pleasure of playing the fish.

For the backpacker—who cannot afford the weight of a landing net—playing the trout to exhaustion is more than just sport. Exhaustion greatly reduces the chance of escape. The trout should be maneuvered to the terrain most closely resembling a beach. The critical moment comes when the leader is grasped a few inches from the no-longer-flopping trout and it is gently beached, deposited several yards inland, and pounced upon before it can flop back into the water. Careless landing technique may cost the beginner one trout in two. The seasoned angler rarely loses a fish.

KILL ONLY FOR FOOD

Of course, small trout or fish not needed for food should not be landed at all. The exhausted fish should be grasped gently but

firmly underwater with one hand while the barb is backed out with the other. If the maneuver cannot be managed underwater, the hand grasping the fish should first be wetted to prevent it injuring the skin or ripping off the scales. Injured trout of any size should never be released. Nearly all trout taken on flies may be released unharmed, while nearly all fish taken on bait are injured by removal of the hook.

Once a trout has been landed, it should promptly be killed. Putting my index finger in the mouth, I quickly bend the head all the way back until it touches the back, breaking the neck and killing the fish instantly. After rinsing off the dirt, I usually lie the trout on a rock in the shade to let the breeze dry first one side then the other before putting it in my creel or on my stringer.

A creel should be well filled with grass or leaves to assure ventilation. Trout that are allowed to grow warm or stay wet or go uncleaned will lose texture and flavor in a matter of hours and will begin to spoil soon after. But by proper care and handling, I have often kept trout without refrigeration for three and four days in camp with no loss of freshness or flavor. By getting the trout dry to the touch almost immediately, and not allowing the sun to warm it, I can carry it in my creel for three or four hours before cleaning without risk.

Cleaning trout is simple enough. I insert a sharp pointed knife blade in the vent and with short, rapid sawing strokes slit open the body cavity all the way to the base of the jaw. After cutting across from one gill opening to the other, I break the colon loose from the vent, and pull the viscera and gills loose. Then, running my thumbnail down the inside of the backbone, I remove the last blackness of the kidney and the job is done. After thoroughly rinsing the fish inside and out, and promptly drying all surfaces, it is ready for cooking, refrigeration, or several days storage in a dry, cool place.

TROUT RECIPES

There are innumerable recipes for preparing trout, but fresh trout fried in butter is hard to beat. For years I have carried a plastic bag containing varying portions of corn meal, cornstarch, salt, pepper, garlic and onion salt, and other spices. After dampening the fish and putting it in the bag for a quick shaking, it is ready for the buttered skillet. Crumbling a little leftover bacon bar over the frying fish enhances the flavor—so does a squirt of lemon juice. I am fond of smoked trout, but the process is not suited to most backpacking trips. Trout wrapped in aluminum foil and baked in ashes, on the other hand, is easy and saves the weight of a skillet. So does trout toasted on a stick.

When it comes to catching trout, there is no substitute for persistence. Almost anyone, equipped with reasonably efficient tackle and situated on reasonably stocked trout water, should eventually catch trout if the necessary effort is put forth. As one of my old fishing partners used to remind me: "You can't catch fish unless your line's in the water." He fished with great determination—and considerable imagination—and always caught fish.

The innocent angler should beware of guidebooks that promise marvelous fishing. Wild trout simply cannot be promised. The excellence of the fishing varies with the skill of the angler, recent fishing pressure, feeding activity, phase of the moon, available food, time of day, weather, season—and, of course, that great imponderable, luck.

Trout fishing has many allures. The chance of a big fish lends excitement to every cast. So does the yank of a striking trout. But what keeps me fishing is the pleasure of exploring the dependably fine country that trout call home.

SIXTEEN

A Sample Trip

We Watch the Weather... Assembling Food and Gear...
Three Little Kits... I Pick a Pack... What to Wear...
Fishing Gear... Menu Planning... Heading for the Trailhead...
Underway at Last!... Setting Up Camp... Building the
Bedsite... Dinnertime!... Evening Recreation...
Warm by the Campfire

In an effort to tie together the material on gear and technique, I provide here in some detail a composite narrative of a trip I take almost every spring, this time with my wife, Deanne. The trip begins at my cabin on Upper Echo Lake on the edge of Desolation Wilderness on the crest of the California Sierra at 7400 feet. Three little lakes offering three species of trout provide us with a destination. While none of them are reached by trail, access is not difficult, partly because we use a canoe. Probably most important is that the lakes are nestled in a small watershed with western exposure, so the swimming is good at a time when many of the lakes in Desolation are still frozen. So this is often my first trip of the year into the area.

I knew the three lakes would be thawed by early May, that insect activity would start the trout feeding on flies by mid-June, and that the nearby Boy Scout Camp did not open until immediately after the fourth of July weekend. To avoid the holiday campers, yet find the water warm enough for swimming, it seemed clear that the last week in June was the time to go. It would be the dark of the moon, which meant poor nighttime visibility, but probably better fishing. The only possible drawback was that mosquitos were likely to be active; since the country was open and well-drained, and since we meant to be prepared for insects, this was a negligible factor. (There are places, of course, where the mosquito menace is the *most* important factor in determining when to go.)

We decided to allow ourselves three days and two nights. Trip length was determined after considering several alternatives. The hike would be comparatively short, the country we wanted to see quite small; and there was a limit to what we could do to amuse ourselves. On the other hand, there would be several hours of driving each way and possibly an hour of canoeing. Alloting only two days and one night would mean going in one day and coming out the next; that would be too rushed. Four days and three nights was likely to lead to boredom. So we settled on three days— the average length of trip for recreational backpackers—sometime during the last week of June.

Normally, the next step is to work out a menu, buy the food and assemble the necessary clothing and equipment. But, since food, clothes, and gear were already at the cabin in preparation for this and other trips, we postponed deciding what to take and turned to the decision of when precisely to go. The problem was weather. Few backpackers can afford to wait for perfect weather, but far too many see their trips spoiled for lack of knowledge about likely storms.

WE WATCH THE WEATHER

On June 26 at Echo, the sky was threatening all day, the wind was from the southeast and the barometer was low and steady. The forecast on the portable radio was for "thunderstorms afternoon and evening" over the central Sierra. It rained a little in the afternoon and that night it snowed. The outlook was distinctly unfavorable.

On the twenty-seventh, the forecasts were for "fair and warmer," and the temperature climbed a little at Echo. The morning of the twenty-eighth the barometer was beginning to rise, and although scattered thunderstorms were still forecast afternoon and evening, these represented only the tattered remnants of the passing storm and would probably be weak and brief. Since the fourth of July weekend was almost upon us, we decided to leave the next day.

Most of my equipment is packed in cartons under a built-in bunk in my cabin. The first step in preparing for a trip is to prop

deciding what to take

open the bunk lid and fish out the notebook containing my latest checklist. It may be possible to remember everything needed on short notice without such a list, but before I made lists I nearly always left something vital home.

I like to postpone final choices and making up my pack until the last possible minute at the trailhead, so I begin by finding two empty cartons: one for food and community gear and the other for my own personal gear. Items on my list in general use, and therefore not stored beneath the bunks I usually skip over the first time around.

Because in years past the weather has ranged from sweltering to below freezing at this time of year, we decided to take our big Sierra Designs Double Mummy bag. Under it we'll rely on the two-inch thick comfort of our Camp Rest foam-filled air mattresses. Whether we take along a tent or merely a lightweight tarp will depend on the weather. We'll wait until the last minute at the trailhead to decide, but I'll need to inspect our Warmlite tent before-hand to make sure it's clean and ready to go.

Cooking gear is the next consideration and I decide on the Coleman Peak One stove because of its easy simmering, wide burner, stability, and capacity. A full tank will see us through the trip so extra fuel can be forgotten. I fire up the stove to make sure it's not clogged, fill the tank and put it in the gear box. In my own box goes a large, single-bladed jackknife (the blade is sufficiently pointed to clean trout, yet broad enough to spread butter) and my folding aluminum spoon-fork. With it goes my large plastic cup marked with lines at every quarter cup. Since weight is not vital, I add an almost weightless aluminum measuring cup as well.

Although our menu is still to be determined, I know we will want a big pot for soups and stews. A teakettle will function as a second pot. The single burner of the stove limits the possibilities (thereby simplifying menu planning). I put in the gear box a $2\frac{1}{4}$-quart Sigg kettle, the lid of which has been fitted with a small knob so that it can be lifted with aluminum hot pot tongs, and my squat one-quart teakettle.

ASSEMBLING FOOD AND GEAR

For carrying water to camp and making fruit drinks, I choose a wide-mouthed polyethylene quart bottle. For this weekend-sized trip my half-empty shaker containing a mix of various salts and pepper does not require refilling. One quart of milk will be more than ample so I open a quart packet of powdered Milkman and empty the contents into my plastic milk squirter bottle (originally a mustard dispenser). After tightly plugging the spout from within with a matchstick, this, too, goes in the gear box.

From my container box comes a plastic squeeze tube that was boiled clean after the last trip. I make sure the cap is screwed on tight, and fill it approximately half full of apricot-pineapple preserves through the open bottom. After cleaning the opening with a wet cloth I fold it over, leaving plenty of room in the bottom, and force on the plastic clip. I give the tube a hard squeeze to make sure it will not leak under pressure in my pack (it never has), then I wipe off the remaining stickiness and toss the tube in the food box.

GORP
is good
any ol'
time.

powdered
milk in a
plugged
mustard
dispenser

It cannot be denied that margarine keeps better than butter, but we much prefer butter, and with minimal precautions it will always stay fresh for the three to five days I am usually out. Butter and margarine are heavy and many think of them as luxuries, but they are high in food energy and probably the most palatable source of badly needed fat. I find it possible to consume an almost unlimited quantity: in soups, stews, on crackers and frying trout, and even, like the Himalayan Sherpas, in my tea. So I select a large, wide-mouthed plastic jar and take two quarter-pound cubes of fresh butter out of the refrigerator and set them on the kitchen table to warm to a workable consistency.

A Ziploc bag will be sufficient to hold the half-pound package of cholesterol and fat-free Jalapeno Nu-Tofu cheese I find in the refrigerator. Ziplocs have become as indispensable for backpacking as produce plastic bags used to be. Out of the pantry I pick a selection of both kinds in several sizes. I hope to need them for bringing home trout. I stuff them all into the bottom of my pack. A Chore Girl, dish cloth, and a half-empty 1-ounce tube of Paket biodegradable hand and dish soap go into a small plastic bag, which is closed with a twisty. I find half a roll of toilet paper secured with a rubber band, and since that looks like plenty I throw it in the box. Paper towels are more easily used in the wind, and they also serve as dish towels and hot pads, but I could not find a partial roll and a full roll is much too bulky for three days.

LITTLE KITS

Next comes our first aid kit packed in a screw-top plastic icebox jar. It contains a dozen assorted plastic Bandaids, a pair each of 2 × 2- and 3 × 3-inch gauze pads, a 1-inch roll of adhesive (not plastic) tape, a roll of 3-inch Kling gauze, and a clean washcloth. There are a few lumps of foam, a sheet of Molefoam and a pair of nail scissors to cut them. Taped to the lid is a needle and a backed razor blade. Scattered about are matches.

My personal kit is packed in a plastic zippered pouch. There was a time when I painstakingly gathered the contents for every trip, but it soon became evident that it would be easier to keep a kit permanently assembled. Mine contains a toothbrush, a tiny flat plastic container of dental floss, a spare tube of chapstick, 1-ounce tubes of Sea & Ski suntan lotion and Desenex athlete's foot ointment, half a roll of anti-acid tablets, a stub of pencil, and the remains of a tube of glacier cream. The little packet weighs 3 ounces, and I put it directly into an outside pocket of the pack.

I PICK A PACK

I decide to carry my internal frame Gregory Polaris pack because it comfortably hugs my back, has more than adequate capacity, and will be easier to manage than a frame pack on the cross-country section of the trip. Mosquitos in the area may be moderately active so I toss in the box a half-empty bottle of Jungle Juice. With it go a Petzl Micro headlamp and a Mini Mag flashlight—after I test the batteries.

The best existing map of the area we are visiting is the seven and a half minute USGS topographical map. I have an old, but still serviceable copy that shows not only the area we will visit but also the surrounding territory, so we can identify the peaks we will use as landmarks. To orient the map, we will need to know directions, so I dig out a liquid-filled plastic-cased compass that weighs only half an ounce and put it in the gear box.

With it goes a 4 × 6-inch spiral notebook with a section of pencil pushed snugly through the spiral binding. Pencil and paper also make it possible to leave notes for other party members in camp or on the trail. And my notebook pages have served as emergency toilet paper, started fires in rainstorms, and supplied mountaintop registers. My notebook and pencil weigh 2 ounces.

WHAT TO WEAR

Next, I turn to the selection of clothes. First comes a long-sleeved Hickory shirt because there are going to be bugs. Over the shirt in the evening (or in the wind) goes an unlined pullover nylon shell anorak with a drawstring on the hood, elastic at the wrists, a drawstring at the bottom (over the hips), and a front zippered pouch into which both hands can be stuffed. The anorak weighs only $7\frac{1}{2}$ ounces and is rarely left home.

Beneath the Hickory shirt goes a short-sleeved mesh polo shirt that is superior to a T-shirt or undershirt in almost every way; it is cooler and drier in hot weather, warmer and drier in cold weather, lighter and more easily washed and dried enroute. I also prefer it as a pajama top. To protect against the possibility of really cold weather, I also put in the box my 4-ounce Stephenson VB shirt, which of course can also serve as windshell, raingear, pajama top, and emergency garment.

Since I plan to hike in shorts and also spend a good deal of time sunning and swimming (possibly in public) I select a boxer-style bathing suit with pockets. In the evening I'll need protection from bugs and cold so I add to the pile the trousers with the wrap-around zipper and velcro waist that were modified for me. While the trousers are before me I fold a yard-long strip of toilet paper and button it into a back pocket. Into a front pocket goes a clean bandana, which may also function as a wash rag, pot holder, towel, neckerchief, etc. A pair of nylon running shorts and a two-piece set of medium-weight Patagonia Capilene long underwear will supply warmth and versatility.

This takes care of all but the extremities. I have tried a good many different hats and sun shades. In the warm and friendly summer Sierra I am concerned with sun protection and maximum ventilation, not rain protection. Summer days are long and the high-altitude sun beats down relentlessly, so that a hat brim that partially shades the nose and neck and ears can make the difference between developing a protective layer of tan or a painful sunburn. For the country we will visit I choose an old, shapeless, once-white cotton tennis hat that weighs 2 ounces. The underside of the $2\frac{1}{4}$-inch brim is dark green for reduced glare, and fully a third of the crown is nylon netting that provides good ventilation. Since I rarely wear dark glasses, I always take a hat when I go out overnight.

The hiking won't be strenuous or the load heavy so my ultra light Hi-Tec Sierra boots will be more than adequate, even if we decide to do a little cross-country scrambling. Since they require no waterproofing (or break-in) I merely tug on the laces to make sure they're strong before tossing them in my box, along with two pairs of wonderful Thorlo Trekking socks. For backup protection against a cold spring storm, I put in a synthetic watch cap, lightweight mittens, and Stephenson VB glove liners and fabric VB socks. My footwear is completed with a pair of featherweight foam rubber sandals (Zoris) to protect bare feet in camp. Having selected clothing to cover all contingencies, I make a pile of what I plan to wear the next morning—which is everything except the boots, spare socks, nylon shell, and VB shirt—and put the pile on my bed, where it cannot be missed.

FISHING GEAR

The fly rod I plan to take is two-piece, 7-foot, 2-ounce Fenwick of furruleless fiberglass. The attached Phlueger Medalist reel is loaded with 50 feet of level backing, a tapered fly line, and a $7\frac{1}{2}$-foot leader tapered to a $1\frac{1}{2}$-pound tippet. I reel the No. 12 mosquito dry fly to the tip of the rod, disjoint the two sections and fasten them side by side—the tip protected by the butt—with stout rubber bands at each end.

Though reduced to $3\frac{1}{2}$ feet the rod will still stick a foot above my pack, but I am accustomed to making the necessary allowances, and this arrangement leaves me ready to cast within 30 seconds of stopping. Because the rod does not fit well in a box, and because leaned against the wall it is easily forgotten, I set it inside the open pack.

In a pocket of my pack goes a small circular plastic sectional fly box that comfortably holds a dozen flies. Fastened to it with a stout rubberband are two extra cellophane-enclosed tapered leaders, the top one holding my fishing license. I also toss in a small tin of Muselin for dressing my line, leader, and fly to make them float.

My Olympus XA 35mm camera weighs 9 ounces loaded with a 36-exposure roll of ASA 400 Kodacolor (without case, which is the way I carry it). I find the camera empty and have no spare film, so I write myself a note to buy a roll on the way to the trailhead. The camera goes in my box while the note stays on the kitchen table. As protection against adversity I fill a small plastic bottle with about 4 ounces of 151 proof rum and put it in an outside pocket of the pack.

Late in the afternoon Deanne sits down to help decide what we'll take to eat. I carry several boxes of backpacking food out to the back porch, and while she picks through the collection to see what looks good, I retrieve the notebook and pencil. We will need provisions for three lunches, two dinners, and two breakfasts.

MENU PLANNING

We discuss our preferences (within the limits of our food supply) and decide on the following: for breakfast both mornings there will be delicious fresh fruit for maximum energy. From the large supply Deanne keeps on hand, I select four bananas, two apples, a large bunch of seedless grapes, a mango, some cherries, and two oranges. For backup and morning snacks there are raisins and air-dried bananas and pineapple. All of this is packed in plastic bags.

For dinner we decide on freeze-dried AlpineAire Chicken Rotelle, consisting of pasta, chicken and sour cream sauce with vegetables for one night, and beef stew, which I have offered to concoct that evening, for the other. Both meals will start with soup and we select foil packets of Lipton ham and pea, and mushroom, each of which will yield four full cups. I empty about 6 servings of bulk freeze-dried apples into a plastic bag and add a heaping tea-spoon of cinnamon and half a teaspoon of nutmeg before knotting the top. Dessert one night will be Backpacker's Pantry cheese-cake; the other night we'll have applesauce, which always tastes good in the wilds.

Lunch always seems the hardest meal to plan for. To the but-ter, Nu-Tofu cheese, and jam already packed, we add two avoca-dos, a small peeled red onion, a bell pepper, a quarter pound of salted wheat crackers, a half pound loaf of thin sliced Westphalian pumpernickle bread, sesame sticks, oriental cookies, and salted al-monds and peanuts.

Provisions are completed by adding enough pre-sweetened lemonade powder to make two quarts, a 3-ounce plastic bag of "trout dip," a mixture of corn starch, corn meal, salt, pepper, onion and garlic salt, and probably other now forgotten ingredi-ents. Having suffered in the past from taking too little or leaving home something vital, I spread all the food on the table grouped by meals, and we give it a hard look. Satisfied now, we dump everything in the food box and turn on the portable radio for the hourly weather report.

Scattered afternoon and evening thunderstorms are still fore-cast locally, with fair weather both to the east and west. The late afternoon sky, though more than half filled with billowing, black-hearted thunderheads, is not particularly threatening, and the barometer has continued to rise.

Back in the kitchen, I find the butter has softened and after removing the wrapping I have little difficulty pressing the cubes into the plastic jar. After screwing the lid down tight I put the jar in the refrigerator, along with the cheese. Then before I forget, I write boldly on a large sheet of paper "Butter and cheese in icebox" and put this reminder on top of everything else in the food box.

That evening, I spread out on the kitchen table the various ingredients for my stew. In order to make some record of my creation, I decide to make two identical dinners, combining ingre-dients in a double plastic bag for the one we take, and keeping them separate in individual small bags for the one I leave behind. That way, if the stew is successful or needs obvious modifications, I am in a position to measure portions and make adjustments.

The ingredients I choose are: dehydrated potato cubes and mixed carrots and peas, a beef bouillon cube, half a package of in-stant gravy, dehydrated mushrooms, half a quart package of Milk-man, 3 ounces of freeze-dried ground beef, salt, beef-flavored TVP,

canoeing across the lake saves many miles of walking.

pepper, and fresh onion and garlic. It is my intention to cook this in the uncleaned soup pot for added flavor, and to add half a cube of butter—if we can spare it. I knot the top of the doubled bag and toss it in the food box. Everything, now, is ready to go.

HEADING FOR THE TRAILHEAD

The following morning dawns cloudy and threatening and the weather forecast is unchanged, but the barometer has continued to rise. Our packs, fishing rod, and the two boxes—including the butter and cheese from the refrigerator—are stowed in the outboard motorboat at my dock. We have decided, both to add variety to the trip and to save $3\frac{1}{2}$ miles of hiking, to canoe the mile and a half width of the lake from the end of the road. So we tow the canoe from my dock down lower Echo Lake to the resort, where I buy a roll of film. With the canoe lashed on top of the station wagon, we load up and start off.

making the stew from scratch

Our principal concern is still the weather, which remains murky as we drive west and then north along the western slope of the range, listening for a change in the forecast. At the end of the gravel road on the shore of a large mountain lake, we unload the car under an overcast sky, launch the canoe and spread the food, cooking equipment and all other community gear on a shelf of granite. I invite Deanne to divide the food; she says "no thanks" but she would appreciate my giving her weight rather than bulk since her pack is small. Although she is a woman, she carries a full share because she's only 15 pounds lighter than I am—and 20 years younger. By now it is nearly noon and we decide to eat lunch here rather than pack it away and start out hungry.

We sit on a glacially polished slab, looking out across the lake to the mountains in the east as we make all kinds of sandwich combinations from the cheese, jam, and buttered crackers. After eating our fill of nuts and finishing a quart of lemonade, we close the plastic bags and pack all the lunch food in a large heavy-duty plastic garbage bag. Hefting an item of community gear (or food) in each hand, I quickly divide everything into two piles of roughly equal weight, taking the bulkier pile for myself.

By this time, we are happy to note, a band of blue sky has appeared in the west, and is steadily growing larger as the gloomy cloud mass moves slowly to the east, so we decide to leave the tent behind and take the lightweight tarp so we can see the stars.

I jam the big sleeping bag into the bottom of the Gregory Polaris, then pack the remaining gear into color-coded stuffsacks before packing them into the upper compartment, keeping the heaviest items close against (but not poking into) my back. Since the day is warming steadily, I take off my trousers and switch to shorts before closing up my pack and checking all zippers and lashings. At the top of my pack are my trousers and shell parka in easy reach in case of insect attack, or a sudden change in the weather. We won't be carrying any water for the short hike to camp, so we take a last drink from the water bottle that stays in the car.

I rub a little #15 sunscreen on my face and the back of my neck, put on my boots, and carry my pack, mattress, and fishing rod down to the canoe. Deanne loads the canoe while I return to lock up the car. After pocketing a couple of dimes because I know there are pay phones at nearby trailheads, I lock my wallet in the car, then hide my keys under a nearby rock, thus saving pocket room, a few ounces and the possibility of losing either valuable. As I climb into the canoe I tell Deanne where the keys are to protect against emergency, then I settle myself in the stern, and as we paddle slowly out into the lake. The last of the preparations can finally be forgotten. The trip, itself, has begun.

UNDERWAY AT LAST!

The small, heavily laden canoe moves slowly through the light chop, but the wind is with us and we cross the lake in less than an hour—an estimate, since Deanne shares my unwillingness to wear a watch in the woods. We drag the canoe some distance up the bank and hide it, well separated from its paddles, in some brush to discourage borrowers. I lash my fly rod to the pack by means of two nylon cords attached to the right side, and lash my full length foam mattress to the top of the pack by two more loops of cord.

We put on our packs and move up through the brush for a hundred yards before finding the well-marked trail that follows the lakeshore. By now the western half of the sky is blue and clear and I know it will be hot in the bright sunlight, so I take off my shirt and stuff it in the top of my pack. For a while the trail climbs gently away from the lake, but when it turns to the east toward a pass and grows steeper, I tell Deanne to go ahead. From past experience I know her comfortable pace uphill is faster than mine, and there is no need for either of us to travel at an uncomfortable speed. I know she will be waiting at the pass when I arrive.

As she takes off, I stop to adjust my shoulder straps to make the Polaris ride more comfortably and to prevent my shoulders from growing sore. A hundred yards farther I stop again, and this time I get it right. As the pitch steepens, I automatically shorten my stride and cut my speed to maintain an unchanged energy output. After a little while my hips begin to ache, reminding me to loosen my hipbelt and tighten my shoulder straps to put a larger portion of the weight on my shoulders. On the steepest stretch my knees start to hurt, but after three limp steps the discomfort goes away.

When I reach the pass, Deanne is waiting in the shade, sitting on a rock, looking out over the lake-dotted granite basin to the east. I take off my pack and join her. Both of us are better acquainted with the basin as viewed from the opposite direction, so we try to identify all the visible lakes and peaks before bringing out the map and compass. I need to be sure I am properly oriented because the route from this point to the lake is mostly cross-country. After a snack of dried pineapple we put on our packs and start off.

When we reach the turnoff area, I hunt until I find the small, unobtrusive duck that I built beside a tree the previous year. The cross-country trip is pretty and easy, passing up a broad grassy draw and dropping over a little rise to the small, sparkling lake. Tucked in a shallow depression in the rolling granite woodland, the lake is flanked by a thicket of willow on one shore and a small, glacially polished dome on the other. We take off our packs in a choice campsite on a little peninsula between two bays. Apparently, we are the first visitors of the year, and there are only a few mosquitos—both excellent signs. The little peninsula has no fringe of marsh to harbor insects, and the parklike stand of pines upon it serves to break the wind, but lets through enough air for good ventilation.

I show Deanne a tilting slab that forms a beach on the more sheltered bay and, after testing the temperature of the water, we immediately take off our boots and dive in, wearing our shorts and shirts to wash them. After an exhilarating swim we peel off our wet clothes, rinse them, wring them out, and stretch them to dry on a flat topped boulder. We lie on the hot slab, talking and dozing and watching the clouds for perhaps an hour before putting on our dry shorts and returning to set up camp.

SETTING UP CAMP

I unload my pack onto a convenient ledge and remove the big down bag from its stuffsack, give it a shaking and spread it opened in the sunshine to regain its loft. Meanwhile, Deanne has unrolled the twin air mattresses and opened their valves to let the foam inside re-fill with air. We gather all the food that might be of interest to birds or mice or squirrels and zip it into my pack. Deanne folds down the legs of the little stove and selects a little bench to serve as a

foam bags and pads expand very quickly.

kitchen while I take the butter and cheese cans and our quart water bottle down to the lake. The tins I partially submerge and secure with rocks; the bottle I rinse and fill with water. I was drinking the water here for many years before Giardia was "discovered." There are no documented cases of Giardia in the region, so we will continue to drink the water without boiling, filtering, or adding chemicals.

My feet are fully restored by a swim and an hour going barefoot in the sun, so I put on my spare pair of heavy socks and my sandals. Next, I set about making my bed. I want a level spot well-shaded in the east from the morning sun, where the ground is soft enough to be shaped to the necessary contours.

BUILDING THE BEDSITE

I find an ideal patch of granite sand in the lee of a boulder and scoop a shallow depression about $2\frac{1}{2}$ feet long and $3\frac{1}{2}$ feet wide with tapered sides and a relatively flat bottom, placing the excavated material in a mound on the end I propose for my head. To test the result, I lie down on my back, make mental notes for repairs, then roll over on one side to check the fit again.

When our bedsite is ready, we cover it with half of the 8 × 8-foot tarp. Then we blow the Camp Rests tight, close their valves and fit them into the depression on the tarp. The double mummy is zipped closed, fluffed again, laid on the twin mattresses, and the other half of the tarp is gently folded over to make a dewproof sandwich. Into it we tuck all the items we might possibly need in the night. Now we can forget our bed until it's time to crawl inside.

My experience the previous year was that the fly fishing was good after the sun went down, but not before. Since the lake surface is still, with no sign of feeding fish, we decide to eat early and fish until dusk. While Deanne drags in some old logs and rearranges already blackened rocks into a campfire circle, I tear open the foil package of ham and pea soup, empty it in the large Sigg pot, along with the quart of water from the bottle, and set the covered pot on the stove. I light the stove, taking care to hold the lighted match to the burner *before* turning on the gas, then turn down the flame.

I take the teapot and the water bottle down to the lake and fill them, coming back with the butter can. While the soup is cooking, I get the salt and pepper shaker, sugar, pot tongs, forks and spoons, applesauce, and Chicken Rotelle and spread them on the ledge near the stove. Then I empty the dried applesauce (with sugar, cinnamon and nutmeg previously added) into the teakettle and add enough water so that, after stirring, all the apple bits are wet and rehydrating. I put the lid on, leaving it to soak, then lift the lid of the big pot with the tongs to give the soup a vigorous stir, using the opportunity to add about a third of a cube of butter.

DINNERTIME!

Moments later the soup comes to a boil and I turn down the flame until the boiling subsides to a slow bubble. The recipe calls for five minutes of simmering, but at a mile and a half above sea level I let it go more than twice that long before calling Deanne. Using the aluminum pot tongs as a handle, I pour it in our plastic cups. By now it has cooked to a thick consistency that makes a spoon helpful, but we still get nearly two delicious cups apiece.

The moment the last cup is poured I scrape the remains of the soup loose so they cannot burn, add the water required for the Chicken Rotelle and empty the package into the pot. This is contrary to the directions, but provides better hydration of the meat at this altitude (6800 feet). While we are waiting for the stew to cook, we go to work on the succulent applesauce. When the casserole begins to bubble I turn down the flame to a low simmer, stirring from time to time to prevent scorching. Since the flavor seems a trifle bland, and to add caloric power, I add Fines Herbes seasoning, my salt and pepper mix and a gob of butter. Then I rinse the applesauce from the teapot and refill it with lake water.

Meanwhile, Deanne has been cutting the zucchini into sticks. We eat them raw as an appetizer while we fix dinner. When the Chicken Rotelle is ready, we pour it into our cups and eat until we're full. By now the teapot is boiling. I turn off the stove and drop a tea bag in the teapot. While the tea is steeping, Deanne takes the three cups to the lake, fills them with water, loosens the clinging food with a spoon and tosses the resulting garbage into the bushes 100 feet back from the lake. In the meantime, I am similarly cleaning our stew pot, after saving the leftover stew in a plastic bag.

Though I am too full of dinner to think of eating, I know something sweet will taste good after we come in from fishing, so I empty the cheesecake mix into the still wet pot and add the required water. After stirring briskly for a minute or so, I cover the pot and put it aside to thicken. Unlike jellos, which need an icy rill or a snowbank to help them set, it needs only a little time. I put a good-sized rock on the lid as insurance against disturbance, and, after a cup of hot tea apiece, we are ready to go fishing.

Since fly casting at dusk around the shore of a Sierra lake can present difficult footing, I change back into my boots, put on long trousers over my shorts, and my long-sleeved shirt over the polo shirt. And since my skin has an unusual attraction for insects of all kinds I rub repellent on my face, hands, neck, and ankles. It takes me less than half a minute to assemble my rod since reel, line, leader and fly were never removed. Carrying my nylon shell and flashlight in addition to fly box, leaders, license, and muselin, I make my first casts in the little bay where we draw our water. Deanne strolls over to watch.

EVENING RECREATION

The sun has now set, but only just, and it is still light and warm. There are only a few clouds to be seen in the east and the breeze is hardly sufficient to ruffle the darkening water. There are only a few rises and these suggest small trout. I cast to several avidly feeding fish, but the rises merely move away from the fly, confirming my suspicion. The year before there were fair numbers of fat 11-inch brook trout. Could they have frozen out during the previous winter? Or have their tastes turned from flies to the fingerlings that evidently had been air planted since my last visit?

Out of the corner of my eye, I see the widening circle of a larger rise. I turn back into the woods and circle toward it, making my way to the water's edge behind a good-sized tree. On my third cast to the area of the rise there is a strong underwater strike and I set the hook. The fish runs for deep water, taking line off the reel, then surges toward the shore and I am alarmed to feel it rooting on the shallow rocky bottom, trying to tear the hook from its mouth. I lean out over the water and lift with all the weight I think the leader will safely stand. The fish comes to the surface, beginning to tire, and within another minute I have safely beached a deep-bodied brook trout of over 13 inches.

In less than an hour I hook and play nearly a dozen good trout, keeping four of the best and returning the rest unharmed. By now it is nearly dark, but Deanne volunteers to clean the catch. She straps on the Petzl headlamp and adjusts the beam to focus brightly on her hands. Using the Mini Mag I help her, burying the entrails well away from the water in thick brush, where they probably will be enjoyed by a garter snake, and the washed trout are hung from a willow stringer threaded through gill and mouth, which in turn is hung from a limb on the west side of a small pine so the fish will not catch the morning sun.

WARM BY THE CAMPFIRE

The night air has grown chilly and our wet hands are cold, but Deanne's campfire blossoms quickly and after a sip of rum we are soon warm and relaxed by the fire. Since both of us are thirsty, I make up a quart of lemonade, which is promptly consumed. Hiking in the dry air of the summer Sierra often results in a daily water loss through perspiration of several quarts. By evening, even after frequent drinks during the day, the hiker craves liquids and sweets. We therefore plan on drinking a quart or two apiece every evening to maintain body fluids. Menus, of course, must be planned accordingly.

It is our habit to sit up late beside the campfire, talking and watching the flames until we're so drowsy that we go to sleep promptly and stay asleep until the morning sun has warmed the air. We polish off the cheesecake and a fresh quart of water before our fire burns low. When we find our way to bed, the tarp is as wet from condensation as though it had rained. We wiggle into the big mummy bag, which quickly warms, then we lie snug and cozy, talking about the day, enjoying the night and watching the stars until we fall asleep.

In the two days that follow, we spend our time swimming in the little bay, dozing in the sun on the slab beside the water, and hiking cross-country to fish and swim in two nearby lakes. The storm has vanished entirely and the humidity quickly drops so there is far less dew on the second evening. In the other lakes we

cleaning up the lakeshore can be satisfying.

have good luck, finding a few large brook trout in one and a dense population of smaller cutthroat, brook and rainbow in the other. Between the lakes, we climb a high dome that yields an excellent view of the surrounding country.

For dinner the second night, we enjoy my stew, augmented by fresh onion, mushrooms, and garlic. Deanne kindly rates it as equal to the Chicken Rotelle. At least it was easy to prepare. We simply added water and the fresh-cut vegetables, brought it to a boil, added more water and let it simmer. After dinner we scale a second dome and find an abandoned trail on the far side, marked by ducks, which we idly follow until darkness forces us back to camp.

On the third day, the eve of the fourth of July weekend, we pack up, and before leaving camp try to obliterate all signs of our passing, except for a little charcoal inside a ring of already blackened rocks. Carrying five good trout in the cool interiors of our packs, we return to the trail and make good time back to the canoe on the shore of the big lake. Then we paddle upwind for an hour against a brisk chop to the opposite shore and the car. Driving home through the mountains to the cabin, my reluctance at leaving the wilderness is nicely balanced by my anticipation of a hot shower and a trout dinner.

GOING BACK

When I get back
to the high bright world
of the windblown sun
and the meadowed rock
things will be all right.

When I return
to the mountain wild
on a turning trail
through a summer rain
my rhythm will return.

When I can escape
to a land left wild
on a still starred night
drowned deep in peace
my life will turn around.

When I get back
to the wilds again
and the easy peace
of a dreaming fire
I'll be content again.

Sources

AIR LIFT Mattresses
BASIC DESIGNS
5815 Bennett Valley Rd.
Santa Rosa, CA 95404

ALPINEAIRE
P.O. Box 926
Nevada City, CA 95959

ANDEAN OUTFITTERS
P.O. Box 220
Ridgeway, CO 81431

ASOLO/KENKO
INTERNATIONAL, INC.
8141 W. 1-70 Frontage Road
N. Arvada, CO 80002

BACKPACKER'S
PANTRY, INC.
1540 Charles Drive
Redding, CA 96003

L.L. BEAN
Freeport, ME 04032

BIBLER TENTS
5441-D Western Ave.
Boulder, CO 80301

BLEUET Stoves
CAMPING GAZ
2151 Las Palmas Dr.
Carlsbad, CA 92009

BRUNTON COMPASS
620 E. Monroe Ave.
Riverton, WY 82501-4997

BUCK KNIVES
P.O. Box 1267
El Cajon, CA 92022

CAMPMOR CATALOG
P.O. Box 997-K
Paramus, NJ 07653-0997

CAMP TRAILS
P.O. Box 966
Binghampton, NY 13902

CARIBOU
MOUNTAINEERING
46 Loren Ave.
Chico, CA 95928

COLEMAN OUTDOOR
PRÓDUCTS
250 N. St. Francis Ave.
Wichita, KS 67201

COLUMBIA ACTIVE WEAR
6600 N. Baltimore
Portland, OR 97203

DANA DESIGNS
109 Commercial Dr.
Bozeman, MT 59715

DE LORME MAPPING CO.
P.O. Box 298
Freeport, ME 04032

DOWN HOME Custom Bags
Deadwood, OR 97430

EARLY WINTERS
P.O. Box 4333
Portland, OR 97208-4333

ENVIROGEAR LTD.
(COCOON BAG)
127 Elm St.
Cortland, NY 13045-2388

EUREKA TENTS
P.O. Box 966
Binghamton, NY 13902

FEATHERED FRIENDS
2013 Fourth Ave.
Seattle, WA 98121

"FIT FOR LIFE"
by Harvey and Marilyn Diamond
Warner Books, 1987

GERBER KNIVES
P.O. Box 23088
Portland, OR 97223

W.L. GORE & ASSOCIATES
1-800-431-GORE

GREGORY MOUNTAIN
PRODUCTS
100 Calle Cortez
Temecula, CA 92390

HARVEST FOODWORKS, LTD
40 Hillcrest Dr.
Toronto, Ontario M6G 2E3
Canada

(HES) HOMEOPATHIC
EDUCATIONAL SERVICES
2124 Kittredge St.
Berkeley, CA 94704
Inquiries: (510) 649-0294
Orders only: 1-800-359-9051

HI-TEC SPORTS USA
4801 Stoddard Road
Modesto, CA 95356

JANSPORT
10931 32nd Place
W. Everett, WA 98204

KELTY PACK, INC.
1224 Fern Ridge Parkway
Creve Coeur, MO 63141

KNAPSACK TOURS
5961 Zinn Drive
Oakland, CA 94611-5003

LOWE ALPINE SYSTEMS
P.O. Box 1449
Broomfield, CO 80038

MARMOT
MOUNTAIN WORKS
2321 Circadian Way
Santa Rosa, CA 95407

MERRELL FOOTWEAR
P.O. Box 4249
Burlington, VT 05406

MOONSTONE
MOUNTAINEERING
5350 Ericson Way Suite C
Arcata, CA 95521

MOSS TENTS
P.O. Box 309
Mt. Battie St.
Camden, ME 04843

MSR/MOUNTAIN
SAFETY RESEARCH
P.O. Box 24547, Terminal Station
Seattle, WA 98124

MOUNTAIN HOUSE FOODS
OREGON FREEZE DRY
P.O. Box 5037-45
Portland, OR 97208

MOUNTAINSMITH
15866 W. Seventh Ave.
Golden, CO 80401

NEW ZEALAND TRAVELERS
P.O. Box 605
Shelburne, VT 05482

NICHOLS EXPEDITIONS
590 North 500 West
Moab, UT 84532

NIKE Boots
1 Bowerman Dr.
Beaverton, OR 97005

THE NORTH FACE
999 Harrison St.
Berkeley, CA 94709

OLICAMP
(SCORPION STOVES)
P.O. Box 306
Montrose, CA 91020-0306

OPTIMUS/SUUNTO
2151 Las Palmas Dr.
Carlsbad, CA 92009

PATAGONIA—Mail Order
P.O. Box 8900
Bozeman, MT 59715

PEET BROS.
P.O. Box 2007
Ocean, NJ 07712

QUEST TENTS
254 E. Hacienda Ave.
Campbell, CA 95008

RECREATIONAL
EQUIPMENT (REI)
P.O. Box 88125
Seattle, WA 98138-2125

RICHMOOR NATURAL HIGH
P.O. Box 8092
Van Nuys, CA 91409

RIACHLE MOLITOR USA
Geneva Rd.
Brewster, NY 10509

SCHRADE CUTLERY
Rt. 209 N
Ellenville, NY 12428

SIERRA CLUB
730 Polk St.
San Francisco, CA 94109

SIERRA DESIGNS
2039 Fourth St.
Berkeley, CA 94710

SIERRA WATER PURIFIER
2801 Rodeo Rd., Suite B-518
Santa Fe, NM 87505

SILVA COMPASSES
CAMPION, INC.
P.O. Box 966
Binghampton, N.Y. 13902

SOLUNAR TABLES
Box 207
Montoursville, PA 17754

SPORTIF
445 East Glendale
Sparks, NV 89431

THERM-A-REST
4000 First Ave. S.
Seattle, WA 98134

THOR-LO SOCKS
THORNEBURG HOSIERY CO.
P.O. Box 5440
Stateville, NC 28677

TOUGH TRAVELER
1012 State St.
Schenectady, NY 12307

USGS MAP SALES
Federal Center
Box 25286
Denver, CO 80225

VASQUE BOOTS
314 Main St.
Red Wing, MN 55066

VICTORINEX KNIVES
151 Long Hill Crossroads
Shelton, CT 06484

WALRUS INC.
929 Camelia St.
Berkeley, CA 94710

WARMLITE (Stephenson)
RFD #4
Gilford, NH 03246

WENGER PRECISE
INTERNATIONAL
15 Corporate Dr.
Orangeburg, NY 10962

"WILDERNESS RANGER
COOKBOOK" $9.95
San Juan National Forest Assoc.
P.O. Box 2261
Durango, CO 81302

WILDERNESS EXPERIENCE
20721 Dearborn St.
Chatsworth, CA 91311

Index

About the Author

Long a tinkerer with backpacking equipment and a searcher after comfort in the wilds, Robert S. Wood is the author of the backpacking best-sellers *Pleasure Packing* and *The 2 Oz. Backpacker.* His latest book is *Dayhiker, Walking for Fitness, Fun & Adventure.*

He has been hiking for 40 years in his beloved Sierra, the Cascades, Mexico, Europe, Alaska, New Zealand, South America, and Australia. As a journalist he wrote and edited for a number of magazines, including *Life, Time, Sports Illustrated, Sierra, Wilderness Camping,* and *Outside.*

Since fortunate investments permitted early retirement, he has devoted his time to wilderness travel, here and abroad, river rafting, hiking, and personal growth—and writing eight books about his adventures. A native of Berkeley and a forestry graduate of U.C., he now divides his year—with wife Deanne and daughter Angela—between homes in the Sierra foothills and the Big Island of Hawaii and a summer cabin on the edge of Desolation Wilderness.